Identity without Selfhood proposes an original conception of identity and subjectivity in the context of recent post-structuralist and queer debates. The author argues that efforts to analyse and even 'deconstruct' identity and self-hood still rely on certain core Western techniques of identity such as individuality, boundedness, autonomy, self-realisation and narrative. In a detailed study of biographical, media and academic representations of Simone de Beauvoir, Mariam Fraser illustrates that bisexuality, by contrast, is discursively produced as an identity which exceeds the confines of the self and especially the individuality ascribed to de Beauvoir. In the course of this analysis, she draws attention to the high costs incurred by processes of subjectification. It is in the light of these costs that, while drawing substantially on, and expanding, Foucault's notion of techniques of the self, the argument presented in the book also offers a critique of Foucault's work from a Deleuzo-Guattarian perspective.

MARIAM FRASER is a lecturer in the Department of Social Sciences at Loughborough University. She has published and given papers developing post-structuralist and queer theories of the self and is currently extending this work into the area of aesthetics. This is her first book.

Identity without Selfhood

Cambridge Cultural Social Studies

Series editors: JEFFREY C. ALEXANDER, *Department of Sociology, University of California, Los Angeles, and* STEVEN SEIDMAN, *Department of Sociology, University at Albany, State University of New York.*

Identity without Selfhood

Simone de Beauvoir and Bisexuality

Mariam Fraser

CAMBRIDGE
UNIVERSITY PRESS

PUBLISHED BY THE PRESS SYNDICATE OF THE UNIVERSITY OF CAMBRIDGE
The Pitt Building, Trumpington Street, Cambridge CB2 1RP, United Kingdom

CAMBRIDGE UNIVERSITY PRESS
The Edinburgh Building, Cambridge CB2 2RU, UK   http://www.cup.cam.ac.uk
40 West 20th Street, New York, NY 10011–4211, USA   http://www.cup.org
10 Stamford Road, Oakleigh, Melbourne 3166, Australia

First published 1999

Printed in the United Kingdom at the University Press, Cambridge

Typeset in Monotype Times 10/12.5 pt in QuarkXPress™ [SE]

A catalogue record for this book is available from the British Library

Library of Congress cataloguing in publication data

Fraser, Mariam.
Identity without selfhood: Simone de Beauvoir and bisexuality /
Mariam Fraser.
     p.   cm. – (Cambridge cultural social studies)
Includes bibliographical references and index.
ISBN 0 521 62357 X (hardback). – ISBN 0 521 62579 3 (paperback)
1. Bisexuality.   2. Identity (Psychology)   3. Self (Philosophy)
4. Beauvoir, Simone de, 1908–   .   5. Foucault, Michel.   I. Series.
HQ74.F73   1999
306.76′6–dc21   98–38427   CIP

ISBN 0 521 62357 X hardback
ISBN 0 521 62579 3 paperback

Dedicated, in loving memory, to J.H.T.F.

The room fills with a twilight of words
Strung with violet light

I have my identity and I have my sex: I am not new yet.

Kathy Acker, *In Memoriam to Identity*

Our only chance is to explore the idea of resisting the self …

Roy Boyne, 'War and Desire'

Contents

Acknowledgements

I would like to thank the Department of Sociology at Lancaster University, where this book began, and the Department of Social Sciences at Loughborough University, where it was finished, for providing stimulating and challenging environments to work in. Very special thanks to Lynne Pearce, Phillip Goodchild and Andrew Quick for all their help and warm encouragement and also to Nikolas Rose, who sharpened my understanding of Foucault and of my own argument. To Angela McRobbie, Natalie Fenton, Sumiko Mushakoji and Katie MacMillan, all of whom read early drafts and who offered support and friendship, thank you. Thanks also to Katie for writing and kindly giving me permission to reproduce lines from 'A Twilight of Words'. I am grateful to Clare Hemmings, Ann Kaloski and Merl Storr for generously sharing with me their thoughts and references on bisexuality, and to Catherine Max for her patience throughout. I am especially indebted to my parents, Farideh and Robin, to Stephanie Lawler, to Celia Lury and to Steven Warburton who have all, in their different ways, been an inspiration to me.

Introduction

[W]e demand that sex speak the truth . . . and we demand that it tell us our truth, or rather, the deeply buried truth of that truth about ourselves which we think we possess in our immediate consciousness.

Michel Foucault, *The History of Sexuality*, Volume I

In *The History of Sexuality, Volume I,* Foucault suggests that the acquisition of sexual identity is closely bound up with the acquisition of selfhood. In the modern era, sexuality is perceived to lie at the heart of the self, such that to 'come to terms' with the truth of sexuality is to come to terms with the truth of the self. In this respect, identity and selfhood are conjoined.

It is with the almost inextricable relation between identity and selfhood that this book is concerned. The sexual identity in question here is bisexuality, the self that of Simone de Beauvoir. A proliferation of newspaper, academic and biographical representations[1] all comment on, and in that commentary are constitutive of, a self which is attributed to de Beauvoir, such that it is perceived to be her property and her responsibility. Significantly however, while *de Beauvoir,* as I will show, is differently constituted in each of the three fields of cultural production, the representation of bisexuality remains, for the most part, consistent: it is inchoately produced across all three 'genres'.[2] This suggests that the discursive possibilities of bisexuality are either limited or enabled by the very same techniques and practices which produce de Beauvoir as an intelligible and coherent self. I will argue that it is the multitude of techniques by which de Beauvoir is produced as an individual that *simultaneously* serve to erase bisexuality, again and again, as an identity which pertains to the self.

The textually mediated figure of de Beauvoir then, provides the vehicle through which to explore the ways in which identity and selfhood come to be wedded, and the occasions when they might be separated. It is for this reason that the focus of this book lies not on discourses which address sexuality *per se,* but on those which attend to selfhood in all its various aspects. Thus with the exception of a brief analysis in the following chapter, I will not, on the whole, be examining in any real detail the recent theoretical and political interventions into sexuality debates which have been made by writers who identify as bisexual and/or who are interested in bisexuality. The burgeoning attention conferred on bisexuality does indicate however, that bisexuality is not *always* an identity without selfhood, as I suggest here. As chapter 1 will illustrate, it is clear that bisexuality can, and frequently is, claimed as a property of the self.

Nevertheless, although this recent explosion of literature on bisexuality is clearly a site where bisexuality is explicitly produced (and reproduced), it is also the case that sexual identities are constructed in spheres where sexuality itself is not the immediate and principal issue at stake. In the texts that I analyse here, texts which focus on a variety of cultural formations and identities which are constitutive of the self, bisexuality is not understood to be anchored to de Beauvoir's body or to be housed in her soul where it might reveal the 'truth' of her self. Instead, bisexuality exceeds the individuality ascribed to de Beauvoir in a number of ways. This, then, is the double axis on which the analysis here rests and the tension which it explores: how is it that de Beauvoir is produced as a self? In representations of de Beauvoir, what contemporary notions of selfhood, one of the aspects of which might or might not be individuality, preclude the possibility of de Beauvoir being perceived as 'bisexual'?

It is through an exploration of the variety of ways that sexuality *and* selfhood are produced that the analysis herein, although confined to a single individual, has implications *beyond* the singularity of de Beauvoir. Throughout this book I will be exploring some of the well-documented 'techniques of the self' which constitute the boundaries of what is considered, in the West,[3] to be 'intelligible' selfhood. These techniques may work in conjunction with each other, they may contradict each other, or they may simply produce the self in different ways (for example, temporally or spatially).[4] By exploring those techniques which render the figure of de Beauvoir intelligible, it is possible to illustrate:

the connections between the truths by which human beings are rendered thinkable – the values attached to images, vocabularies, explanations and so forth – and the techniques, instruments and apparatuses which presuppose human beings to be certain sorts of creatures, and act upon them in that light.

(N. Rose 1996: 296. See also Foucault 1988a)

Even contemporary feminist and queer theories of the self, as I will illustrate in chapter 2, are not always entirely distanced from conceptions of selfhood which are often understood to include, for example, boundedness and individuality. In this respect the study of bisexuality here goes some way to demonstrate what is at stake in recent analyses of the self and why it is that sexuality, in particular, often lies at the cutting edge of these debates.

The book will draw, principally, on Deleuze's analysis of Foucault (1988). The conceptual associations between the two thinkers have been strengthened by Deleuze's claim that Foucault's work has changed 'what it means to think' (Deleuze 1988: 120) and Foucault's announcement that 'this century will be known as Deleuzian' (Foucault 1977: 165). Rosi Braidotti suggests that: 'With the Foucault–Deleuze connection philosophy becomes creative, affirmative, critical work' (Braidotti 1991: 67) and that no account of Foucault's work would be complete without reference to Deleuze because he, 'more than any other, accompanied and in many ways pursued the Foucauldian project well beyond the aims intended by its initiator' (Braidotti 1991: 66). Braidotti's assertion is confirmed in this book: I will be suggesting that while Foucault's work provides a useful analysis of techniques of the self, his own conception of the self, an aesthetics of the self, is not ultimately sufficient to account for 'bisexuality' as it is produced here. The study of the ways in which bisexuality *fails* to be constituted as an identity bound to selfhood, also renders the *cost* of intelligible selfhood, to the self which is produced through a variety of techniques, explicit:

It is . . . a question of the thousand petty humiliations, self-denigrations, deceptions, lies, seductions, cynicisms, bribes, hopes and disappointments, that are the price, the other side, of these 'civilising' processes.   (N. Rose 1996: 322)

It is in this light that the epigraphs which frame this book were chosen and the conclusions at the end of the analysis will be drawn. It is in this light also, that I have attempted to avoid reinstating a one-to-one relation between desire and selfhood and, rather than claim that de Beauvoir is 'really' bisexual, consider what possibilities are engendered by the notion of an identity without a self. I have employed Deleuze and Guattari's understanding of desire to do this because, significantly, they offer a conception of desire where subjectivity is not posited as its ultimate arbiter.

1

Identity and selfhood

It is not unusual in much contemporary, and particularly post-structuralist, social and cultural theory to preface any analysis of 'identity' or 'subjectivity' with the caveat that these are subject positions without essence and, to a greater or lesser extent, to assert that selfhood itself is socially and/or discursively constructed. These claims, which might loosely be situated under the umbrella of 'deconstruction', have been of special interest to those who seek to politicise the self and, in so doing, to expose the naturalised and universalistic notion of the self for what it is.[1] Feminists such as Rosi Braidotti, for instance, argue that it is precisely because 'systems of knowledge and scientific discourse at large' (Braidotti 1994: 152) conflate the specifically White masculine point of view with the generally human standpoint, that a history of Western feminism from Simone de Beauvoir's work in the 1950s through to 1990s feminist post-structuralist theory, has constantly questioned, revised and produced concepts of identity and difference.[2]

While the move away from a notion of identity as fixed and immutable has been welcomed, particularly because it calls attention to differences within and among 'women', it has nevertheless produced its own share of tensions. Feminists have shown that there is much pleasure to be had in 'having' an identity, and that sometimes having an identity, or passing as a particular identity, is not a question of pleasures, but of life and death (Phelan 1993). Patricia Waugh (1992) notes that the deconstruction of concepts such as identity, history and agency is itself a privilege; they must exist before they can be dismantled. While broadly in favour of the destabilisation of identity, Braidotti herself has also noted that: 'contemporary philosophical discussions on the death of the knowing subject . . . have the immediate effect of concealing and undermining the attempts of women to find a theoretical voice of their own . . . in order to deconstruct the subject one must first have gained the right to speak as one' (Braidotti quoted in Benhabib 1995a: 32). Waugh and Seyla Benhabib also point out that post-modern theories are themselves not free of the 'patriarchal metanarratives' (Waugh 1992: 199) which they seek to deconstruct: 'it [should] be important to note right at the outset that much of the post-modernist critique of Western metaphysics itself proceeds under the spell of a metanarrative, namely . . . that "Western metaphysics has been under the spell of the 'metaphysics of presence' at least since Plato . . ."' (Benhabib 1995a: 24). Nevertheless, the problems with, and within, these theories might not necessarily have a bearing on the question of whether feminism should or should not build alliances in this area. Alice Jardine for example, argues that it would be a 'fatal mistake' (Jardine 1985: 257) to dismiss modernity entirely since it offers a number of theoretical concepts which may be useful to feminist theories and practices. Elizabeth Grosz too, suggests that feminists should acknowledge rather than disavow 'patriarchal frameworks, methods, and presumptions' and, further, that it is the '*immersion* [of feminism] in patriarchal practices (including those surrounding the production of theory) [which] is the condition of its effective critique of and movement beyond them' (Grosz 1995: 57).

The 'deconstruction' of identity then, raises a number of issues for feminists and has forced further reflection on the concept of 'feminism' itself, as well as on the category 'women' which is usually assumed to be its foundation. For example: although the act of deconstruction – and especially the deconstruction of the notion of an 'essence' of identity – has been acknowledged to have 'radical' implications (not least because it reveals that processes of knowledge production, and knowledges themselves, are not neutral), it is also the case that identity and selfhood remain the privileged terrain from which a politics can be articulated (such as the identity 'woman', for example, in feminist politics).[3] In response to this paradox, Gayatri Spivak has suggested that although 'it is absolutely on target to take a stand against the discourses of essentialism . . . strategically we cannot' (Spivak 1984/5: 184). And indeed, the value of strategic essentialism was recently illustrated when a number of anti-gay politicians and activists in America revealed themselves to be eager to situate homosexual identities in the arena of voluntary choice rather than biological essence:

The response of antigay politicians and activists to the recent wave of biological reports on sexual orientation has been a uniform 'It ain't so!' When former Vice President Dan Quayle was asked in 1992 about the brain and genetic studies, he said 'My viewpoint is that it's more of a choice than a biological situation . . . it is a wrong choice.'   (LeVay 1996: 249)

If homosexuality is a choice, rather than an inherent essence, then it may also be figured as a 'wrong' choice (as Dan Quayle puts it). A further implication here is that, *as a choice* (rather than a biological or genetic attribute), homosexuality may be 'unchosen'. Biological essentialism – and the assertion of an identity which cannot be wilfully 'detached' from the self – may therefore be used to shield lesbians, gays and bisexuals from the wave of anti-gay discrimination. As culture and choice are themselves deployed as essences, biology and genetics are transformed from that which oppresses to that which can protect homosexuals.[4]

It is in the face of such stark and reductive dismissals of identity once its 'essence' – whatever form that essence might take[5] – has been disputed, and in an attempt to maintain *both* an anti-humanist position *and* some working notion of 'identity', that some feminist theorists have turned their attention to Michel Foucault's work. In the short but important article 'What is enlightenment?' (Foucault 1991a), Foucault outlines the reasons for his rejection of humanism and situates his own work against it. Although arguing that 'not . . . everything that has ever been linked with humanism is to be rejected' (Foucault 1991a: 44), he is critical of the way that humanism, leaning 'on certain conceptions of man' (1991a: 44) – such as the conception that human consciousness is 'the original subject of all historical development' (Foucault quoted in Deleuze 1988: 21) – subsequently colours and justifies these assumptions 'to which it is, after all, obliged to take recourse' (ibid.). Nevertheless, while Foucault argues that the subject cannot be understood to be the originary source of discourse, this stance does not lead him to dispense entirely with an analysis of identity and selfhood. On the contrary, in what has become known as his genealogical phase (Foucault 1991b), he addresses the production of subjectivity and argues that discourse is constitutive not only of statements but of the subject itself, as both the target and object of power. In other words, the speaking subject, as a discursive site, is implicated in the very same power relationships that allow the theoretical text to function.

It is this redefinition of discourse, where discourse constitutes the bridge between the material and the theoretical (Braidotti 1991: 78–9, 88–9), which has been one of the most productive and significant features of Foucault's work in the context of post-structuralist feminist theory. For this reason, it is worth considering it in more detail.

Foucault's neo-materialism

The shift from the textual to the material corporeality of the subject, Deleuze argues, begins when Foucault focuses his attention not just on 'the primacy of the statement in knowledge' (Deleuze 1988: 33), as in *The Archaeology of Knowledge* (1992a), but also on 'the form of the visible, as opposed to the form of whatever can be articulated' (Deleuze 1988: 32).[6] In *Discipline and Punish* (Foucault 1979b) for example, the penal code is understood as that which *articulates* criminality, while the prison itself makes the criminal *visible* and itself constitutes a visibility, the Panopticon: 'a visual assemblage and a luminous environment' (Deleuze 1988: 32). Hence the visible, a further dimension of discourse, does not refer simply to what is, literally, 'seeable' (such as the material form of the prison or empirical bodies), but is also productive of what we are and are not able to visualize: 'For example, at the beginning of the nineteenth century masses and populations become visible, and emerge into the light of day' (ibid.). In this respect, unformed matter is formed into substances, which 'are revealed by visibility' (Deleuze 1988: 77).

According to Deleuze then, *Discipline and Punish* marks a turning point after which the visible and articulable are linked – by knowledge as well as by power, which are themselves bound to each other. Knowledge does not appear where power relations are suspended; rather, all knowledge expresses or implies a power relation. Because power has no essence (no independent form or content), its domain is strategic: power is a *strategy*, or non-formalised relation, whose effects are attributed 'to dispositions, manoeuvres, tactics, techniques, functionings' (Foucault quoted in Deleuze 1988: 25). While the domain of power is *strategic*, that of knowledge, by contrast, is *stratic* (Deleuze 1988: 112). Knowledge arranges, regulates and normativises. Concerned with forms, it forms substances (formed matter, which is revealed by visibilities) and formalises functions (which are revealed by statements).

Foucault develops the notion of a 'diagram' which is 'a display of the relations between forces which constitute power' (Deleuze 1988: 36). Two forms of regulation, description-scenes and statement-curves (which correspond to two systems: that of light and that of language, visibles and articulables), realise the diagram of forces. Thus:

> The *diagram* is no longer an auditory or visual archive but a map, a cartography that is coextensive with the whole social field . . . It is a machine that is almost blind and mute, even though it makes others see and speak.   (Deleuze 1988: 34)

It is the very blindness and muteness of power, and that it does not 'reveal' anything of itself (any hidden depth or meaning), which incites *us* to see and to speak.[7] This is because in itself power is only 'virtual, potential, unstable' (Deleuze 1988: 37); it is affirmed, realised, or 'integrated' (ibid.) only when it is carried out. And conversely: 'Seeing and Speaking are

always already completely caught up with power relations which they presuppose and actualise' (Deleuze 1988: 82). Power is therefore productive
before it is repressive, it may incite, induce, seduce and provoke:

> What makes power hold good, what makes it accepted, is simply the fact that it
> doesn't weigh on us as a force that says no, but that it traverses and produces things,
> it induces pleasure, forms knowledge, produces discourse. It needs to be considered
> as a productive network which runs through the whole social body, much more than
> as a negative instance whose function is repression.   (Foucault 1991c: 61)

Foucault's redefinition of power as productive, as a microphysics which
informs the whole social field, coupled with his emphasis on the way that
knowledge forms substances as well as formalises functions, lends what
Braidotti calls a 'neo-materialis[t]' (Braidotti 1991: 265) aspect to his work:
'materialism [is redefined] in such a way as to include the bodily materiality of the subject' (Braidotti 1991: 89). The term *assujettissement* describes
subjectification as both an active (subject of) and passive (subjected to)
process connected to power and knowledge through discourse. The
definition of truth too, is extended. Not only a system which produces and
regulates statements, truth is now inextricably linked to power: '"Truth" is
linked in a circular relation with systems of power which produce and
sustain it, and to effects of power which it induces and which extends it. A
"regime" of truth' (Foucault 1991c: 74).

This redefinition of discourse enables Foucault to consider the material
effects of processes of subjectification while at the same time, because the
subject is understood to be produced through a matrix of power relations,
displaces the concept of an essential and transcendent self, a humanist self
which 'runs in its empty sameness throughout the course of history'
(Foucault 1991c: 59). From now on, the self is perceived to be the site of an
historical problem where even the question 'What kinds of human beings
have we become?' (N. Rose 1996: 294) represents a historically and culturally specific project. Lois McNay suggests that in the final phase of
Foucault's work: 'Established patterns of individualization are rejected
through the interrogation of what are held to be universal, necessary forms
of identity in order to show the place that the contingent and the historically specific occupy within them' (McNay 1994: 145).

It is this focus on the self and particularly processes of individualisation,
without recourse to humanism, which enables Foucault, as Elspeth Probyn
argues, to develop 'a mode of theory that is not organized around individuals but that with force offers us a space where we can take seriously how
we are individuated' (Probyn 1993: 136). Thus for example, Foucault
reveals that the author appears in discourse at a 'privileged moment of

individualization in the history of ideas, knowledge, literature, philosophy and the sciences' (Foucault 1991d: 101). This means not that an act of volition on the part of the individual produces that individual as an author, but rather that the subject position 'Author' contributes to the production of individuality (see chapter 3 especially). As Rosalyn Diprose says, 'the operation of power is ahead of conscious intervention' (Diprose 1994: 29). Hence even if the individual were to attempt to overturn the 'traditional image' (Foucault 1981: 59) of the author, by setting out, for example, 'to write a text on the horizon of which a possible oeuvre is prowling', it would still be from 'some new author-position' that this 'trembling outline' (ibid.) would be cut. Critiquing reflective Cartesian consciousness, Foucault displaces the centrality of the self in favour of 'a process of knowledge production where . . . the code precedes and is independent of the message' (Braidotti 1991: 89).

That power relations can penetrate the body without first having been mediated by consciousness indicates that Foucault's analysis of subjectivity extends further than the analysis of the stratic or formalised relations of knowledge and the relations between forces (power). Foucault identifies a third axis, 'the axis of ethics' (Foucault 1991a: 48), which is folded force and which constitutes subjectivity:

What I want to show is how power relations can materially penetrate the body in depth, without depending even on the mediation of the subject's own representation. If power takes hold on the body, this isn't through its having first been interiorized in people's consciousness.   (Foucault 1980b: 186)

Whereas in his earlier works Foucault defined the subject as derivative of the statement, in his later work the 'interiority' of the subject, and indeed the subject itself, is understood as an in-folding of the outside or the folded inside of the outside. The fold, therefore, is not something other than the outside, nor does it reflect the outside. Instead, it is 'precisely the inside *of* the outside' (Deleuze 1988: 97), a 'doubling' movement whereby the fold relates 'back to itself' and in this folding back, a relation to the self emerges ('subjectivation'). In other words, subjectification is *constitutive of interiority*. Deleuze writes:

This is what the Greeks did: they folded force, even though it still remained in force. They made it relate back to itself. Far from ignoring interiority, individuality or subjectivity they invented the subject, but only as a derivative or the product of a 'subjectivation'.   (Deleuze 1988: 101)

How did the Greeks do this, what Deleuze calls 'subjectivation'? In his analysis of Greco-Roman philosophy in the first two centuries AD, of

Christian spirituality and of the monastic principles developed in the fourth and fifth centuries of the late Roman Empire (Foucault 1988b), Foucault demonstrates: 'the *problematizations* through which being offers itself to be, necessarily, thought – and the *practices* on the basis of which these problematizations are formed' (Foucault quoted in Probyn 1993: 122). In other words, Foucault makes explicit the way that the self under examination is itself the *result* of the processes which attempt to explore and/or describe it. Confession is no longer the only instrument which produces truth (as implied in the first volume of *The History of Sexuality*);[8] Foucault turns his attention to the *variety* of techniques which enable individuals to affect 'their own bodies, their own souls, their own thought, their own conduct' (Foucault quoted in Probyn 1993: 120). Hence subjects not only perform operations on their own bodies and thoughts, but also, in so doing, transform and modify themselves. I will outline some of these operations briefly, since the implications *for* the self, of techniques – such as self-reflection, writing and confession – *of* the self, will be examined throughout this book.

Greco-Roman and early Christian techniques of the self

In Greek and Roman texts the injunction to care for the self is 'a *real activity* and not just an attitude' (Foucault 1988b: 24. My emphasis.). The Greeks developed a 'mirror relation' (Foucault 1988b: 31) to the soul, believing that the truth lay within it, while the Stoics subjectificated truth through a mnemotechnical formula: they memorised their teachers' statements and converted them into rules of conduct. The constant writing activity undertaken during this period served to intensify and widen the experience of the self. Foucault argues therefore, that writing about the self was an established practice long before either the Reformation or romanticism.

Although the method through which the Stoics subjectificated truth was different to that of the Greeks, for them too, these practices constituted a permanent principle of action, which were, additionally, subject to examination: 'Is this truth assimilated enough to become ethics so that we can behave as we must when an event presents itself?' (Foucault 1988b: 36). Notably, in what Foucault describes as a 'pre-Freudian machine of censorship' (Foucault 1988b: 38), the self was to watch over and weigh up its own representations of its thoughts in order that they may be controlled. In a similar vein, monastic techniques of the self required the self to scrutinise its thoughts continually (in order that they might always be directed toward God) and, in order to purify them, to continually verbalise them to a higher authority: 'scrutiny is based on the idea of a secret concupiscence. [. . .] It implies that there is something hidden in ourselves and that we are always in a self-illusion which hides the secret' (Foucault 1988b: 46). Hence confession becomes a mark of truth (Foucault 1988b: 48).

While Stoic care of the self was a private matter, for the Christian it was a public event: one was obliged to disclose one's faults, temptations and desires 'either to God or to others in the community and hence to bear public or private witness against oneself' (Foucault 1988b: 40). Penitential behaviour included not only self-recognition and self-revelation but also self-punishment: 'To prove suffering, to show shame, to make visible humility and exhibit modesty – these are the main features of punishment' (Foucault 1988b: 42). Two paradoxes emerge: firstly, renunciation of the self was possible only through a knowledge of the self and secondly, confession, while necessary in order to rub out sin, simultaneously exposed 'the true sinful being of the sinner' (ibid.). The point of confession therefore, was to break with one's past identity and impose the truth through violent rupture and dissociation: 'Self-revelation is at the same time self-destruction' (Foucault 1988b: 43). Foucault argues however, that a 'decisive break' (a discontinuity)[9] occurs in the eighteenth century, after which time techniques of the self no longer require a renunciation of the self, but are instead employed to 'constitute, positively, a new self' (Foucault 1988b: 49).

Not only did the Greeks invent the relation to the self, they also linked this relation to oneself to sexuality (Deleuze 1988: 102). Indeed, it is the concentration of normative knowledge around sexuality that indicates that it is an especially dense transfer point of power. Sexuality gives rise to 'scientia sexualis' and all the concomitant processes of individuation (for example, the identification of the homosexual as a species) and also ties the subject 'to his own identity by a conscience or self-knowledge' (Deleuze 1988: 103).[10] Hence while Foucault does not identify sexuality *itself* as a technique of the self (I will return to this point below), he does suggest that, in the modern age, the processes of subjectification, and especially individuation, that take place in the search for the 'truth' of the self are often anchored around the search for the truth of sexuality:

Between each of us and our sex, the West has placed a never-ending demand for truth: it is up to us to extract the truth of sex, since this truth is beyond its grasp; it is up to sex to tell us our truth, since sex is what holds it in darkness . . . A double petition, in that we are compelled to know how things are with it, while it is suspected of knowing how things are with us.   (Foucault 1990a: 77–8)

What is significant here, and central to the thesis developed throughout this book, is Foucault's emphasis on the way that sexuality and selfhood are understood to be entangled in each other. The 'double petition' to which he refers implies that sexual identities, in the modern era, are bound to the self, a self which is (principally) intelligible precisely because it is both possessed of, and possessed by, sexuality.

Bisexuality

I want to pause here, briefly, to illustrate the ways in which the constitution of selfhood and processes of individualisation, in contemporary Western societies, may be closely tied to sexuality – and specifically, in the following examples, to bisexuality. I choose to focus on bisexual identities firstly because, although I will be questioning the assumed relation between (bi)sexuality and selfhood throughout this book, it should nevertheless be acknowledged, at the outset, that individuals who identify, and are identified as, 'bisexual', can and do 'exist'. And secondly, it is largely because this existence has only very recently been acknowledged, celebrated, and also criticised, that bisexuality is particularly interesting, and yields itself to rich analysis (as much of the current literature on the subject indicates). In a paper given at a recent seminar series, Merl Storr reminded her audience that it was, as far as she could remember, only in 1992 that the first academic conference in the United Kingdom included the word 'bisexual' in its subtitle. At that conference however, bisexuals found themselves:

having to defend not just the viability of bisexual politics or theory but the very existence of bisexuality as an adult sexual orientation: 'bisexuality just *isn't* a sexual orientation', Elizabeth Wilson blithely informed one bisexual woman who challenged her from the floor.   (Storr 1997a: 2. *See also* Hemmings 1993)

By contrast, today, judging by the numerous publications on bisexuality (see Hemmings 1997, Morris and Storr 1997 and Storr 1997a for summaries of this literature) – and especially Marjorie Garber's massive tome *Vice Versa: Bisexuality and the Eroticism of Everyday Life* (1996) – the 'existence' of bisexuality as a 'viable' sexual orientation, whether sympathetically received or not, is largely accepted.

So what might the 'truth', as Foucault puts it, of bisexuality be? Some researchers have implied that it is a 'riddle' (Weinberg, Williams and Pryor 1994: 4) (which presumably requires solving). Although this position suggests an ignorance of bisexuality, or even ignorances, given that knowledge and power are conjoined in discourse, no knowledge of bisexuality can be 'pure' or 'free' from the power/knowledge relations that produce it.[11] Indeed, Eve Sedgwick contends that 'far from being pieces of the originary dark, [ignorances] are produced by and correspond to particular knowledges and circulate as part of particular regimes of truth' (Sedgwick 1994:

25). To suggest that bisexuality is a riddle then, is not to place it beyond knowledges of sexuality nor is solving the riddle of bisexuality beyond the fecund propagation of truths. Indeed, the notion of bisexuality as *the* riddle might be no more than another exploitation of *the* secret which must be spoken of *ad infinitum* (Foucault 1990a: 35).

Given the riddled status of bisexuality, it is tempting to invoke a conspiracy of oppression *par excellence*, tempting to try to 'liberate' bisexuality from veils of misrepresentation, misrecognition or 'misinformation' (Blasingame 1992: 49) and to 'expose' its hidden truth. Various examples of this sentiment are manifest in literature on bisexuality (Hutchins and Kaahumanu 1991; Weise 1992; Eadie 1993). Here, the constituted (bisexual) self is a given, even if it is presently invisible: 'invisibility is, for the present, how we [bisexuals] experience oppression' (Baker 1992: 266). This central presupposition – that the bisexual self, although invisible, öbjectively 'exists' – forces the question as to how such oppression has come about. A narrative subsequently emerges, wherein bisexuality's apparently singular and unique history (Baker 1992: 265) is perceived to offer a radical and emancipatory potential which other sexuality identities, including queer, do not: 'Bisexuality alone calls these assumptions ["the dichotomization between politics and desire"] into question' (Weise 1992: xi); the 'bisexual community would pose a significant and unique challenge to the dual gender system and the limitations inherent in compulsory heteromonosexuality' (Baker 1992: 266); 'The queer community was established on a set of norms of what constituted queer . . . If we only replicate the system that has oppressed us, then are we as progressive as we would like to think we are?' (Blasingame 1992: 49).

These perspectives suggest that, although the self-identified bisexual, or bisexuality, stands in an isolated, and even lonely, position with respect to lesbian, gay and queer theory and politics, it is precisely this distance which has enabled it to maintain an autonomy from the tarnishing processes, authorities and legitimisations which enable 'other' identities to be adopted. This is an approach to bisexuality which implicitly relies on a narrativisation of being: the (bisexual) self is understood to run continuously throughout history, while a 'core', very often perceived to be individuality, remains 'static' even though external events change, and even if external events act 'on' the self in some way.[12] Inevitably bringing contemporary presuppositions about the self to its analysis, the existence of the bisexual subject is assumed, where*after* the theory seeks 'to recreate the conditions that have made its existence possible' (Simondon 1992: 297).

Rather than try to understand what the (bisexual) self 'is' or how it came to be what it 'is' through time, an alternative trajectory will be fashioned here which seeks to understand the '*a priori* of our existence as subjects' (N. Rose 1992: 161). Beginning from the Foucauldian premise that it is the processes of subjectification (the processes by which force is folded), rather than the subject itself, which has a history, I will be taking the self to be no more (or even, no less) than an aggregate of the very techniques which seek to describe it.[13] No form of bisexuality therefore, can be understood in isolation from the techniques which constitute selfhood; bisexuality is not 'free' from the authorisations and legitimisations which enable identities to be claimed. Indeed, the very ability to lay claim to the identity 'bisexual' suggests that bisexuality is entangled in processes of subjectification. As Foucault writes in *The Use of Pleasure,* his analysis 'of desiring man is situated at the point where an archaelogy [*sic*] of problematizations and a genealogy of practices of the self intersect' (Foucault 1992b: 13). Thus both knowledge (problematisations) and experience (practices) of the self, as well as the knowledge and experience that forms a relationship between the two, are inculcated, organised and acted upon by the self itself. And because problematisations and practices of the self fold force – and this is why Foucault's description of the fold is particularly important in the context of this book – they are themselves *productive of* selfhood.

This production of selfhood is especially evident in some of the late 1980s and early 1990s literature on bisexuality. Many of the articles in anthologies such as *Bi Any Other Name* (Hutchins and Kaahumanu 1991) and *Closer to Home* (Weise 1992) are, as partial or full confessions, constitutive of a subject who declares the truth of the self. In the following extract for example, a number of techniques of the self, some of which are described by Foucault (see above), are deployed by the individual in order to construct the self as 'bisexual':

It was not easy for any of us. My wife and I went through many traumas and sleepless nights coming to terms with my bisexuality. I experienced feelings of guilt and other emotional issues . . . For a long time I was unfulfilled in my bisexuality. One day I decided to change all that. I contacted the local gay and lesbian newsletter, and with their encouragement, wrote an article about my bisexuality. I received over sixty supportive, affirmative letters and phone calls . . . Today . . . I have a relationship with a bisexual man who is supportive of my chosen lifestyle. He and my wife are friends. I feel freed of my own bondage and this has freed me creatively. I am writing more and more, and with greater clarity . . . I now wear my bisexuality as a badge of honor and no longer carry it as a liability . . . I believe that it is time to become more visible, to have a group identity and pride.   (Brewer 1991: 142–3)

Here, guilt and remorse are relieved, as in the early Christian techniques of the self, through public confession. This confession does not contribute to the renunciation of the self however, but rather serves to 'constitute, positively, a new self' (Foucault 1988b: 49), and marks a transition from shame to 'pride'. Another key feature which enables this shift is the empathy and mutual recognition of others which contributes not just to the identification of one bisexual identity, but to the production of a 'bisexual community', a community which demands recognition and visibility. The 'freedom' that confession occasions is perceived to bring with it still more 'freedom' (for the author of the extract) to magnify the self through writing (a well-documented technique of the self). The confession itself is a narrative which brings all these techniques together to produce a 'bisexual' self.

This extract is indicative of *only a tendency* in the literature on bisexuality. Nevertheless, the tendency to claim bisexuality as a 'legitimate', if not 'authentic', subject position is a potent one, and one which I would argue sets limits for bisexuality. While the extract clearly illustrates Nikolas Rose's claim that 'in making our subjectivity the principle of our personal lives, our ethical systems, and our political evaluations, [we believe] that we are, freely, choosing our freedom' (N. Rose 1989: 11), at the same time, the *costs* of the 'freedom' to 'be' bisexual are also clear. *Assujettisement* (whereby the self is actively subject of and passively subjected to regimes of power/knowledge) serves only to bind the self all the more tightly into discursive networks of knowledge and power. Processes of stratification – where, endowed with an origin, interiority and depth, a subject is produced through the positions made available by discourse – give rise to what Deleuze would call 'molar' entities, entities whose forces are congealed into binary oppositions, such as those of men and women or homosexual and heterosexual. For Deleuze and Guattari: 'Bisexuality is no better a concept than the separateness of the sexes. It is as deplorable to miniaturize, internalize the binary machine as it is to exacerbate it; it does not extricate us from it' (Deleuze and Guattari 1988: 276). Deleuze and Guattari appear to confine bisexuality to androgyny and then suggest that it holds within it the two molar entities of male and female.[14] Although the author of the above extract is not referring to bisexuality-as-androgyny, it is arguable that the account nevertheless sediments desire into an identity which binds and folds force to produce the 'bisexual' subject and the interiority conferred on it.[15]

Jonathon Dollimore – considering the often hostile responses from parts of the lesbian and gay community to those who would call themselves bisexual – describes the 'psychic, social and political investments' (Dollimore 1996: 524) that impel the consolidation of identities (a consolidation that may be as compelling, as the above extract illustrates, for bisexuals as for lesbians and gay men):

identity politics are often most invested when the fortunes of a minority have improved, but not securely; in some cases identity remains precariously dependent upon that improvement, and in a context where hostility not only remains, but has actually intensified, in part as a response to the increased social visibility which the emerging identity entails.[16] Identity politics are inseparable from a consolidation of this ground recently gained and precariously held. Such consolidation is inevitably also a struggle for survival, which includes a struggle for the means of continuing visibility.   (Dollimore 1996: 524)

It may be the privileging of identity in relation to other sexual identifications that makes the move to claim an 'authentic' bisexual iden-tity especially attractive. Nevertheless, bisexual theory and politics has gone through, and continues to go through, a considerable number of twists and turns. Morris and Storr point out that debates around bisexuality are no longer concerned primarily with 'speak[ing] out' (Morris and Storr 1997: 1), but are also characterised by a variety of features which include a val-orisation of 'fluidity' and a desire to interrogate some of the problems invoked by bisexuality in the very moments that it appears to be most radical. Thus while it should be acknowledged that confessional 'personal stories' – the title of the second section of *Bisexual Horizons* (Rose and Stevens 1996) – still have a highly visible (and understandably significant) place in the literature, it is also the case that recent theoretical interventions seek to destabilise some of the assumptions on which Western selfhood rests in elegant and sophisticated ways. Maria Pramaggiore's and Donald Hall's (1996) introductions to the edited collection *Representing Bisexualities: Subjects and Cultures of Fluid Desire,* for example, deploy the very term which is frequently used to berate bisexuality and bisexuals as a trope through which to question the relations between gender, sexuality, sexual objects and desire:

Fence-sitting – an epithet predicated on the presumption of the superiority of a temporally based single sexual partnership – is a practice that refuses the restrictive formulas that define gender according to binary categories, that associate one gender or one sexuality with a singularly gendered object choice, and that equate sexual practices with a sexual identity.   (Pramaggiore 1996: 3)

The productive force of an 'epistemology of the fence' (D. Hall 1996: 11) is explored in various guises throughout the collection. Many of these essays trace not what bisexuality 'is' (they are not concerned with a narrativisation of being), but the effects of the term within discourse: what does (and what can) bisexuality (be made to) 'do'? Similarly, the introduction to the Bi Academic Intervention's (BAI) (1997) collection *The Bisexual Imaginary: Bisexuality and Representation* explicitly draws attention to, and theorises, the specifically *ironic* use of 'derogatory' terms, such as 'fence-sitting', in recent bisexual theory and activism. Irony, they argue, 'is a particular – though by no means exclusive – bisexual approach to representation' (BAI 1997: 10), enabling well-worn sexual tropes to be recycled and regenerated for a bisexual culture which suffers from a poverty of images. The San Francisco bisexual magazine *Anything That Moves* for example:

plays on both biphobic and bi-positive discourses. Here bisexuals are able to take a common insult and make it 'mean' differently: it's a joke, pleasurable and playful for many bisexuals, but open to abuse, misunderstanding or even incomprehension from outside.
(ibid.)

Significantly, the use of irony offers a path to negotiating *both* the impulse to claim an authentic identity *and* to deconstruct the very concepts of authenticity and identity. 'Ironic authenticity' thus represents something of a signature tune for bisexuality as it struggles to find a place on the broader map of contemporary sexualities: 'such an identity is "on the edge" of authenticity and artificiality . . . The bisexual imaginary is both iconic (setting up an image) and ironic (destabilizing that image), without ever having to choose between the two' (BAI 1997: 11). As in Pramaggiore's and Hall's book, this collection is characterised by a focus on the discursive efficacy of 'bisexuality' – in genealogy (Storr (1997b) argues that the term 'bi-sexuality', in Havelock Ellis's and Richard Von Krafft-Ebing's work, illustrates the mutually constitutive role of sex and 'race'), in literature (see for example Ann Kaloski (1997) on the position of bisexuality in Nancy Toder's *Choices*) and in visual culture (Jo Eadie (1997), for instance, demonstrates how bisexual characters, in two contemporary films, 'carry' anxiety).

Although Dollimore does not direct his criticisms of bisexual 'postmodern' theorising (what he calls 'wishful theory') at the collections that I have mentioned here, he might nevertheless claim of these too, that they posit bisexuality as '[u]nstable, yes, but not in a self-threatening way: this is a liberating, dynamic state of unfixity, and one which seems oddly secure in its very instability' (Dollimore 1996: 526). There is some truth in this insofar as bisexuality, while frequently perceived as a bug that disrupts various dualisms, is often (although not always) considered to be an identity tied to a self (a self which is produced, in large part, through the very identity which is apparently disruptive). However, this is not Dollimore's concern. Instead, he 'warns' that:

when identity is destabilized by desire we should not underestimate the potential cost. It is then that we can become flooded by apprehensions of loss endemic to our culture and which it is partly the purpose of identity politics to protect us against.

In this sense too, identity can be as much about surviving, even evading desire, as about expressing it.   (Dollimore 1996: 531)

Dollimore urges 'us' not to underestimate the cost of the loss of identity. But perhaps it is the very high costs of identification itself which are themselves underestimated. Nikolas Rose suggests that in contemporary modern Western society: 'we are *condemned* to make a project out of our identity' (N. Rose 1992: 153. My emphasis.). While this may sound like a reincarnation of the existential 'burden' of freedom, Rose is in fact arguing, like Foucault, that although 'the great promise or the great hope of the eighteenth century . . . lay in the simultaneous and proportionate growth of individuals with respect to one another' (Foucault 1991a: 47), the concomitant growth in 'the acquisition of capabilities and the struggle for freedom' (Foucault 1991a: 47–8) has in many instances been matched by an intensification of disciplinary knowledge and power. This point is not necessarily best illustrated through an analysis of texts which are directly concerned with the issue of sexuality (*especially* if they claim that (bi)sexuality destabilises the self), but of those which implicitly – and sometimes (although rarely) explicitly – engage with the production of intelligible and plausible selfhood. It is here that high costs of subjectification are made clear.

Simone de Beauvoir

I have argued that (sexual) identities do not emerge in isolation (in and of themselves), but are rather produced in conjunction with a variety of cultural formations which are linked to the self. While different practices enjoin the self to develop a different relation to her or himself, these practices 'are neither merely *different versions* of a self, nor do they *sum into* a self' (N. Rose 1997: 136). Thus 'individuality', 'subjectivity', 'identity' (and even materiality, as the following chapter will show) are all understood to be contingent techniques of the self none of which either work in identical ways or make up the totality of the self under study. Individuality in particular, and the concomitant processes of individualisation, are key practices whose longstanding endurance has been documented by a variety of theorists (including Michel Foucault, Nikolas Rose, Zygmunt Bauman, and feminists, such as Sandra Bartky, Celia Lury and Elspeth Probyn). It is because of this emphasis on the individual in discourses of selfhood and sexuality that it is appropriate to consider not the assumed or taken-for-granted individuality of the (bisexual) self, but the way that the production of bisexuality is bound up (or not) with the *construction* of individuality.

The significance of the figure of Simone de Beauvoir to the analysis of bisexuality here is now apparent. 'De Beauvoir' is employed as a vehicle through which to explore some of the techniques which constitute the self: *individuality, femininity, responsibility* (for herself and for others) and *the ability and willingness to choose* are among the techniques which render 'de Beauvoir' intelligible. Not only these, but shame, self-knowledge and con- science are also examples of techniques through which de Beauvoir's inter- iority is folded, and the self ascribed to her rendered stable (such that the relations between forces are fixed and regularised). As noted above, Foucault (and Deleuze) take the notion of folded force as a general definition of the self[17] – I will also draw on this concept throughout the book. In short, with the exception of parts of chapter 7 and chapter 8, the majority of my argu- ment will focus on the *techniques* which fold force and which are productive of the selfhood, and particularly the individuality, attributed to de Beauvoir.

A brief note here then, about the concept of 'techniques of the self', which I will be employing in two different capacities. My first use of the term is closely allied to Foucault's own understanding, where 'techniques' refer to specific practices (such as confession or diary writing) which are deployed by individuals upon their own selves in order to transform them- selves (towards a desired state, such as wisdom, virtue, authenticity). This is the effect of self on self, as Deleuze would have it (Deleuze 1988: 97–105). I am also however, referring to the way that *narratives* are employed as a technique through which the individual is rendered (and renders itself) intelligible. Although Foucault draws attention to the writing activity undertaken by the Stoics, as well as the role of confession in early Christianity, he does not explicitly comment on the link between these tech- niques and the emergence of narrative as a notable technique of the self. Nikolas Rose however, argues that the minutely detailed documentation of spiritual pilgrimages, and of 'the lives and writings of those such as St Bonaventura, Meister Eckhardt, Thomas à Kempis and others' (N. Rose 1989: 219), were early examples of narratives which are today found, for example, in the 'modern literature of psychotherapeutics' (ibid.). This sug- gests that narrative emerged alongside the early Stoic and Christian tech- niques of writing and confession as a *techne* which was 'crucial in the development of the modern Western self' (N. Rose 1989: 218).

While the Stoics' writings and Christian confessions point to an early use of narrative in the production of selfhood, Huck Gutman argues that: 'it is with Rousseau that a genuinely modern temper . . . first comes clearly into view' (Gutman 1988: 101). Saint Augustine's *Confessions*, Gutman argues, although 'an enormously important work in that history of the gradual emergence of a visible self' (Gutman 1988: 103), is concerned less with Augustine's own spirit and more with the spirit of God. Rousseau's

Confessions, by contrast, are concerned entirely with the development of an individualised self in its autonomy:

the reader of the *Confessions* understands that its immense significance, its aura of newness, has to do with its documentation of the emergence of that subject which was theretofore largely hidden: 'For a long time ordinary individuality – the everyday individuality of everybody – remained below the threshold of description'.

(Gutman 1988: 116)

One of the means by which Rousseau 'lower[s] this threshold' (ibid.), and establishes a relation to the self, is through narrative. Not only, Gutman argues, does Rousseau 'create himself as a character with a history' (Gutman 1988: 106) but he also recognises 'that it is in time, through temporal succession, that the self comes to be what it is' (Gutman 1988: 101).

History and temporality are two features which Paul Ricoeur identifies as central to narrative identity (Ricoeur 1991b). Ricoeur's theory of narrative identity will be exploited in chapters 3 and 4 to explore the way that the question 'who is de Beauvoir?' is answered and how, in that answer, the sexual-narrative-identity ascribed to de Beauvoir is constituted. Chapter 3 will look at those events which are perceived to warrant enumeration and which are subsequently configured into a plot such that de Beauvoir's story is rendered meaningful and her individuality established. However, assuming that a 'meaningful life is one that aspires to the coherency of a story with a plot' (White 1991: 144), chapter 4 will consider the implications of and for events which are *not* incorporated into the narrative of de Beauvoir's life. In this context Ricoeur's distinction between identity-as-selfhood and identity-as-sameness is especially apt because it illustrates that, where bisexuality is concerned, identity-as-selfhood is not always a given.[18]

Within the framework of narrative then, particular presuppositions about what it is to be 'human', particular beliefs and understandings, are employed to constitute the self *as* a plausible self. Such narratives are historically and culturally specific.[19] I would suggest that in Western society today, for example, narratives which relate (to) sexual identity are especially common. This may partly be a result of the women's and the gay and lesbian liberation movements and partly because of the high profile of the psychotherapeutic industry throughout the course of the twentieth century (Plummer 1995). 'Stories' about one's (sexual) practices (and fantasies, desires, etc.) are told and recounted (in more or less literal or intentional ways) in order that the self may perceive itself (and be perceived) to 'have' a particular sexual identity. Hence although Foucault does not refer to sexuality *itself* as a technique of the self, insofar as sexuality is often – through narrative – construed as a problem upon which the self consciously reflects, and a practice which is carried out by the self (sometimes, as chapter 6 will demonstrate, in order to transform itself), sexuality might itself increasingly be understood to be just such a (narrative) technique.

There are two reasons for choosing the figure of Simone de Beauvoir specifically as the cipher through which to study representations of bisexuality and the construction of selfhood. Firstly, de Beauvoir has had a 'visible' persona in the West (particularly Western Europe) for a large part of this century. She was a central figure in two cultural movements (existentialism and feminism), played an active part in feminist and French (inter)national politics until the end of her life, and continues to be seen, by some, as a French national icon (see chapter 5 especially for an analysis of the perceived relation between de Beauvoir's national identity and her sexuality). Secondly, de Beauvoir was a prolific writer for almost fifty years, reaching not only academic readers but also readers of newspapers, journals and women's magazines. All her major works reached a mass audience (Moi 1994: 74):

Challenging established hierarchies and conventions, they [de Beauvoir's major works] often provoked intensely enraged responses ranging from profound admiration to violent hostility. By producing a highly public persona for their author, her autobiographies added fuel to the controversies.   (ibid.)

The 'controversies' surrounding de Beauvoir's personal life are numerous: she was the ninth woman in France to pass the *agrégation* in philosophy (Moi 1994: 1) and among the first generation of women to attend the *Ecole Normale Supérieure*. She neither married nor had children (although towards the end of her life she adopted Sylvie Le Bon) and, after only a few years teaching, was able to earn an independent living by writing. Her 'open' relationship with Jean-Paul Sartre has been a source of contention almost from the moment it began as, more recently, have her relationships with women.[20] One of the consequences of leading such a colourful and *public* life is that the figure of de Beauvoir has generated an enormous amount of literature not only engaging with her work, but also with her life: in 1994 there were 'over forty full-length studies . . . hundreds of scholarly essays . . . and . . . massive newspaper and magazine coverage' (Moi 1994: 74).

The 'celebrated'/celebrity figure of de Beauvoir therefore, whose life spans most of the twentieth century, appears at the crossroads of feminism, high/low culture, existentialism, the media and the academy. As a (feminist) thinker, and woman who did (or did not, some argue) break with the traditions of femininity, 'de Beauvoir' has been, and continues to be, a productive field of enquiry for writers in many fields (academic and media, as well as popular biography). This is the case even, perhaps especially, when such writers are engaged in a critique of her life and work.

It is important to repeat however, that I am not concerned with the 'truth' of de Beauvoir, with the significance of her relationships (to her), or with the 'reality' of her life. My intentions are not to explore competing representations of de Beauvoir in order that I may 'disclose', after analysing them, the final and authoritative 'truth' of her self. Instead, de Beauvoir is employed as a *cipher* through which well-documented techniques of the self, and particularly techniques pertaining to sexual identity, may be examined. Similarly, existentialism is important here only insofar as commentators understand it to have had a significant role in shaping the self that they ascribe to de Beauvoir. Toril Moi for example, whose book *Simone de Beauvoir: The Making of an Intellectual Woman* (1994) is one of the texts that I explore throughout this analysis,[21] claims that de Beauvoir's belief in existentialism had a number of specific implications for 'her' psyche. In this respect, the perceived role of existentialism in de Beauvoir's life is seen to constitute her in particular ways (see chapter 3 especially). As with de Beauvoir herself then, existentialism *in itself* is not the issue here. My aim is not to discover the 'truth' (of a self), but rather to consider the ways in which truth is produced through discourse and to examine in detail the implications of this production.

So what is produced? I would argue that this book engages with texts which, in exploring and problematising the figure of de Beauvoir, her life and her work, are themselves productive of ways of being. The same may be said of my own analysis and, in this respect, this account is an infinitely regressive study of discourses of sexuality and selfhood. Hence although Foucault suggests that at the horizon of commentary 'there is perhaps nothing but what was at its point of departure – mere recitation' (Foucault 1981: 58), I am more inclined to agree with the notion that it nevertheless allows for 'the (endless) construction of new discourses' (Foucault 1981: 57).[22]

Bisexuality and Simone de Beauvoir

The combined analysis of the discursive production of de Beauvoir and of bisexuality indicates, firstly, that bisexuality, in various forms, has a presence in most of the texts considered here and, as such, may be perceived neither as an aporia nor an absence. Secondly, it confirms that de Beauvoir is constructed as a sexual being – although her sexual identity is only constituted as lesbian or heterosexual. Between these two axioms a number of questions hover: what has the figure of Simone de Beauvoir to do with the bisexualities manifest in the texts if she is not explicitly identified to be, or even implicitly constituted as, 'bisexual'? Is it the case that the 'truth' of bisexuality is not something which de Beauvoir possesses, nor something which she is possessed by? How is it, then, that de Beauvoir's *individuality* is nevertheless important to constructions of bisexuality?

Foucault's analysis of the role of confession and writing in the production of 'truths' and of the way in which techniques of the self are now employed in order to constitute rather than renunciate the self, will be central themes throughout the book. The relation between self-recognition, self-revelation and self-punishment (particularly with regard to shame and remorse) will also be examined throughout, as will the very *public* nature of disclosure. Indeed, it is through the act of imputed disclosure that de Beauvoir is produced as a sexual entity, and through this act that 'her' truth is known (see especially chapter 5). What I will also be concerned with however, are the *kinds* of 'truths' that are able to be extracted from de Beauvoir's confession and, given the specific discursive conditions through which the self is produced, whether it is possible for bisexuality to contain the kernel of 'de Beauvoir's' truth within it.

While many of the techniques of the self which Foucault identifies are relevant to this analysis, the construction of bisexuality and of de Beauvoir is not confined to those identified by him. For instance, although sexuality is understood to be one of the principal ways through which a relation to the self is established, it may not *always* be central. Deleuze suggests that sexuality does not have an exclusive monopoly on assemblages of desire (on assemblages such as the self). In *Dialogues* he writes: 'We do not believe in general that sexuality has the role of an infrastructure in the assemblages of desire . . . No assemblage can be characterised by one flux exclusively' (Deleuze and Parnet 1987: 101). This is not to deny the differentiation by sex in the constitution of the self. Nevertheless, as Rose argues, all relations to the self, including sexuality, must be open to historical investigation (N. Rose 1997: 138). Presuppositions about the self in general (whether they refer to sexuality or not) appear to preclude bisexuality. Chapters 3 and 4 for example, will consider the way that the narrative structure in four accounts of de Beauvoir's life and work produces an effect of continuity between past and present and how this serves *both* to ascribe individuality to de Beauvoir *and* to preclude her from being produced as 'bisexual'. Chapter 5 explores the implications of the presupposition that sexual identity and selfhood are linked, when press representations of de Beauvoir locate the source of her relationships with both men and women not 'in' her self, but in history, in a particular lifestyle and/or in existential philosophy. In chapter 6, the roles of choice and responsibility, and their relation, are construed as techniques of the self which, coupled with assumptions about bisexuality, serve to erase any possibility that bisexuality might be a property of the self. In short, although the issue of precedence is open to question, it is arguable, simply, that sexuality is not produced in isolation from other techniques of the self, which may not be expressly linked to it.

In sum: to assume that the bisexual self stands as evidence of the truth of bisexuality, or that bisexuality is evidence for the truth of a bisexual self, is to take too much for granted. Most importantly, and this goes to the heart of my argument, it is to assume that a (bi)sexual identity *must* be anchored to a self, must reside within, and be expressive of, the self who possesses it. (Or, as in the 'double petition' described by Foucault, is possessed by it.) And yet this analysis of bisexuality indicates that the self does not always bear the great weight of sexuality, and that (bi)sexuality does not always author the self, or at least aspects of it, in the way that lesbian and heterosexuality are frequently perceived to do (whether this is desirable or not). Indeed, the position of bisexuality in these texts suggests that desire will not necessarily be bound to an individual who is 'defined by her form, endowed with organs and functions and assigned as a subject' (Deleuze and Guattari 1988: 275).[23]

As Elspeth Probyn notes, 'the question of "what are we?" marks the exigencies of acting and behaving and belonging within the present as it problematizes the task of contemporary cultural criticism' (Probyn 1993: 109). To theorise identity then, is not merely an exercise in abstract problematisation, but also engenders an active relation to the self. All *excavations* of the self, including this one, also *participate* in the discursive productions of selfhood. Even those discourses which seek to 'deconstruct' the self – such as the post-structuralist feminist work with which this chapter began – will assume some features at least (materiality for example) to be constitutive of selfhood. This will be the focus of the following chapter. It is important in the context of this study because, as I will argue throughout, the presuppositions which create a basis for explications of selfhood are also often those which preclude, displace and erase bisexuality as an identity which 'belongs' to the self.

2

Identity and embodiment

I have illustrated already that Foucault 'does not write a history of subjects but of processes of subjectivation' (Deleuze 1988: 116). Hence the notion of the 'subject' does not refer to a fixed or static entity but rather to a 'practice of being', a production enabled by techniques which do not remain consistent over cultures or through history.[1] As such, Foucault's genealogy provides a useful tool with which to explore the minefield of contemporary theories of the self, and their implications, while simultaneously avoiding the temptation to offer yet another '"just so story" of how the human being got its individuality' (N. Rose 1996: 301). With this in mind, and drawing principally on Foucauldian themes which have been taken up and adapted by feminist theorists, this chapter will examine the extent to which questions of sexuality have become caught up with questions of how the self acquires individuality.[2]

Just as the theoretical reflections which will be outlined below both *recognise* the individuality of the self and also work *against* it, so this study will be concerned *both* with the ways that representations of de Beauvoir ascribe individuality to her – which, by implication, indicates that individualisation is constitutive of intelligible selfhood (Strathern 1992; Haraway 1991) – and *also* with the way that techniques of the self, particularly that of individuality, may preclude the possibility of de Beauvoir being perceived as a 'bisexual individual'. In this respect, the following analysis of de Beauvoir and of bisexuality would be impossible without, and is indebted to, feminisms and queer theories which have opened up the relation between an individual and its identity in order that all three (the individual, the identity and the relation between them) are available as a site of political contestation.

This chapter will also, however, be concerned with the way that theorists who attempt to displace foundations, or at least to call them into question, are no less likely to invoke a series of presuppositions with respect to the self than those who seek to maintain them in some form. While feminist and queer theorists often reject the notion of a 'fixed' self, they neverthe- less frequently assume a number of features to be necessarily constitutive *of* the self (even if this self is contingent). Indeed, that which is productive of selfhood is often brought sharply into focus in the context of post- structuralism, as what can and cannot afford to be theorised *out* of 'self- hood' is debated. The following analysis will pay particular attention to the ways that, in the practical application of Foucault's work, the very pre- suppositions which were to be dismantled are frequently reconfigured. Interestingly, and perhaps because of their shared trajectories, some of the charges brought against queer theory and activism might also be brought against Foucault. As I will argue, the politicisation of identity, and the notion of Foucault's 'aesthetics of the self', have been complicated by the emergence of theories which share similar themes and draw on similar tropes, but which are not situated within the same radical context: for example, techniques of the self which emphasise the body on display, in performance and 'self-care' strategies. Further, these practices often operate within a conjunctive and celebratory, rather than critical (or at least reflexive) relation to spectacular society and consumer culture.

Assujettissement

As noted in chapter 1, a number of feminists face the challenge of both undoing an essential or 'natural' conception of the self while simultane- ously maintaining the category 'women' which feminism ostensibly requires. Denise Riley puts the dilemma thus:

> 'women' is a volatile collectivity in which female persons can be very differently positioned, so that the apparent continuity of the subject of 'women' isn't to be relied on . . . for the individual, 'being a woman' is also inconstant, and can't provide an ontological foundation. Yet it must be emphasised that these instabilities of the category are the *sine qua non* of feminism, which would otherwise be lost for an object, despoiled of a fight, and, in short, without much life.   (Riley 1988: 2)

In this context, Foucault's analysis of discourse and the concept of *assujettissement* has proved useful, insofar as it enables the material effects of discourse to be taken seriously (effects which are productive of the subject), but at the same time recognises the changing conditions of dis- course, so rendering these effects contingent. The very notion of 'women' as a foundational category which is fixed through time and across different cultures is therefore called into question.

It is into the heart of the presupposition that an identity such as gender is somehow fixed for all time that Judith Butler's theory of performativity intervenes. *Bodies That Matter* (1993) asserts that material bodies – 'real' bodies, including those which appear to be irrevocably marked by 'their' identities – have a temporal as well as a spatial dimension.[3] 'Matter' will no longer be conceived 'purely' as a site or a surface, a space on which signs are available to be read by those who might 'master', empirically, the visual field (Tyler 1994: 219). Instead, matter is understood to be *a process* of materialisation which itself constitutes the static 'matter' of bodies. Materialisation, Butler argues, is the regulatory, heterosexual, norm which produces the effect of a coherent person possessed of a gender identity: '"Intelligible" genders are those which in some sense institute and maintain relations of coherence and continuity among sex, gender, sexual practice, and desire' (Butler 1990: 17).

In the course of developing her argument, Butler dramatically exploits the entry into the material realm that Foucault's analysis of power and discourse offers. Arguing that there is no 'unmarked' body which exists prior to and subsequently receives the 'stamp' of gender, Butler's reliance on the concept of *assujettissement* is strikingly clear: 'Subjected to gender, but subjectivated by gender, the "I" neither precedes nor follows the process of this gendering, but emerges only within and as the matrix of gender relations themselves' (Butler 1993: 7). By drawing on the Foucauldian conception of power, Butler ensures that the notion of a do-er is not displaced only to be replaced by a concept of power which, in its turn, 'does to', or which is itself transformed into the 'enabling source': 'This view informs the misreading by which Foucault is criticised for "personifying" power' (Butler 1993: 9). As noted in chapter 1, power relations do not exist 'above' the material world, as a kind of supra structure, but instead take place 'within the very tissue of the assemblages they produce' (Deleuze 1988: 37). Hence while the 'evidence' (and especially the visual evidence) might point to the inert and unchanging stasis of matter, matter is instead understood to be discursively constituted.

This move to displace the self as the originary source of power (in favour of one which is produced through power/knowledge regimes) has, however, been found to be problematic. According to Seyla Benhabib for example, Butler debunks 'any concepts of selfhood, agency and autonomy' (Benhabib 1995a: 21). If we are produced through discourse then how, Benhabib asks, are we to change our selves? In the face of an apparently imminent surrender to discursive regimes which are 'beyond' the self, Benhabib argues that: 'Theoretically, we should be reluctant to cut the branch on which we sit . . . hence my call for reflection on foundations'

(Benhabib 1995b: 118). Benhabib's insistence on the need for 'intentional-ity, accountability, self-reflexivity, and autonomy' (Benhabib 1995a: 20) renders explicit features which she perceives to be at the heart of 'selfhood'. To be rid of foundations, she argues, would also be to dispense with these desirable – or at least necessary – attributes.

Yet Butler's theory does offer an alternative account of agency and, significantly, one which does not require recourse to a subject who is the source of agency. A key feature of her analysis, and the one which most cen-trally addresses critiques such as Benhabib's, is that matter is repeatedly produced through performativity, that which 'brings into being or enacts that which it names, and so marks the constitutive or productive power of discourse' (Butler 1995b: 134).[4] Crucially, performativity is not a singular act, but rather a reiteration of acts:

This is doubtless related to Lacan's claim in *The Four Fundamental Concepts of Psychoanalysis* that every act is a repetition. In this sense, the 'doer' will be produced as the effect of the 'deed', but it will also constitute the dynamic hiatus by which further performative effects are achieved.   (Butler 1995b: 135)

The combination of Foucault's analysis of discourse and the Lacanian concept of repetition adds to the force of Butler's argument insofar as it enables her to offer an account of agency without returning to a notion of a transcendental subject. Power, Butler argues, does not 'cease' after the subject is constituted; the subject is 'subjected and produced time and again' (Butler 1995a: 47).[5] If the subject *appears* to have 'an identity' (which is fixed or static) however, this is only because reiteration 'conceals or dis-simulates the conventions of which it is a repetition' (Butler 1993: 12).

That acts necessarily require reiteration, signals that identification is never actually achieved. And it is precisely the incompleteness of the pro-cesses of subjectification, and the necessity of reiteration, that is the condi-tion of agency within discourse. While the subject may not 'choose', freely, what it is 'to be', gender performativity nevertheless involves:

deriving agency from the very power regimes which constitute us, and which we oppose. This is, oddly enough, *historical work*, reworking the historicity of the signifier, and no recourse to quasi-transcendental selfhood and inflated concepts of History will help us in this most concrete and paradoxical of struggles.
(Butler 1995b: 136)[6]

In other words, for Butler, it is into the instability wrought by the discursive necessity of reiteration, that the (materiality of the) signifier might be reworked. Thus queer, for example, as the site of collective contestation: 'is, in the present, never fully owned, but always and only redeployed, twisted, queered from prior usage and in the direction of urgent and expanding political purposes' (Butler 1993: 228). Butler accounts for agency therefore, but without locating its source either in the subject, in power or in 'History'.

Although Butler argues that 'the temporary totalization performed by identity' is a 'necessary error' (Butler 1993: 230), this does not imply that processes of subjectification do not have real material effects. In this respect, Butler answers Benhabib's critique that to be rid of foundations is to dispense with the self entirely. Butler, like Foucault:

> elaborates a poststructuralist ontology of the subject. She claims, *pace* Benhabib, that it is not sufficient to view the subject as *situated* vis-à-vis a setting or context that is external to it. Instead, we should see the subject as *constituted* in and through power/discourse formations.   (N. Fraser 1995a: 66)

Butler's use of psychoanalysis is, however, a departure from Foucault and does not sit easily with his later work on techniques of the self.[7] Nevertheless, the use of psychoanalysis not only contributes to Butler's theorisation of agency, but is also employed in order that she might negotiate the self/other dualism.[8] I will consider this briefly here, because it is in Butler's challenge to the self/other dualism, and the political conclusions that she draws from this analysis, that the extent to which she seeks to *maintain* rather than *reject* the notion of the self (as theorists such as Benhabib suggest that she does) is illustrated.

Rather than suggest that heterosexuality and homosexuality are in opposition (that self and other are separate and oppositional), Butler argues that each is produced through a disavowal of the other:

> The abjection of homosexuality can take place only through an identification with that abjection, an identification that must be disavowed, an identification that one fears to make only because one has already made it, an identification that institutes that abjection and sustains it.   (Butler 1993: 112)[9]

The notion of an abjected 'outside', an abjected 'other', is in fact '"inside" the subject as its own founding domain' (Butler 1993: 3). In short then, the subject is not produced in autonomous isolation, but rather assumes its shape through, and is therefore dependent on, an identification with an 'other' (which is subsequently disavowed). Although Butler's analysis centres on the role of the 'heterosexual imperative' in enabling 'certain sexed identifications and foreclos[ing] and/or disavow[ing] other identifications' (Butler 1993: 3), she also suggests that to reverse this logic and posit a coherent lesbian or gay identity over and against heterosexuality would constitute a political error. This tactic, Butler argues, serves only to strengthen and sustain heterosexuality in its rejection of it: 'Here it should become clear that a radical refusal to identify with a given position suggests that on some level an identification has already taken place' (Butler 1993: 113).

Far from rejecting the self, Butler argues that the 'I' which is produced through, and which is dependent on, repudiation is a 'weak self', and one whose 'posture of autonomy' (Butler 1995b: 140) is further weakened by disavowal:

My objection to this form of disavowal is that it weakens the sense of self, establishes its ostensible autonomy on fragile grounds, and requires a repeated and systematic repudiation of others in order to acquire and maintain the appearance of autonomy.   (Butler 1995b: 140)

Even this brief sojourn into Butler's analysis suggests that it is far more than merely the explicit formulation of the processes by which the gendered subject is materialised through discourse. So far, the discussion has made references not only to 'the body's sex', but also to 'the subject', to 'the speaking I', to 'the self' as well as to 'performing identity'. It is precisely this multitude of terms which constitutes one of the most problematic aspects of Butler's work. Nancy Fraser, writing of *Bodies That Matter*, notes that:

Butler's tendency, when discussing subjectivity, [is] to shift too quickly and without adequate differentiation among various conceptual levels – from, for example, the structural-linguistic level (at which she invokes a quasi-Saussurean account of the function of the shifter 'I') to the psychoanalytic level (at which she invokes a quasi-Kristevan account of the *intra*psychic process of individual, ontogenetic subject-formation via abjection) to the institutional level (at which she invokes a quasi-Foucauldian account of the constitution of various different and distinct *subject-positions* at various different and distinct institutional sites).

(N. Fraser 1995b: 163)

Seyla Benhabib goes still further than Fraser in her critique of Butler, and suggests that 'even if Butler would like to distinguish gender-constitution from identity-constitution' (Benhabib 1995b: 110), she nevertheless offers a complete 'theory of self' (Benhabib quoted in Butler 1995b: 133). Butler herself argues however, that 'if I were to offer a "theory of the self", which I do not, it would not be reducible to a theory of gender' (Butler 1995b: 133). Instead, Butler defines 'the subject' as a 'category within language and, hence, distinct from what Benhabib will call a "self"' (Butler 1995b: 135). Despite Butler's objections to the contrary however, and although it remains largely undefined, she nevertheless does make reference to, and even suggests what she would like to see constitute, 'the self': 'My call, then, is for the development of forms of differentiation which lead to fundamentally more capacious, generous, and "unthreatened" bearings of the self in the midst of community' (Butler 1995b: 140).

It is not the intention of the discussion here to sift through and to determine once and for all the precise meanings associated with each of the categories (for example, embodied subject, subjectivity, identity) which have been employed. Rather, the point is to highlight the way in which, when these concepts are *not* made explicit, a number of presuppositions regarding 'the self' almost inevitably emerge. As illustrated above for example, Butler argues that the subject is a category in language and *therefore* distinct from 'the self'. In other words, Butler implies that the self is produced through *more* than language alone. Nevertheless, her analysis of the subject clearly makes a contribution to the notion of intelligible 'self-hood', insofar as the reader assumes that the subject represents at least one *aspect* of the self. Further, even though Butler does not assume that the materiality of bodies constitutes *the sum of* the self, it does appear to be a constituting factor in the production of the self. This point will be explicated more clearly through the following analysis of Diana Fuss's (1991) introduction to the collection of queer essays called *Inside/Out*.[10]

Boundedness

Fuss argues that recent lesbian and gay theorising has been in part motivated by the desire to work on and over boundaries such as self/other in order to expose the mechanisms of the inside/outside dialectic. This binary opposition, 'inside/outside', has been recognised as:

> the very figure for signification and the mechanisms of meaning production. It has everything to do with the structures of alienation, splitting, and identification which together produce a self and an other, a subject and an object, an unconscious and a conscious, an interiority and an exteriority.   (Fuss 1991: 1–2)

Queer theorists question where the limits of borderlines such as subject/object, interiority/exteriority lie and, in particular, seek to challenge the self/other dualism. This latter arrangement presumes, as noted above, that the self is an autonomous, 'self-sufficient' entity. Psychoanalysis offers a means by which to deconstruct this knowledge of the self insofar as it posits an unbridgeable divide between conscious and unconscious: without access to the unconscious, the conscious self is irrevocably 'split', rather than 'whole'. Not only does queer recognise the instability of the psyche, it also attempts to deconstruct its boundaries:

> To protect against the recognition of the lack within the self, the self erects and defends its borders against an other which is made to represent or to become that selfsame lack . . . [However] [h]eterosexuality can never fully ignore the close psychical proximity of its terrifying (homo)sexual other, any more than homosexuality can entirely escape the equally insistent social pressures of (hetero)sexual conformity.   (Fuss 1991: 3)

In other words, by theorising the nuances of intrasubjectivity in the constitution of the self, queer theorists argue that the 'other', upon which the self depends in order that it might 'protect against . . . lack', is not outside but rather, as Butler also notes, 'inside' the self itself. Thus: 'the denotation of any term is always dependent on what is exterior to it' (Fuss 1991: 1).

Queer theory's agenda then, in part, is to 'undo' what has already been 'done'. As Steven Seidman puts it:

The point of departure for queer theory is not the figure of homosexual repression and the struggle for personal and collective expression or the making of homo-sexual/gay/lesbian identities but the hetero/homosexual discursive or epistemologi-cal figure. The question of its origin is less compelling than a description of its social textual efficacy.   (Seidman 1995: 130)

In order to untangle the effects and implications of the discursively pro-duced homosexual self however, that self (even if it is a 'necessary error') must first be assumed. In other words, much of queer theory concerns itself with the relations between forces which have *already* been fixed by state-ment curves and regularised by description scenes: it addresses itself to the discursive formations – literally, formed substances and formalised func-tions – of power/knowledge, rather than to the flow of forces *per se*.[11] Revealingly, for example, Fuss argues that the homosexual began to 'haunt' the heterosexual at the very same moment that it was 'born' as a 'species' (Fuss 1991: 4): 'the first coming out was also simultaneously a closeting; . . . the homosexual's debut onto the stage of historical identities was as much an egress as an entry' (ibid.). Queer theorises the ghostly, abjected figure of the homosexual because it has *already* been identified, revealed in the shim-mering light, as a species or 'personage'.[12]

The recent literature on bisexuality (frequently written by self-identified bisexuals) and the visibility of proliferating bisexual groups in Britain sug-gests that, like the homosexual, the bisexual self has also 'achieved' the status of a 'personage'. Yet it is also the case that techniques such as individuality, and even materiality, which are often taken for granted where the homosexual self is concerned (indeed, without them such a self might not be articulable), cannot always be assumed in the context of bisexuality. In the texts that I will be analysing throughout this book, no 'bisexual self' is produced through discourse, flows of forces do not congeal to form a bounded, 'bisexual entity' which might subsequently be available for (re)figuration.[13] It is arguable then, that even though queer's use of psycho-analysis offers a critique of the self as a unified 'whole', queer theorists still assume, even in a most limited sense, that some notion of 'boundedness' is a necessary feature of intelligible selfhood. Indeed, Fuss argues that the boundaries between inside and outside 'cannot be easily or ever finally dispensed with' (Fuss 1991: 1).[14] This implies that the self is always, at some level (although perhaps not that of the psyche?), divided from the non-self, or the other. What is important here is that Fuss implies that boundaries are constitutive of the self and that *ultimately* the self is, after all, produced through those boundaries which distinguish inside from outside. Given that the boundaries of the self are not located in the psyche (both Butler and Fuss use psychoanalysis to provide a persuasive analysis of intrasubjectivity),[15] the question remains as to where these other boundaries are located.

Fuss argues that theories of performativity are concerned with 'the imaginative enactment of sexual redefinitions, reborderizations, and rearticulations' (Fuss 1991: 7). These loops and linkages of queer theories and theories of performativity are exemplified by the 'four knot' pictured on the cover of *Inside/Out*:

The undecidability of this simple topology may be its greatest appeal . . . It visualizes for us in the very simplicity of its openings and closures, its overs and unders, its ins and outs, the contortions and convolutions of any sexual identity formation.
(Fuss 1991: 7)

Notably, Fuss adds that the topology 'is nonetheless embodied, sexualised' (ibid.). In other words, whatever the imaginative, or psychic contortions and convolutions of sexual identity formations, they are nonetheless anchored to the (presumably) individual human body.[16]

The assumption that any sexual identity formation is embodied casts an interesting light on the implications of Butler's analysis as it has been taken up elsewhere. Butler herself warns of the dangers of leaving 'matter', and its relation to sexuality, untheorised:

We may seek to return to matter as prior to discourse to ground our claims about sexual difference only to discover that matter is fully sedimented with discourses on sex and sexuality that prefigure and constrain the uses to which the term can be put.
(Butler 1993: 29)

While the impetus behind Butler's work is to reveal the discourses through which 'matter' is materialised, and even though Butler herself, as noted above, objects to the suggestion that her theory of gendered bodies constitutes the totality of 'the self', it appears that the contemporary emphasis on embodiment has led it to attain a privileged status in the analysis of sexual identity and, relatedly, the 'self'.[17] Sexual identity is understood always to be embodied, and is rendered a constitutive aspect of the self. And yet not all sexual identities are necessarily anchored in material corporeality, as I will argue. Bisexuality is sometimes understood to reside outside of the self ascribed to de Beauvoir, while at other times it is produced between the surfaces of other sexual identities (which are embodied). Perversely then, insofar as sexual identity is *assumed* to be embodied, embodiment remains an *under*-theorised aspect of sexuality and selfhood.

Some of the most interesting questions that Butler herself asks are: 'For whom is outness a historically available and affordable option? . . . Who is represented by *which* use of the term [queer], and who is excluded?' (Butler 1993: 227). Some bodies, Butler points out, in some instances, are 'invisible'. Outness, for example, might be affordable only to certain classes, or to people of a particular race, ethnicity or religion. But not only are some bodies invisible, outness might also not be available to those bodies which do not 'materialise' visibly. In this respect, the material and the visible are linked, insofar as the accent on materiality often brings with it, perhaps inadvertently, an emphasis on the visible (by which I mean what is, literally, 'seeable').[18] It is with this issue in particular that the following section will be concerned: who can, and cannot, afford to engage in a politics of visibility? And for what reasons might this not be available to everyone? Some of the criticisms that have been targeted at queer theory and activism in this context also, notably, bear a striking resemblance to those directed at Foucault's 'aesthetics of the self'.

Aestheticisation: of identity, of politics

An issue raised by contemporary queer theories and political strategies concerns the extent to which the emphasis on materiality translates into a politics which leans heavily on the visible performance of the queer body. For example:

the hyperbolic 'performance' of death in the practice of 'die-ins' and the theatrical 'outness' by which queer activism has disrupted the closeting distinction between public and private space have proliferated sites of politicization and AIDS awareness throughout the public realm.   (Butler 1993: 232–3)

The theatrical performance of death serves a political aim: it politicises the division between the public and the private sphere in order that AIDS become a highly visible concern for everyone, rather than a stigmatised and private affair. In this respect, the visibility of the queer body itself assumes a political value wherein the theatrical is not *opposed* to the political but rather emphasises 'the increasing politicisation *of* theatricality' (Butler 1993: 233).[19] Similarly, Lisa Walker argues that one of the reasons that the figure of the butch has been celebrated is because her '"blatant" representation of sexual deviance' (Walker 1993: 882) stands in stark contrast to the 'assimilation or the imitation of heterosexual stereotypes for the purpose of camouflage, that is, closetry, being "in the closet"' (Grahn quoted in Walker 1993: 882). The butch lesbian renders her sexuality visible (through clothes, gestures, perhaps through bodily physique) by putting it on 'display'. She, like the drag artists that Butler analyses in *Gender Trouble* (1990), destabilises the inside/outside binary that is productive of coherent gender identities. That is, drag is a double inversion of the assumption that the 'outer' male or female body is an expression of the 'inner' masculine or feminine self.

As with queer, Foucault's 'aesthetics of the self' is posited to counter the obsessive contemporary search for the 'inner' truth or 'essence' of the self. Foucault's emphasis on aesthetics is intended to 'free the moral imagination from the mere imitation of reality and establish, in Bachelard's words, "imagination in its living role as the guide to human life"' (McNay 1994: 147). In order to 'liberate' the imagination, Foucault argues that the self must be denaturalised, and must style itself anew:

> [Arts of existence are] those intentional and voluntary actions by which men not only set themselves rules of conduct, but also seek to transform themselves, to change themselves in their singular being, and to make their life into an œuvre that carries certain aesthetic values and meets certain stylistic criteria.
>
> (Foucault quoted in McNay 1994: 136)

Rather than suppressing desire, Foucault, drawing on Ancient Greek ethics, claims that desires can and are to be transformed by the individual (Diprose 1994: 30).[20] These practices of transformation constitute what is now variously known as the arts or aesthetics of existence. Such arts, which privilege the self as the site of possible change, accord with Foucault's belief that contemporary society no longer believes in 'grand narratives' and therefore that any ethics must arise from a more localised basis. His microphysics of power, which illustrates the normalising effects of power at the micro-level, also befits this analysis. Nevertheless, Foucault has been criticised for not taking account of feminist work which demonstrates, for example, that while dieting, exercising, body-building and so forth can all be considered an aesthetics of existence, they are also perceived to be practices of the self (carried out on the body) which 'might be described, in Foucault's terms, not as operations of power, but as closer to states of domination' (Thacker 1993: 18).[21] In other words, as Lois McNay argues, Foucault's aesthetics of the self has been found to be problematic insofar as it fetishises aesthetic practices and implies that it is the practice of self-stylisation *itself* – without regard to its context or its implications – that constitutes the basis of his ethics.

Foucault's notion of an aesthetics of the self can by no stretch of the imagination be collapsed with queer politics. However, some of the charges brought against Foucault do bear more than a passing resemblance to those directed at queer theory and, in particular, the political campaigns it is often seen to give rise to. One of the reasons for this may be because both attempt to marry politics with aesthetics. The theatrical performance of queer politics for instance, has been seriously complicated by high profile identity projects which also assume the form of aesthetic lifestyles, but which are based on a rather different agenda. Some have questioned ACT UP's, for example, 'obsessive relationship with its own image in the media' (Saalfield and Navarro 1991: 362) and asked whether the queer aesthetic represents any more than an exercise in conspicuous 'lifestyle' consumption: 'Is going to an ACT UP demo like buying Calvin Klein underwear?' (ibid.). This is an important question because, as McNay writes:

in a society in which the behaviour of individuals is often governed by an incitement to consumption, it may be necessary to determine the point at which the construction of one's life as a work of art ceases to be an act of conspicuous consumption – or in Bourdieu's terms a sign of 'distinction' – and becomes a gesture of resistance.
(McNay 1994: 155)

Michel Maffesoli argues that lifestylisation – and a parallel can be drawn here with both Foucault's arts of existence and with queer – represents 'a synergy between the ethical and the aesthetic' (Maffesoli 1991: 18). He goes on:

Whether trendy exercises in sensory isolation, or various forms of body-building, or jogging, or Eastern techniques of one sort or another, the body is being constructed as a value . . . even in its most private aspects, *the body is being constructed only in order to be seen*; it is theatralized to the highest degree. Within advertising, fashion, dance, the body is adorned only to be made into a spectacle.
(Maffesoli 1991: 18–19. My emphasis)

To draw attention to the points of resonance between queer and Foucault's aesthetics of the self on the one hand and to self-fashioned lifestyles on the other is not to suggest that they are the same, nor is it intended to diminish the politics of the former two. My intentions here are rather to emphasise the complex context in which they are situated. Insofar as all these projects – queer, Foucault's aesthetics and lifestylisation – have a tendency to be concentrated within the field of visibility, and because they are often based around the theatre of identity, an equivalence may be forced between them whereby their political intentions and effects cannot be distinguished. Theorists of the spectacle (Debord 1977; Plant 1990, 1992) might argue not only that each represents *a* spectacle, but also that they are absorbed, without differentiation, into the fleeting whims of *the* spectacle.

Is this emphasis on the visible merely a question of historical context (the emergence of queer among a proliferation of lifestyles), or is the reappropriation of queer into, and by queer of, consumer culture and spectacular society integral to queer theory and politics itself? At one level, this is surely confined to the contextual, a 'problem' which can itself be exploited. Thomas Yingling for example, following Baudrillard's lead, suggests that:

AIDS activism has not been coopted into the great institutional machinery of culture that currently recodes sign value as use value . . . but instead insists upon forcing spectacle itself into political use – hence the resurrection of agit-prop, street theater, poster art, etc.   (Yingling 1991: 296)

Yingling appears to be situating AIDS activism in the tradition of the avant-garde – the Dada, the Surrealists and the Situationist Internationalists for example – which has attempted to cross the boundaries between art, politics and everyday life. Rosemary Hennessey however, argues that the avant-garde itself should be considered in relation to 'the more general aestheticisation of everyday life in consumer capitalism' (Hennessey 1995: 164) and that queer theory and politics, as the latest participant in this trajectory, should explore in more detail the way that the emphasis on aestheticisation obscures the very social relations that make it possible. She writes: 'often trouble-making takes the form of a cultural politics that relies on concepts of the social, of resistance, and of pleasure that keep invisible the violent social relations new urban identities depend on' (Hennessey 1995: 146–7). In this respect, the 'problem' of the emphasis on the visible – and its *dependence* upon a very specific context (which Hennessey suggests is 'the new bourgeois professional class' (Hennessey 1995: 150)) – is integral to queer. At its most general, Hennessey is concerned that both Foucault's aesthetics of the self and queer theory and activism are relevant only to a privileged minority who can afford to turn their lives into a 'work of art'.

Specifically, Hennessey's doubts about queer politics and theories are twofold. With respect to politics (political campaigns), she objects to the emphasis on the commodity as part of a campaign for queer visibility. The intimate relation between Queer Nation, for example, and consumer culture is clear in the names its affinity groups have adopted. These include SHOP (Suburban Homosexual Outreach Program), QUEST (Queers Undertaking Exquisite and Symbolic Transformation) and United Colors (which focuses on queers of colour) (Hennessey 1995: 159). The aim of these groups, Hennessey argues, is not so much to market positive images of queers, but to tap into consumer desire and disrupt the heterosexual pre-suppositions on which this desire rests. Their tactics include 'rewriting the trademarks of corporations that appropriate gay street styles (changing the 'p' in GAP ads to 'y')' and 'parading into suburban shopping spaces dressed in full gay regalia, holding hands, or handing out flyers' in order to 'insert gay spectacle into the centers of straight consumption' (Hennessey 1995: 160). Reworking Marx's concept of commodity fetishism, Hennessey suggests that although Queer Nation exposes the hidden heterosexual meanings invested in commodities, this strategy rests on the illusion that the value of the commodity resides in the physical object itself – its signification, meaning or its role in the production of identity – rather than in the human labour that goes into producing it: 'When the commodity is fetishized, the labor that has gone into its production is rendered invisible' (Hennessey 1995: 162). In other words, a 'bourgeois way of seeing', which rests on the notion of an autonomous aesthetic perception, disguises a story of class inequality which precedes and is productive of the object that seems to have appeared as if 'by magic'.

Hennessey argues that queer theory too, like queer activism, reduces the question of social change to that of cultural representation. For her, queer theory does not 'historicise' the signifier 'queer' so much as (merely) place it in a historical context. The work of historicising, she suggests, requires establishing and tracing connections between social life on a number of different levels (rather than on the discursive level alone).[22] She writes of Butler's analysis of drag for example, that:

> To historicize the meaning of drag among the urban middle class in the United States at the turn of the twenty-first century would be to link it as a discursive prac-tice to the social relations that make it possible and in so doing situate practices specific to a particular social formation in the United States within the larger frame of late capitalism's geopolitics and multinational economy. (Hennessey 1995: 150)

Hennessey argues that Butler's focus on 'the specific and the local (à la Foucault)' (ibid.) disallows this broader historicising. And without this, the conception of identities as performative significations is brought perilously close to the notion of identity as self-fashioning: 'When queer theory reconfigures gender identity as a "style of the flesh", to use Judith Butler's phrasing, . . . it is taking part in the post-modern aestheticization of daily life' (Hennessey 1995: 167).[23] Not everyone, Hennessey argues, can partic-ipate in exposing the fiction of identity, and not all lesbians and gay people are living the glamorous lives that their 'chic commodity images' (Hennessey 1995: 175) suggest.[24] Drawing attention to the relation between queer activism and Foucault's aesthetics of the self, Hennessey argues that 'the answer to why everyone's life couldn't become a work of art could take us somewhere else, to another story, one that makes visible the contradictory social relations the aestheticisation of social life conceals' (Hennessey 1995: 167).

While Hennessey's attack on the contemporary focus on cultural representation in theories of sexuality appears to be one of the most sustained and coherent (see also Hennessey 1993), she is not alone in mounting this kind of critique. Sue O'Sullivan argues that although academic theorising currently confers a primacy on representation and language as constitutive processes in identity, 'style is only skin deep' (O'Sullivan 1994: 95). Danae Clark too, suggests that the emphasis on '"life style" lesbianism' (D. Clark 1991: 185) welcomes homosexuals as consuming subjects rather than social subjects (D. Clark 1991: 192). Most interestingly, she writes: 'This stylisation furthermore promotes a liberal discourse of choice that separates sexuality from politics and connects them both to consumerism' (D. Clark 1991: 193–4). This suggests that anti-essentialist positions – here promoted perhaps unexpectedly by the media in its focus on 'lifestyle lesbianism' – are not in themselves inherently desirable. As Eve Sedgwick notes, the notion that we can choose whatever sexual identity we want to be has facilitated the right-wing prescription that 'gays who wish to share in human rights and dignities must (and *can*) make the free-market choice of becoming *ex*-gays' (Sedgwick 1994: 226). I will return to the issue of choice, in relation to the production both of lesbian identities and of bisexuality, in chapter 6.

Perhaps one of the most interesting critiques of the emphasis on the material and the visible, with respect to the constructions of bisexuality that I will be identifying here, is to be found in Peggy Phelan's work on the politics of performance. Phelan suggests that '[v]isibility politics are compatible with capitalism's relentless appetite for new markets and with the most self-satisfying ideologies of the United States: you are welcome here as long as you are productive' (Phelan 1993: 11). Like Hennessey, Phelan points out that capitalism invisibilises certain social relations (such as women's reproductive labour). She also notes that the contemporary accent on resignification in the production of identities befits the 'fundamental aspiration of the American mythos' (Phelan 1993: 105) which centres on the invention and reinvention of identity.[25] Phelan uses Jenny Livingston's film *Paris Is Burning,* which Butler herself analyses at some length in *Bodies That Matter,* to illustrate this point. She writes:

Part of the appeal of *Paris* for a white, straight audience is its ability to absorb and tame the so-called Otherness of this part of Black and Latino gay male culture. The dreams of economic success, fame, and security articulated by the performers are exactly the same dreams of 'most American men'. The means by which these dreams are realized – self-invention, hard work, and ingenuity – are the same methods celebrated in the careers of Ragged Rick and *Rocky I* through *V*.

(Phelan 1993: 106)

While Hennessey and Phelan share similar concerns, their conclusions are somewhat different. For Phelan the answer to the 'problems' engendered by visibility politics is not, as it is for Hennessey, to start 'from a different place in how we see' (Hennessey 1995: 177), but to value that which is not visibly representable and which is, relatedly, not 'productive'. Linking this to the material, she writes:

what would it take to value the immaterial in a culture structured around the equation 'material equals value?' As critical theories of cultural reproduction become increasingly dedicated to a consideration of the 'material conditions' that influence . . . identities, questions about the immaterial constructions of identities . . . fade from the eye/I.   (Phelan 1993: 5)

The relation between identity, materiality and visibility will be a concern throughout my argument given that I, like Phelan, will be exploring some of the 'immaterial constructions of identities' as well as the implications for and of those identities which do not cohere in material corporeality. Would such an identity be visibly representable? If not, would it be discursively produced as an aspect of 'the self' at all? Perhaps it is not merely the fetishisation of the aesthetic moment itself, but the accent on the self as the locus of change, the privileging of an aesthetic *self* – as 'an antidote to the normalising tendencies of modern society' (McNay 1994: 142) – which is particularly problematic. It is possible that the self which is held to be the vehicle of transformation is itself, as I will argue, normalising.

'What can a body do?'

Rosi Braidotti explicitly considers the contemporary emphasis on both the material body and the visible, situating this focus in a historical context. Arguing that the 'mind–body dualism, of which the thinking of Descartes is the major example, is one of the founding gestures of the modern rational order' (Braidotti 1994: 58), Braidotti suggests that modernity's project seeks not only to critique this dualistic scheme and deconstruct the individualistic autonomy of the Cartesian self, but also sets itself the task of re-evaluating the body itself: 'In many respects, the age of modernity is anti-Cartesian in that it marks the emergence of the material bodily self at the center of our theoretical attention' (ibid.).[26] Following a

Foucauldian schema, Braidotti points out that in the modern age, the body has become 'the site of proliferating discourses and forms of knowledge, and of normativity' (Braidotti 1994: 59). Bio-power, for example, signifies the 'total control and manipulation over the living matter' (Braidotti 1994: 60).[27]

The proliferation of discourses which target the body has occurred on two levels. In the first instance, at the level of clinical anatomy, the body has become an object of knowledge to be measured and described (Braidotti 1994: 59) (in this respect, the body is understood as the sum of its organic parts). In the second, the body is perceived as 'the site of transcendence of the subject, and as such it is the condition of possibility for all knowledge' (Braidotti 1994: 59) (in this context the body is understood to represent more than its anatomical parts). Yet despite this dual emphasis on the body, there is still, Braidotti argues, paradoxically, little agreement as to what exactly constitutes it. This is particularly clear with respect to women's bodies. Taking each level in turn, Braidotti focuses, firstly, on the disappearance of the female body in the new reproductive technologies and, secondly, on its erasure in post-modern discourses of the 'feminine'. Significantly, she links both these issues to visibility.

With respect to new reproductive technologies, briefly, Braidotti establishes a relation between the invisibilisation of the female body *as a whole* and, ironically, the increasing capacity of technology to represent the 'unrepresentable'. She argues that in the biotechnical universe, echograms and echography have scaled new heights in making the invisible (such as the origins of life, tissues and cells) visible: 'the scopic drive is reaching a paroxysm; as if the basic principle of visibility had shifted into a mirage of absolute transparency, as if *everything* could be seen' (Braidotti 1994: 49).[28] At the same time however, Braidotti and Sarah Kember, who analyses the role of photo-mechanical and electronic imaging in the classification of the body, argue that current medical technology obliterates, rather than dominates, the female body which is transformed into no more than a 'vehicle for scientific information' (Kember 1995: 107). For Braidotti, one of the most acute manifestations of this obliteration is the world-wide traffic in body parts or organs. Based on the assumption that all organs are equal to each other and interchangeable, that all organs are *the same*, Braidotti argues that the commercialisation of 'organs without bodies'[29] (Braidotti 1994: 64) invisibilises *differences* between 'real' and 'whole' women, differences (of age, race and class) which have implications for the roles women are called upon to play in the reproductive industry. Like the emphasis on lifestyles and commodities then, the focus solely on the physical object/organ itself, at the expense of the social context from which it emerges, invisibilises differences between individuals which are structured by inequality.

In order to highlight the risks which may attend the emphasis on the visible, Braidotti refers to the relation identified by several feminist philosophers between 'looking' and 'knowing', wherein the desire to see is likened to the will-to-knowledge. She notes that psychoanalysis, for example, relates the scopic drive to knowledge, control, domination and, notably, the body: 'the practice that consists in opening something up so as to see how it functions; the impulse to go and see, to "look in" is the most fundamental and childlike form of control over the other's body' (Braidotti 1994: 67). Although Braidotti does not wish to ignore, or erase, the visible entirely, she is concerned with the way in which the visible has gained priority *over* other ways of knowing. Not only scientific culture, but contemporary Western popular culture too, she argues, rests 'on the fantasy that visibility and truth work together' (Braidotti 1994: 69).[30] This is the 'triumph' of the visual image and visual representation, which functions as though 'the scopic . . . were indeed the most adequate way of re-presenting the act of knowledge' (ibid.).

The fraught relationship between visibility, knowledge and the female body (in particular) in scientific and popular culture finds its parallel in philosophy. Braidotti writes:

In a complex reversal, the 'feminine', which traditionally was the dark continent of discourse, emerged as the privileged symptom and sign of and, in some cases, even as the solution to the crisis of the subject. The postmodern discursive inflation about the 'feminine' . . . fails to raise the question that is crucial to feminist practice, namely: 'what does this have to do with real-life women?' Just like the body, the 'feminine' is re-presented as a symbolic absence.   (Braidotti 1994: 47)

It is precisely because of this erasure of 'real-life women' – both at the level of clinical anatomy and in contemporary philosophising – that Braidotti's analysis of what she calls 'nomadic subjectivity' places the material embodiment of 'real' women at its heart. Braidotti defines 'nomadism' as a political project which seeks not only to oppose the 'false universality of the subject' (Braidotti 1994: 158), but also to 'affirm and enact different forms of subjectivity' (ibid.). Her starting point however:

remains the political will to assert the specificity of the lived, female bodily experience, the refusal to disembody sexual difference into a new, allegedly postmodern, antiessentialist subject, and the will to reconnect the whole debate on difference to the bodily existence and experience of women.   (Braidotti 1994: 174–5)

Drawing on Deleuze as well as Foucault, Braidotti clearly and usefully, unlike Butler, distinguishes between identity, (political) subjectivity, the self and the body (although all four are interrelated). What is especially interesting here is that *despite* these clear distinctions, and her explicit focus on some of the consequences of the contemporary emphasis on the visible, the implications of Braidotti's trajectory are strikingly similar to those theories of identity outlined above.

The term 'Woman', Braidotti argues, refers to: 'a female, sexed subject that is constituted, as psychoanalysis convincingly argues, through a process of identification with culturally available positions organized in the dichotomy of gender' (Braidotti 1994: 162). Although related to subjectivity, identity 'bears a privileged bond to unconscious processes' (Braidotti 1994: 166). As in the analyses considered above, Braidotti is concerned, as part of the process of politicisation which deconstructs autonomous individualism, to confront the supposed self-sufficiency of identity. Thus she argues that identity is relational, 'in that it requires a bond to the "other"' (Braidotti 1994: 166). The distinction that Braidotti draws between identity and subjectivity enables her to account for complexities, multiplicities, 'for contradictory moments, for confusions and uncertainties' (Braidotti 1994: 166) not only between women, but within women as well: 'I stress this because far too often in feminist theory, the level of identity gets merrily confused with issues of political subjectivity . . . Unconscious desire [associated with identity] and willful choice [associated with subjectivity] do not always coincide' (ibid.).

The distinction between subjectivity and identity also enables Braidotti to engage with 'women' without focusing on the individual woman/subject as a fixed or totalising category. For her: 'the "I" [the synthesis of both the historically anchored subject and split identity] is a grammatical necessity, a theoretical fiction that holds together the collection of differing layers, the integrated fragments of the ever-receding horizon of one's identity' (ibid.). In one respect at least then, a comparison may be drawn between Braidotti and Butler in that each consider identity to be a fiction or 'necessary error' (Butler 1993: 230).[31] However, because Braidotti distinguishes between subjectivity and identity, her analysis does not lend itself to the criticism frequently targeted at Butler which is, as noted above, that the social is erased except insofar as it is constitutive of the subject. Although Braidotti, like Butler, focuses predominantly on the micro-level (the local and particular), her theory does also, as I have indicated, allow her to examine the effect on women of scientific, technological and popular cultural discourses.

Braidotti defines the self as 'an entity endowed with identity' (Braidotti 1994: 165), which is 'anchored in . . . living matter, whose materiality is coded and rendered in language' (ibid.). According to Braidotti then, the 'self' is at least three things. Firstly, it includes identity, subjectivity and materiality. Secondly, it is at some level fractured, insofar as identity is 'a play of multiple, fractured aspects of the self' (Braidotti 1994: 166). Finally, identity and materiality, as in Butler's analysis and much queer theory (see above), are closely tied[32] and related to language. The body itself 'refers to a layer of corporeal materiality, a substratum of living matter endowed with memory' (Braidotti 1994: 165). Overall then, despite the fictive 'I', the self appears to be coherent and individualised. Indeed, one of the features of 'real-life women', no matter how fractured, is a sense of individual integrity. Much of feminism is (justifiably) concerned with those moments where this integrity has been violated (as Braidotti demonstrates in her discussion of reproductive technology). So although the 'identity' of the self is split and relational (the self requires 'others', at the level of identity, in order to establish a relation to itself and therefore cannot be seen as *wholly* self-sufficient), the self itself is nevertheless an 'entity' which is by definition a distinct existent rather than a quality or relation. In this respect, Braidotti's 'self' might be described just as Butler's 'I' is: as a 'bounded and distinct kind of being' (Butler 1995b: 140), embedded in material corporeality. How is the self-sufficient independence of 'the self', which includes materiality, subjectivity and identity, to be disrupted when only one aspect of it (identity) has been rendered relational? It is arguable that in Braidotti's analysis, even if identity, an aspect of the self, is constituted through relation rather than division, the boundaries of the self *per se* are not necessarily destabilised. Rather, the self is placed in relation to other individualised and bounded selves of the same form. Perhaps inevitably then, the aim to create 'new images of female subjectivity' (Braidotti 1994: 158) is itself bound by the problematic of the embodied subject which precedes the theory.

A notable feature of Braidotti's analysis is that theoretically her position does not lead to the conclusion that 'the body' must necessarily always be collapsed with corporeal materiality, or even with matter itself. To adopt a Deleuzian definition of a body, which Braidotti does, is to understand the body 'as pure flows of energy, capable of multiple variations' (Braidotti 1994: 165). In *Dialogues,* Deleuze outlines a concept of bodies understood not as forms or functions, but as affects[33] distributed on a plane of immanence.[34] Drawing on Spinoza, he writes:

> *'What can a body do?',* of what affects is it capable? . . . Spinoza never ceases to be amazed by the body. He is not amazed at having a body, but by what the body can do. Bodies are not defined by their genus or species, by their organs and functions, but by what they can do, by the affects of which they are capable.
>
> (Deleuze and Parnet 1987: 60)

Because bodies are about the ability to affect and be affected, there may be greater differences between a plough horse and a racehorse than between a plough horse and an ox (Deleuze crosses the boundaries between species here): 'This is because the racehorse and the plow horse have neither the same affects nor the same capacity for being affected; the plow horse has affects in common, rather, with the ox' (Deleuze 1992: 627. See also Foucault 1994: xix). In Deleuze's analysis, a body may be anything: 'it can be an animal, a body of sounds, a mind or an idea' (Deleuze 1992: 629). At least two implications follow. Firstly, a body may *or may not* take the form of a 'human individual'. The subject for example, as it is defined by Deleuze (and Guattari), is no more than a *temporary* coagulation of forces. Elizabeth Grosz explains:

the subject is not an 'entity' or thing, or a relation between mind (interior) and body (exterior). Instead, it must be understood as a series of flows, energies, movements, and capacities, a series of fragments or segments capable of being linked together in ways other than those that congeal it into an identity.   (Grosz 1994: 197–8)

Secondly, given that a body might be something like a 'body of sounds', it is possible that it may not be anchored in materiality at all. Nikolas Rose draws attention to a similar point in relation to the fold which, he argues, is useful only if 'the lines of these folds do not run through a domain coterminous with the fleshy bounds of the human individual' (N. Rose 1997: 143). In other words, identities do not, necessarily, have to be 'bounded by the enclosure formed by the human skin or carried in a stable form in the interior of an individual' (N. Rose 1997: 144). Qualifications such as these are particularly apt in the context of this study of bisexuality, which indicates that an identity may not always inhere in the human body. Hence Deleuze's understanding of the body, one which goes some way to displace the corporeal solipsism which can be found in Foucault's, as well as in Foucauldian, analyses,[35] will implicitly inform the following analysis and will be explicitly considered in chapters 7 and 8.

In the first chapter I introduced a number of concepts in Foucault's genealogy which have enabled feminists both to critique 'the false universality of the subject', as Braidotti puts it, and at the same time to explore processes of subjectification. Set against some conceptions of bisexuality and of the self, particularly those which rest on a narrativisation of being, this provides the theoretical framework within which my own analysis will be situated. What I have done in this chapter is further to consider how feminists have developed and critiqued Foucault's work, and to examine some of the implications which may follow from this: the inadvertent accent on visibility, following the privileging of material corporeality, is a case in point. I have also been concerned with how even those theories which attempt to displace the concept of an essential or transcendental self maintain a number of presuppositions about what is exactly constitutive of the self. In particular, the chapter has focused on the way that, while *aspects* of the self have been rendered relational (psychoanalysis especially enables the theorisation of intrasubjectivity), many of the boundaries, not least the boundaries of the human body itself (although this does not constitute the whole of the self), remain intact. Thus while identity is in many of these accounts understood to be a 'necessary error', it remains, as Carole-Anne Tyler argues, central to the theorisation (and practice!) of selfhood:

Poststructurally savvy, we 'know' that coming out is a naively essentialist notion. Since we are always already caught up in a system of conventional differences that preclude the recovery of a 'genuine' difference, we can only reverse the discourse that has produced us and embrace the identity we have assumed as if it represented what we really are.   (Tyler 1994: 222)

What I want to begin to question now is whether all identities are in fact available to be 'embraced' by the self, and whether it might be possible that an identity could be separated even from *representing* what 'we really are'. In short, I will be looking at whether it is possible for an *identity without selfhood* to be produced through discourse. While the vehicle of this analysis is the textually mediated figure of Simone de Beauvoir, again, it should be emphasised that the techniques which are ascribed to her, and which are constitutive of 'de Beauvoir's self', are not unique *to* her. An analysis of a figure from another historical period, class or ethnicity, would certainly illuminate a different constellation of techniques from those which contribute to the production of de Beauvoir *as* 'de Beauvoir' (a White, bourgeois, French feminist/writer/author/philosopher/lover . . .) However, given (as these two chapters have illustrated) the durability of some techniques of the self which have been documented in contemporary Western social and cultural theory, a large part of the analysis, it seems reasonable to assume, would remain consistent. And as Foucault's genealogy of desiring man [*sic.*] suggests, these knowledges of the self, as well as the knowledge that forms a bridge between knowledge and experience, are themselves productive of selfhood, of identity, and of the relation between identity and selfhood. It will be in the light of the analysis of selfhood – 'de Beauvoir's' – and of identity – bisexuality – that I will return to the issue of what Tyler calls '"genuine" difference', as difference is understood by Deleuze, in the final two chapters.

3

Telling tales

> [T]o own the facts of one's own life is not self-evidence, it is *war* – a war
> ... over the possession of – or rather, the constitution of what will pass
> *as* – the truth.   Jacqueline Rose, *The Haunting of Sylvia Plath*

Before considering the different ways in which bisexuality is precluded
(chapter 4), displaced (chapter 5)[1] and erased (chapter 6) as an identity
which is understood to 'belong' to de Beauvoir, it is worth examining the
processes through which particular identities *are* attributed to her, such that
they are perceived to be a 'property' of her self. Two techniques in particular, both of which play a significant part in establishing de Beauvoir as a
'unique' individual, will be examined here. These are the author function
(Foucault 1979a, 1991d) and narrative (Ricouer 1980, 1991a, 1991b).[2]

Although I will be arguing that the author-function is a key mechanism
by which critics are able to ascribe individuality to de Beauvoir and,
further, to identify the site where the 'truth' of 'her' self is located, I am not
suggesting that this is because de Beauvoir is, after all, the subject of
enunciation. Instead, as an author, de Beauvoir fills 'one of [the] possible
positions' (Deleuze 1988: 55) made available by discourse. For Foucault,
the 'Author' functions as one of the internal procedures by which discourses are controlled, it 'limits . . . [the] . . . element of chance [in discourse]
by the play of an identity which has the form of individuality and the self'
(Foucault 1981: 59).[3] An analysis of the author function is privileged here
because, as I will illustrate, even though s/he is supposedly 'dead' (Barthes
1992), the issue of the author's 'originality', creativity and even 'genuis' is
still very much a matter of concern in contemporary Western culture.
Indeed, Kate Fullbrook and Edward Fullbrook's biography explicitly sets
out to 'prove' that it was de Beauvoir who was the 'originator' of existential philosophy.

This chapter will begin then, by exploring the implications of Foucault's assertion that 'a text always bears a number of signs that refer to the author' (Foucault 1979a: 22).[4] I will argue that de Beauvoir's life stands not merely as an explanation for any 'unevenness' in the *text* (as Foucault anticipates that it might) but, further, that psychoanalytic readings of de Beauvoir's texts are perceived to shed light on her *life*. However, while the attention paid to the relation between de Beauvoir's biography and her texts is central to the production of her self, this is possible only if there is a technique by which the biography itself is rendered intelligible. One of the ways that this occurs is through narrative emplotment. As I will illustrate, narrative and the author-function work in tandem, enabling (through the configuration of the plot) the inconsistencies of the text to be ascribed to the author's 'development' and (through the author-function) allowing the author, an individual, to 'exist' as a discursive production. Hence Paul Ricoeur's theory of narrative identity, with its accent on temporality, complements Foucault's analysis of the author-function.[5] Ricoeur's thesis also, importantly, at once highlights the centrality of the identity of the individual in the production of the self and also enables a more detailed analysis of the different ways that this identity is established through narrative. The second part of this chapter will explore three of these ways. Finally, true to narrative form, the chapter will end by considering the specific moments where narrative closure occurs in the biographies (moments which are central to the production of narrative identity), and will look briefly at the implications of de Beauvoir's death as it, too, serves to constitute her individual identity.

The author-function

Among the discursive features which preserve the status of the author is the notion of a 'work'. How else are the limits of the texts under analysis to be defined, Foucault asks, if not by a concept which designates a unity that only the author may account for? 'What is necessary to its composition if a work is not something written by a person called an "author"? [. . .] is everything he wrote and said, everything he left behind, to be included in his work?' (Foucault 1979a: 16). This relation, between author and work, is the central focus of this first part of the chapter. While it may be that the concept of a work is, for some critics, something that does not require explicit analysis (I will explore such commentaries first), a number of them draw fine distinctions between de Beauvoir's published and unpublished writings in order to locate, more 'precisely', the truth of her self (in the latter). This is the focus of the second section. A third implication of the author-function will also be examined, one which unfolds when commentators privilege *any* texts, published or unpublished, over and above the author's 'intentions'. This, significantly, has the effect of conferring an authority on the critic, an 'expert knowledge', which is exercised over, and disciplines, the author. Such authority is particularly clear in Toril Moi's use of psychoanalysis, which maintains the individuality of the author de Beauvoir and, additionally, develops it into subjectivity.

Life and work

De Beauvoir's life frequently informs readings of her work to the extent that the work is understood to 'belong' to her not merely because it goes under the name 'Simone de Beauvoir', but because it is everywhere stamped with what is perceived to be the mark of her own individual biography. Michelle Le Doeff, for example, in an article published in the academic journal *Feminist Studies*, writes:

> Without laying any but the lightest stress on it, one may recall that *The Second Sex* is also a labor of love and that de Beauvoir brings as one of her morganatic wedding presents a singular confirmation of the validity of Sartrian [*sic*] philosophy – your thought makes it possible to think the feminine condition, your philosophy sets me on the path of my emancipation, your truth will make me free.
>
> (Le Doeff 1980: 279–80)

De Beauvoir's relationship with Sartre so impresses upon Le Doeff's reading of *The Second Sex* that this apparently influential text is not merely read alongside her life but, more significantly, her life serves as witness in a court which judges the work (Deleuze and Parnet 1987: 8–9). Le Doeff implies that de Beauvoir has in some way failed both the test and the text: she thought the feminine condition, she found the path of emancipation, she tried to free herself, but all this *through*, and even *for*, Sartre. The name 'de Beauvoir' therefore, is 'more than an indication, a gesture, a finger pointed at someone, it is the equivalent of a description' (Foucault 1991d: 105). This description refers *specifically* to a *specific* individual: 'de Beauvoir' is not just the writer of *The Second Sex*, just as *The Second Sex* is not simply written by someone called 'de Beauvoir'. Instead, *The Second Sex* highlights the singularity of de Beauvoir's individual life and, conversely, de Beauvoir's individual life is expressed in *The Second Sex* (according to Le Doeff, it is an expression of her relationship with Sartre). Thus both life and work reinforce each other such that neither could belong to anyone but 'de Beauvoir' herself.

More than ten years after Le Doeff's article, the emphasis on de Beauvoir's life, and particularly Sartre's role in shaping that life, appears to have hardly altered. In the introduction to a special edition on Simone de Beauvoir in the academic journal *Signs*, Margaret Dietz has occasion to note that 'Anglo-American studies of Beauvoir took a dramatic turn in the 1980s' (Dietz 1992: 80). Significantly, the ten books written between 1981 and 1990 that Dietz cites, as well as the numerous interviews, are concerned with *both* de Beauvoir's life and her work. Dietz remarks on the focus of studies on de Beauvoir:

> Regardless of their [academic] emphasis, central to most of these studies is Beauvoir's relationship with Sartre and at least the implicit presumption that this heterosexual relationship, for good or ill, dominated her life and her identity as a woman.   (Dietz 1992: 83–4)

From the very start of this special edition then, critical interest in de Beauvoir's life, in her 'heterosexual relationship', and in the centrality of Sartre in her biography is firmly established. So significant is the author's life in the interpretation of her work, that Dietz suggests that it is de Beauvoir's attitudes in *life* which go some way to account for the (cool) reception of her work: 'Beauvoir's marginal influence in feminist politics was to no little degree a consequence of her almost lifelong ambivalence about feminism as a political movement' (Dietz 1992: 78). In other words, had de Beauvoir been personally less ambivalent towards the feminist movement (she did not publicly call herself a feminist until she was well over sixty), her work may have been more influential in that sphere.

What is especially significant in this context is that the focus on de Beauvoir's life itself propagates the necessity of yet more knowledge of that life in order that her work be given a 'fair trial'. Margaret Simons for example, a contributor to the same *Signs* special edition on de Beauvoir, writes:

> The discovery of lesbian connections in Beauvoir's life raises the question of how these connections might suggest a rereading of *The Second Sex*, which has often been criticized as 'male identified', and the history of the contemporary feminist movement as well.   (Simons 1992: 158)

Here the burden of responsibility conferred on the author has implications not only for the reception of de Beauvoir's work, but on the history of the contemporary feminist movement itself.

Two qualifications might, at this point, be added to Foucault's claim that the author is perceived to be 'manifested equally well, and with similar validity' (Foucault 1979a: 22) across all the works attributed to him or her. Firstly, it is arguable that the *degree* to which the biography of the author is understood to inform and shape the work and, further, critical evaluation of the relationship between life and work, varies according to the gender of the author. Feminist research has shown that women's writing, even when fictional, is frequently perceived to be 'personal' so 'reducing' its status from 'art' to that of confessional exhumation. Toril Moi, for example, notes that a number of critics accuse de Beauvoir of creating fictional characters which are (all!) 'a distasteful expression of her personality' (Moi 1990: 29). And yet, while de Beauvoir's work is understood to exemplify her relentless narcissism, the 'egotism' of writers such as Elias Canetti (whose *œuvre* is similar to that of de Beauvoir's) is turned into a 'virtue' (Moi 1994: 80–1). This, then, is a cultural double standard which Foucault does not acknowledge in his account of the author-function. It is worth noting however, that feminist texts on de Beauvoir, which often consider the author's concern with her 'self' to be a 'virtue',[6] also generate their own share of problems. As the above extract demonstrates, the focus on de Beauvoir as a 'real' individual imputes a heavy responsibility to her which has, in its turn, led her to be harshly judged.[7]

Secondly, it is questionable as to whether the 'truth' of the author is to be found *evenly* distributed across all of his or her work. As noted above, the importance attributed to establishing the 'truth' of de Beauvoir's life in order to evaluate the work more 'accurately' may have the effect of instigating an intensified search for this truth, as well as for its precise location. When this occurs, assumptions as to what is to be included in that curious unity 'a work' is brought sharply into focus. This is the concern of the following section.

The unpublished truths and the published untruths

For Simons, as for a number of other commentators, the 'truth' of de Beauvoir (and for Simons, the 'truth' of her sexuality in particular) may be found in her (previously)[8] unpublished and unavailable journals, letters and manuscripts.[9] Comparing these unpublished texts to de Beauvoir's published memoirs, Simons notes that in the latter, de Beauvoir recounts how she told her friend Stépha 'of her fear of male sexuality' and that she experienced 'a flush of sexual feelings' (Simons 1992: 140) when she and her sister were 'sprawled in the grass of the park' (de Beauvoir quoted in Simons 1992: 143). Simons adds however, that:

a nearly illegible reference to this conversation with Stépha in the 1928 journal refers not to lying entwined with her sister in the grass, but to having Zaza leaning over her bed embracing her. [. . .] As interesting as the evidence of Beauvoir's erotic passion for Zaza is the evidence that she censored it in her autobiography. The journals and letters show Beauvoir's awareness and sometimes concern that her feelings and behavior are lesbian.

(Simons 1992: 143–4)

Although Simons does not explicitly use the term 'truth', her conclusions with respect to the *difference* between the published and the unpublished material nevertheless suggest that it was precisely this that was hidden from the public eye. De Beauvoir's censorship of the published autobiography is not only 'as interesting' as her erotic passion, but is more importantly perceived to *confirm* (the truth of) it. This emphasis on censorship illustrates the significance of repression in the constitution of the self: Simons assumes that that which is hidden is *more true to the self* than that which is revealed.

As in some of the academic texts, so the popular biographies suggest that not everything that has been 'recorded' about de Beauvoir necessarily reveals the 'truth' of her self. Francis and Gontier, for example, preface their account with something of a contract with the reader, promising that they have done their utmost to acquire as much of the truth as possible:

When one writes the biography of a controversial figure, it is not always possible to be certain that one has all the facts or is using the accurate version of events that have been recorded in different or contradictory ways. We did our best to obtain all the information currently available and to consult those witnesses who agreed to meet with us.   (Francis and Gontier 1987: vii)

Reminiscent of an oath in a court of law, this 'sworn statement' is augmented by a legal vocabulary: the biographers speak of 'facts' and 'accurate versions', 'records' and 'witnesses'. This suggests that the truth itself is on trial. An oblique reference to other biographers (those for whom it may not have been 'possible to be certain'), indicates that the battle ground over which the marketing value of popular biographies fight are the 'real facts' of de Beauvoir's life.

Given that the truth may be 'hidden', the biographers establish a hierarchy between the published and unpublished material wherein the latter is perceived to be more 'true' to de Beauvoir than the former. Hence not *everything* written by de Beauvoir is understood to be a guarantor of the truth in itself. Indeed, it is de Beauvoir's skill as a novelist, for example, which suggests to Francis and Gontier that the truth-value of de Beauvoir's published work – autobiographical or not – is open to question (Francis and Gontier 1987: ix–xv). In a neat reversal of the opinion held by many critics, that her novels and philosophical texts are too personal (see above), Fullbrook and Fullbrook argue that de Beauvoir's literary talents as a novelist render her autobiographies 'suspect' with regard to the truth of her life story:

our repeated readings of Beauvoir's autobiographies – a main source for all biographers of the pair [de Beauvoir and Sartre] – revealed just how tightly *structured* they were . . . That such a life had been proposed as her own by a novelist who had the talent to sustain a massive international readership since the 1940s began to indicate to us the need for caution.   (Fullbrook and Fullbrook 1993: 2)

If, as the historian Hayden White argues, the 'authority of the historical narrative is the authority of reality itself' (White 1987: 20) then who, of all recorders, will be more subjective than the subject herself? Fullbrook and Fullbrook's, as well as Francis and Gontier's, suspicion of the published work renders explicit a logic which also lies behind Simons' assertion (above) that the unpublished documents are more true to de Beauvoir's self than the published material. In each case, the very process which 'reveals' the author – that is, the process of publication which makes her available to the reader/public (which 'publicises' her) – also serves to 'hide' de Beauvoir. In other words, the 'real' de Beauvoir is the *private* de Beauvoir, the one who stands, frustratingly, behind the author to whom the (published) texts point.

For both Francis and Gontier and Fullbrook and Fullbrook the unadulterated truth (free from the author's tampering) is to be found elsewhere – principally, in de Beauvoir letters. Fullbrook and Fullbrook argue that de Beauvoir's letters to Sartre yield 'the prize [that] is the correction of one of the great legends of this century' (Fullbrook and Fullbrook 1993: 98).[10] Francis and Gontier, notwithstanding the (considerable) number of resources available to them, also perceive de Beauvoir's letters, which in this instance were written to Nelson Algren, to have a significance against which nothing compares:

The point of departure for this biography was our tracking down of the handwritten, unpublished letters that Simone de Beauvoir wrote to the American author Nelson Algren, with whom she had fallen in love. These 1,442 pages of delicate script[11] recount, sometimes on a daily basis, Simone de Beauvoir's life as well as the lives of Jean-Paul Sartre and their friends. This correspondence, covering the years from 1947 to 1960, is a rich firsthand account of existentialism's golden hours, the turn of events in politics and literature, gossip among the intellectual set, and above all a love story.   (Francis and Gontier 1987: ix)

The letters are a (literally) signed guarantee that Francis and Gontier's biography will furnish an authoritative interpretation of de Beauvoir's life story. They are a 'rich firsthand account' both because the 'reality' of de Beauvoir's experience has been 'found' for the 'first' time and because, written on a 'daily basis' (resembling a diary, a notable technique of the self) they have an immediate and spontaneous quality on a par with the 'truth-full' soul which pours from the psychologist's couch. Further, they are written under the influence of 'love' which implies that they will be intimate and likely to be devoid of self-reflective censorship. Thus aside from sheer quantity, the quality of the letters may also be vouched for: they are unpublished (unedited), handwritten (authentic) and free from the demands of publishing houses.

The issue here concerns the truth: who owns it and under what circumstances. The following extract from Margaret Crosland's biography for example, confirms that although the truth of de Beauvoir may 'belong' to her, she also represents an obstacle to its outing. Crosland writes: 'If Beauvoir's death was an irreparable loss, these posthumous publications [de Beauvoir's letters to Sartre and the *Journal de Guerre*] have allowed deeper insight into her personality and relationships' (Crosland 1992: ix). The apparent *closure* of death *opens* the door on de Beauvoir's life. Armed with the benefit of 'distance' and 'objectivity' (which make available facts that de Beauvoir could never, by definition, possess), Crosland is able to read de Beauvoir's story retrospectively and, in so doing, recover a truth that de Beauvoir herself could hardly have been aware of. If de Beauvoir's life stands in the way of the truth then, her death frees it up to a public who is able to 'own' it as it had never been owned by de Beauvoir herself. Ted Hughes' hope, that 'each of us owns the facts of her or his own life' (Hughes quoted in J. Rose 1992: 65), is naïve in light of the magnificent force by which the death of the author releases the truth of the self.

The suspicion surrounding the truth-value of the published texts, coupled with the status conferred on the unpublished material in this regard, enables the critic or biographer to posit a direct, even rather simple, relation between de Beauvoir's letters and the 'truth' of de Beauvoir. It is not the case however, that the published texts are never perceived to contain the truth of de Beauvoir, but rather that a somewhat more complex procedure is required in order to gain access to it. Foucault argues that the author-function 'does not develop spontaneously as the attribution of a discourse to an individual' but is instead the result of 'a complex operation which constructs a certain rational being that we call "author"' (Foucault 1991d: 110). The following section will consider how it is that critics are able to identify the 'truth' of de Beauvoir across a range of her texts, whether they are published or not.

Truth and the published texts

As I outlined in chapter 1, Foucault regards the act of writing to be a technique of the self, 'one of the most ancient Western traditions' (Foucault 1988b: 27), whereby 'the experience of oneself was intensified and widened' (Foucault 1988b: 28). De Beauvoir's letters to Sartre, like Foucault's description of Marcus Aurelius' letters to Fronto, are frequently seen to provide a detailed, 'careful', as the *Independent on Sunday* (2 February 1992b) puts it, care of the self, a 'record of her days, where she sleeps and with whom' (ibid.). The letters shed light on the truth of de Beauvoir precisely *because* they are a 'description of everyday life': 'these details are important because they are you – what you thought, what you felt' (Foucault 1988b: 29). The role of writing as a technique of the self is especially clearly illustrated in the following extract, taken from a different article, also in the *Independent on Sunday*: 'The burden of Beauvoir's emancipation from French bourgeois society was borne by her with an equanimity for which the process of writing, of self-actualisation, is entirely responsible' (*Independent on Sunday,* 10 June 1990). Here, 'the process of writing' explicitly corresponds to 'self-actualisation'.

For Foucault, it is the *act* of writing which functions as a technique of the self. This kind of writing is distinguished from 'writing' which is of concern in debates surrounding the 'death of the author'. The notion that a text may be interpreted in a number of ways, that it is not 'bound' by the author's intentions and that it does not offer a direct 'reflection' of the author, are some of the features which are said to have 'caused' this 'death'. The author is no longer perceived to be 'an indefinite source of significations which fill a work' (Foucault 1991d: 118) since writing creates 'a space into which the writing subject constantly disappears' (Foucault 1991d: 102). In texts on de Beauvoir however, the author does not often 'disappear' *into* the space created by writing, so much as unintentionally reveal the truth of her self *through* her writings. Where priority is given to de Beauvoir's writings *per se,* the critic may locate the 'truth' of de Beauvoir not only in the unpublished texts (as above) but also in the published texts. In the following extracts for example, taken from the academic journals *Yale French Studies*, *L'Esprit Créateur* and *Women's Studies and Interdisciplinary Journal* respectively, whatever attempts de Beauvoir might make to 'lock [herself] up' are perceived to be futile:

This [the division between being 'generous and long-suffering' on the surface and 'guilty, selfish, passionate and erotic' beneath] is precisely the inscription of herself as a writer that Beauvoir seems most eager to lock up in her writing. But this message has left its mark everywhere in the debased and murdered heroines, in the failed sisterhood, and the hostile mother–daughter relationships in her novels. Women, Beauvoir has said in response to a criticism of her negative presentations of female characters, women are 'divided'. Herself, it seems, most of all.   (Evans 1986: 85)[12]

In spite of all the words that cover what cannot be said, Beauvoir's rationalist discourse does not entirely erase a countertext that transgresses the rules she sets for herself. Those contradictions, and the divided self they reveal, inscribe her work in troubled figures.   (Kaufmann 1989: 31)

Indeed, her tendency to mask her actual feelings is even apparent in her autobiographical works, where an inner voice seems to express feelings which are quite different from, and even contradictory to, her explicit statements.

(Yanay 1990: 227)

In each of these extracts, de Beauvoir's 'writing' is seen to escape her and therefore, without the author intending it, 'reveals' the 'truth' of the author. De Beauvoir is unable to 'erase', 'mask' or 'lock up' her 'self'. Repeatedly, the 'divided self', the 'inner voice' and 'feelings' emerge through what Evans calls de Beauvoir's 'writing', and what Kaufmann and Yanay call her 'work/s'. In one respect then, the author *has* suffered a death of sorts, insofar as her conscious goals are no longer significant in the interpretation of the text (or more precisely, if de Beauvoir's intentions have any significance at all, it lies only in her failure to achieve them). Despite the apparent displacement of the author however, her importance in relation to the work is nevertheless maintained (and even strengthened) insofar as the texts – albeit against the author's conscious wishes – now expose the 'truth' of her self. It is a 'game', as Foucault argues (Foucault 1991d: 102), and one that the author has lost. This authorial loss however, is the critic's gain; s/he now knows more about the author, through her texts, than the author herself does. Hence these critics do not require recourse to unpublished material to identify the 'truth' of de Beauvoir since the 'truth' of herself is revealed through the interpretation of *all* the texts, published or not. The 'unlocking', as Evans might put it, of de Beauvoir's 'writing' confers an authority on the critic who acquires the expert knowledge needed to locate the truth of de Beauvoir's 'deep self'. In short, the privileging of de Beauvoir's writings/novels *per se* does not enable writing to transgress *itself*, but to transgress the intentions of the author. It does not displace the author, or create a 'space' into which she disappears. Instead, it serves to tie the author (and her 'truth') all the more tightly to the text.

So far, this chapter has considered the way that de Beauvoir's work is perceived to 'belong' to her not merely because it is written by her and carries her name, but also because it is understood to 'reveal', in one way or another, the 'truth' of her self. Some commentators locate this truth by marking a clear distinction between published and unpublished texts and by positing a direct link between the 'truth' of de Beauvoir and the unpublished material. An alternative strategy identifies the truth of de Beauvoir across the range of her texts, with little or no distinction between them. Moi's account of de Beauvoir's life and work is interesting in this context because although she agrees that de Beauvoir's letters to Sartre reveal 'a wealth of details' (Moi 1994: 4) not available in the memoirs and, further, that they contain sentences which sometimes emerge verbatim in the novels – whereby '[i]t would be easy to conclude that, all in all, the letters must contain the "real" version of the events' (ibid.) – she nevertheless argues that it would be a mistake to collapse her 'personal writing' (Moi 1994: 244) (which she defines as writing not undertaken with a view to publication) with the 'essence' of de Beauvoir. In other words, Moi notes the difference between the published and unpublished material, but, precisely on the grounds that the unpublished texts *are* personal, argues that: '[because] her letters and diaries represent Beauvoir in her most vulnerable psychological state . . . it is a mistake to take them to reveal the essence of the whole woman' (Moi 1994: 245). Moi is suggesting therefore, that no *singular* text can be collapsed with de Beauvoir. Taking the position of critics who find the truth of de Beauvoir across the range of her texts one step further, she argues, explicitly, that there can be 'no *methodological* distinction between "life" and "text"' (Moi 1994: 3–4).

However, unlike the critics cited above, it is not Moi's intention to iden-tify the 'truth' of de Beauvoir. Indeed, she displaces the very notion of the truth of the self. Moi argues that her book is not a biography, but rather a 'personal genealogy' wherein she 'does not reject the notion of the "self" or the subject but tries instead to subject that very self to genealogical investigation' (Moi 1994: 7).[13] In other words, there is no 'essence' of de Beauvoir; instead, her self is overdetermined by a variety of social, psychological, historical and cultural factors. De Beauvoir 'is' an 'extra-ordinarily complex effect of a whole network of different discourses and determinants' (Moi 1994: 6) *none of which* is reducible to the 'real' de Beauvoir.

This reading is a radical one insofar as, for Moi, de Beauvoir's writings are less indicative of her own 'true' self, than of a self which is determined by a variety of (external) factors. In this respect then, Moi's 'personal genealogy' displaces the individuality which the critics cited above confer on the author. Nevertheless, the following section will explore the way that Moi's use of psychoanalysis, although it destabilises de Beauvoir's *ration-ality*, does not deconstruct the notion of the self *per se*. Indeed, Moi's psychoanalytic readings of de Beauvoir's texts maintain the individuality of the author and even develop it (into subjectivity).

The 'psy' complex

The 'expert knowledges' of the critics cited above indicates that although the truth of de Beauvoir is perceived to 'belong' to de Beauvoir (she is pos-sessed of and by it), she is by no means necessarily the most well equipped to access the truth within her self. De Beauvoir's self requires interpretation, just as the confessional technique of the self demands that the soul's disclosure be heard, scrutinised and evaluated by a higher authority. If this authority no longer assumes the shape of priest, then it has often been replaced, as the examples above demonstrate, by the critic. A critic who employs, moreover, extensive use of what Rose has called the 'psy disciplines' (N. Rose 1997: 139). Rose suggests that the 'generosity' of the 'psy disciplines', the willingness of psy to 'give itself away', has led it to acquire a legitimacy deriving from its claim 'to tell the truth about human beings' (ibid.). Thus it is, Rose argues, that 'it has become impossible to conceive of personhood, to experience one's own or another's personhood, or to govern oneself or others without "psy"' (ibid.). The examples so far bear witness to Rose's thesis, particularly insofar as the 'psychologising' of de Beauvoir does not necessarily require rigorous psychoanalytic interpretation. Commentators refer with ease, and without explanation, to the censorship in de Beauvoir's texts, to her 'divided' self and to her 'inner' feelings. Entire texts are found to be riddled with truths, truths which de Beauvoir consciously tries to hide, but unconsciously – a term which has infiltrated Western culture such that it is employed as an everyday colloquialism – reveals. Again, this highlights the significance conferred on 'repression' in the production of the self; critics ascribe a 'deep' self to de Beauvoir, locating the 'real' de Beauvoir in that which is not conscious. Foucault argues however, that although:

[c]ritics doubtless try to give this intelligible being a realistic status, by discerning, in the individual, a 'deep' motive, a 'creative' power, or a 'design' . . . these aspects of an individual which we designate as making him an author are only a projection, in more or less psychologizing terms, of the operations that we force the texts to undergo, the connections that we make, the traits that we establish as pertinent, the continuities that we recognize, or the exclusions that we practice.

(Foucault 1991d: 110)

The techniques by which the individual author is fleshed out and inscribed with depth is particularly clearly illustrated in Moi's account of de Beauvoir's life and work.

The convergence of life and text befits, indeed stems from, Moi's use of psychoanalysis as one of the main tools of analysis.[14] She writes:

I have always been struck by the fact that Freud, in *The Interpretation of Dreams*, seems unable to distinguish between the psyche and the text: at the same time as he gives us a theory of interpretation, he also gives us a map of the human mind . . . for Freud, the person only reveals herself in the form of a text: to all practical purposes, the Freudian subject *is* a text.   (Moi 1994: 4)

A Foucauldian reading would also find Freud's twofold discovery significant, but for different reasons. In the light of Foucault's analysis of the self, the psyche may be understood as one of the cultural formations which stabilise the fold, which fold force. In this context, the psyche represents not an archive (or even 'a map') of the human mind, so much as a mirror which reflects only 'the images we have conjured up to describe ourselves' (Hutton 1988: 139). In other words, Freud's 'theory of interpretation' *requires* a 'human mind' (housed in a subject who is possessed of a psyche) in order that it (the psyche) be available for psychoanalysis: 'Foucault . . . argues that the self is not an objective reality to be described by our theories [theories such as Freudian psychoanalysis] but a subjective notion that is actually constituted by them' (Hutton 1988: 135). The notion that de Beauvoir 'reveals herself in the form of a text' therefore not only belies the presupposition that a 'self' exists which is able to be 'revealed' but also, in the very process of revelation, is constitutive *of* that self. Arguably, Moi's use of the genealogical method sits uneasily with psychoanalysis insofar as psychoanalysis, in the process of deconstructing the self, simultaneously reconstructs it through its analysis of subjectivity. To this extent Moi, as Rose puts it, engages with a self which is itself '*resultant* of the processes under study' (N. Rose 1996: 299).

Psychoanalysis, like the confessional technique of the self, generates 'an imperative to seek knowledge of the self' (Hutton 1988: 131). However, since the secrets of the psyche are not transparent, this knowledge may be procured only with the aid of a higher authority who is qualified to interpret the soul's spillage.[15] Deleuze writes:

> There were already so many people, so many priests, so many representatives who spoke in the name of our conscience, it was necessary for this race of priests and representatives to speak in the name of the unconscious.
>
> (Deleuze and Parnet 1987: 21)

Although de Beauvoir, the individual, has been 'liberated' (from the tyranny of her 'self') by the theory of the unconscious, she is at the same time subjected 'even further to the technology of knowledge and power' (Braidotti 1991: 83): 'What is controversial in psychoanalysis, in this context, is precisely its implicit alliance with a juridical model of knowledge, which allows it to function in the schema of avowal, confession and interiorization' (ibid.). Psychoanalysis' production of the 'deep', interior, self is therefore one of the techniques, and arguably a dominant one, which stabilises the 'self' even as it decrees its instability.

It goes without saying that Moi was not de Beauvoir's psychoanalyst and that de Beauvoir did not 'confess' to Moi. However since, according to

Moi, the subject '*reveals* herself in the form of a text' (Moi 1994: 4, my emphasis), she is nevertheless able to unveil a 'disclosure' through de Beauvoir's texts. For example: Moi finds a 'logic at work in *L'Invitée*' that 'operates in the interstices of Beauvoir's own reading' (Moi 1994: 96). De Beauvoir, Moi argues, was impelled to write *L'Invitée* in order that she might 'work through some fundamental fantasies of her own' (Moi 1994: 122), fantasies which were overdetermined by a variety of factors (including de Beauvoir's investment in existentialism). Thus despite de Beauvoir's own belief (according to Moi) that *L'Invitée* was inspired by the 'historical unhappiness' (Moi 1994: 124) of the second World War, Moi suggests that in fact the novel signified a defiant 'entry into the literary field in France as an absolute *triumph* over and *liberation* from the realm of the mother' (Moi 1994: 120). Further corroboration for this reading is found in other texts by de Beauvoir: 'I want to show that certain themes raised in the novel also occur in other texts by Simone de Beauvoir, and that when they do, they tend to cluster around the image of a mother figure' (Moi 1994: 119).

To the extent that Moi gains a knowledge of de Beauvoir through her texts, de Beauvoir is subjectified in much the same manner as she would be, had she confessed:

The confession is a ritual of discourse in which the speaking subject is also the subject of the statement; it is also a ritual that unfolds within a power relationship, for one does not confess without the presence (or virtual presence) of a partner who is not simply the interlocutor but the authority.   (Foucault 1990a: 61)

Although the psychoanalytic theory of the unconscious ensures that the subject is no longer 'considered "master" in the house of knowledge' (Braidotti 1991: 84) (thereby providing a powerful critique of the humanist self), by 'reading off' de Beauvoir's unconscious in her texts, Moi herself stands in the master's shoes (and lives in the house of knowledge). In effect, Moi's reading displaces de Beauvoir's own authority over her self, only to replace it with what Rose calls the 'expertise of subjectivity' (N. Rose 1989: 2) represented by 'psy'. The privileging of de Beauvoir's texts, coupled with Moi's ability to know what de Beauvoir cannot (her discourse is beyond her own control), further suggests that Moi's (psycho)analysis is not so far removed from the positions of the critics cited above (who locate the truth of de Beauvoir across the range of her texts, published or not). Insofar as 'confessions' are culled from de Beauvoir's texts, these texts assume a central role in her subjectification.

Moi, as demonstrated above, considers *all* de Beauvoir's texts relevant to her analysis. Although *none* contains the truth, it remains that the texts in their entirety (texts which the author-function ensures are ascribed to de

Beauvoir) contain a psychoanalytic logic which points to de Beauvoir's subjectivity (even though it is not coincidental with itself and cannot be collapsed with any one text or character) as surely as the work points to the author and designates a unity. In short, in Moi's account it is not that the texts bear 'a number of signs that refer to the author' (Foucault 1979a: 22) so much that, aided by the psychoanalytic interpretation, the texts reveal, and are constitutive *of*, an intelligible portrait of the subject. Hence insofar as Moi prioritises writing, and also assumes a subject who is (consequently) able to be psychoanalysed, the individuality of the author is maintained and even elaborated through the explication of a subjectivity. The issue here is not psychoanalysis itself, nor what Moi and other critics 'mean' when they analyse de Beauvoir's writing. Rather, my concern is with the *effects* that are produced in the search for de Beauvoir. Principal among these effects is the production of de Beauvoir herself.

Narrative identity

Having considered the different ways in which the author-function enables the critic to ascribe individuality and subjectivity to de Beauvoir, this second part of the chapter explores how the narrative structures in accounts of de Beauvoir's life contribute to a portrait of intelligible selfhood. Most obviously, Paul Ricoeur's analysis can be used to illustrate how representations of de Beauvoir's life and work do more than offer information about dates and actions/events and instead harness these 'facts' to a narrative which enables their significance to be evaluated in the light of the overall story. Thus although the author-function enables commentators to locate the site of the truth of de Beauvoir, this truth, like the 'logic' that Moi identifies in de Beauvoir's texts, does not spring 'spontaneously' from the work, but is instead produced through narrative. Less obviously perhaps, Ricoeur's analysis will be used to draw attention to the importance of the narrative identity of individuality in the construction of plausible selfhood.

Becoming de Beauvoir

Although biographers frequently claim to be 'invisible servant[s]' at the mercy of material which *of itself* reveals the 'truth' of their subject, a writer of 'real events' is nevertheless able, as Carolyn Steedman points out, to appropriate for him or herself 'the most massive authority as narrator' (Steedman 1992: 613). Ricoeur's theory of narrative makes visible the 'invisible servant' that Steedman describes. It is through 'the act of *following* a story' (Ricoeur 1991a: 21), he argues, that events which would otherwise appear to be random are rendered meaningful. In particular, it is the plot which enables one story to be made out of multiple incidents or, as he puts it, that 'transforms the many incidents *into one* story' (ibid.). The story (the whole) is thereby perceived to be more than the enumeration (the sum of its parts) as each event (each part within the story) 'receives its definition from its contribution to the development of a plot' (Ricoeur 1980: 171). Since all the events come together in the course of the plot (they are configured by the plot), Ricoeur argues that the conclusion is 'the pole attraction of the entire development' (Ricoeur 1980: 174): 'rather than being predictable, a conclusion must be acceptable. Looking back from the conclusion to the episodes leading up to it, we have to be able to say that this ending required these sorts of events and this chain of actions' (ibid.). The implication here is that although the story appears to unfold *naturally*, as though it were an 'inevitable' progression, this is in fact possible only because of 'the teleological movement directed by our expectations when we follow the story' (ibid.).

Significantly, none of the accounts of de Beauvoir's life begin with her childhood (none begin with de Beauvoir's 'beginning'). Instead, they start with a portrait of de Beauvoir at the peak of what she is perceived to 'be'. Margaret Crosland's biography, for example, begins with a representation of de Beauvoir as a socialist-feminist and, befitting this representation, she ends her introduction with a description of a 'single red rose' which lay on de Beauvoir's grave, and which captures all that Crosland believes de Beauvoir stood for. In Francis and Gontier's biography, de Beauvoir is a writer and, more centrally, Sartre's lover. The epigraph which precedes and anticipates the subject of their first chapter is taken from de Beauvoir's *The Prime of Life*: 'I know that no harm could ever come to me from him – unless he were to die before I died' (Francis and Gontier 1987). Fullbrook and Fullbrook's biography begins with an anecdote: Sartre is being interviewed and, 'in his old age', lets slip that 'he had not been de Beauvoir's first lover' (Fullbrook and Fullbrook 1993: 4). The implications of this 'revelation', according to Fullbrook and Fullbrook, are weighty: 'If *this* story was based on a fabrication, then so too might be any of their others' (ibid.). The point of this specific anecdote corresponds to the aim of their biography more generally, which is to demonstrate that the belief that it was Sartre, rather than de Beauvoir, who was the intellectual force behind the relationship and the original source of most of Sartre's ideas, including *Being and Nothingness*, is nothing but a fabrication.[16]

Moi's account too, begins with what she refers to as an 'emblematic' moment (Moi 1994: 16) in de Beauvoir's life. This is a conversation between de Beauvoir and Sartre, described in *Memoirs of a Dutiful Daughter,* after which, Moi argues, de Beauvoir persistently describes herself as Sartre's philosophical Other. For Moi, 'all the essential elements of Beauvoir's "erotico-theoretical" relationship to Sartre and to philosophy' are to be found in this one scene (Moi 1994: 15). Hence her personal genealogy is, for the most part, anchored around this conversation: she will consider the factors, both subjective and objective, which led de Beauvoir to perceive herself in such a way, as well as the implications, both conscious and uncon-scious, of de Beauvoir's position (a woman in an elitist, male-dominated, intellectual environment) as they are revealed in her texts.

By beginning with a significant moment of closure, accounts of de Beauvoir's life demonstrate that narrative time is not merely a forward pro-gression (like the direction captured by the phrase 'the arrow of time') but is also a *recollection* (by definition backwards) *from* the end point:

> The analysis of the plot as configuration has already led us to the threshold of what could be called 'narrative repetition'. By reading the end into the beginning and the beginning into the end, we learn to read time backward, as the recapitulation of the initial conditions of a course of action in its terminal consequences.
>
> (Ricoeur 1980: 183)

Narrative repetition, as I will illustrate below, is a central feature in the pro-duction of narrative identity. The recapitulation that Ricoeur describes is particularly acute in the biographical genre given that the reader is usually familiar with the subject. The initial image of de Beauvoir, captured at her most equivocal, is pregnant with the narrative to follow, a narrative which, necessarily temporal, is condensed into a single trope (the rose, the quote, the interview, the conversation).[17] In each of these examples the symbol of 'de Beauvoir' is caught in the spotlight, typifying the star/hero that is famil-iar, or will become familiar, to the 'public'/reader. To this extent the biogra-phies begin with a device which may be compared to the frames that also 'capture' de Beauvoir (see chapter 5): frozen (as in a freeze-frame), de Beauvoir is as static as the photographs that usually grace a biography's central pages.

The initial representation of de Beauvoir as she 'is' enables the reader to anticipate the direction of the narrative in advance. The reader *expects*, by the end of the story, to understand how it is that de Beauvoir came to (be) herself (and this is, arguably, where much of the pleasure of reading biog-raphy lies). According to Ricoeur's theory of narrative: 'The end of the story is what equates the present with the past, the actual with the potential' (Ricoeur 1980: 186). However, prior to de Beauvoir becoming who she is – prior to the narrative equation between present and past, actual and poten-tial – her progress is inevitably hampered by a 'thousand contingencies'

(Ricoeur 1980: 174). These contingencies do not represent a diversion from the narrative however. Instead, they serve as episodes which make the conclusion all the more convincing: 'This is the paradox of contingency, judged "acceptable after all", that characterises the comprehension of any story told' (ibid.). By way of example, I want to consider briefly how, although each of the four accounts of de Beauvoir's life cast her relationship with Sartre in a different light, their narrative structures are such that *all* the representations are, within their own context, persuasive. This is because the 'contingencies' which precede de Beauvoir and Sartre's infamous 'pact'[18] (and it is the conditions under which this pact is 'signed' that sets the tone of their relationship) contribute to the impression that it is the 'natural' consequence of the preceding events.

Contingencies

The first few pages of Francis and Gontier's biography indicate that de Beauvoir's life story is to be collapsed with a love story. The protagonist's initial 'potential', which the narrative will retrieve and confirm, is her capacity for love. They outline the plot immediately: 'A pretty young girl, the most intelligent among her peers, meets the most brilliant boy around, and there you have it: the ideal couple' (Francis and Gontier 1987: 2). The biography is to portray a love story of literally mythological proportions:

Retold by Chrétien de Troyes or Béroul, this love story would sound like the stuff of legends [. . .] there are no stories more often told than those of the great enduring loves. Why would we remember Cosima and Richard Wagner, or Abélard and Héloïse, were it not that matters of the heart are the most enticing . . . that the story of a couple whom life could not wear down and defeat moves us, intrigues us, and holds us a prisoner of its magic.   (Francis and Gontier 1987: 2)

De Beauvoir's relationship with Sartre is 'enduring', 'legendary', 'magical' and resonates with other well-known love stories. By situating de Beauvoir and Sartre in the context of famous heterosexual lovers, Francis and Gontier demonstrate Ricoeur's thesis that popular stories are not so much a telling for the first time, as a *re*telling, where 'following the story is less important than apprehending the well-known end as implied in the beginning and the well-known episodes as leading to this end' (Ricoeur 1980: 179).

Above all, Francis and Gontier represent de Beauvoir's relationship with Sartre as a brave challenge to bourgeois morality: 'Her attitude was a courageous one; to reject marriage in 1929 was to relegate oneself to the fringes of society' (Francis and Gontier 1987: 103). Given that the relationship is cast as an act of 'revolutionary' (ibid.) daring, Francis and Gontier's biography portrays de Beauvoir's early (sexual) experiences accordingly. De Beauvoir's initial foray into the world of bohemian cafes and bars is perceived to be a positive and fulfilling experience. As soon as she samples the 'magic' and 'the poetry of the bars', she casts off (promptly, and with considerable ease) 'the last ballast of her [bourgeois] social upbringing' (Francis and Gontier 1987: 73). De Beauvoir meets with 'foreigners, homosexuals, and drug addicts' (ibid.), begins 'the search for thrills' (Francis and Gontier 1987: 74), smashes glasses 'with aplomb' (Francis and Gontier 1987: 73) and takes pleasure in dancing with '[c]omplete strangers' (Francis and Gontier 1987: 75). In short, de Beauvoir appears to have found her 'natural' habitat in 'the poetry of the lower depths' (Francis and Gontier 1987: 114) and, insofar as this attraction continues to hold a 'strange fascination' (ibid.) for the rest of de Beauvoir's life – she 'never failed to investigate the quarters of ill-repute' (ibid.) – it constitutes a link which unites the young (the potential) and the adult (the actual) de Beauvoir. It is in the light of these early experiences that de Beauvoir and Sartre's pact appears as the culmination of a sequence of events, the logical result of an attitude which de Beauvoir possessed from the beginning of her life, before she met Sartre. The conclusion therefore, as Ricoeur puts it, is acceptable (if not predictable).

Crosland's account, by contrast, reads very differently. Clearly critical of the pact that Sartre and de Beauvoir devised, Crosland argues that it was Sartre's polygamy that shaped the nature of the alliance: 'It is absurd to regard the two of them as Great Lovers, for Sartre made his own position quite clear: he loved Simone but he was "polygamous"' (Crosland 1992: 78–9). Where Francis and Gontier suggest that de Beauvoir agreed to the pact with Sartre 'because it corresponded to her own convictions' (Francis and Gontier 1987: 103), Crosland argues that it is yet another echo of bourgeois marriage. Thus, without Francis and Gontier's belief in de Beauvoir's (sexual) precocity, Crosland suggests that the bars which de Beauvoir attends in her youth are not exotic, but rather 'sordid dive[s]' which 'bored' and 'sickened' her (Crosland 1992: 61). De Beauvoir is said to retain not only her 'prudery', but also her 'bourgeois aura' (ibid.). She has 'a virgin's fear of men' (Crosland 1992: 62), men who do not 'approach' her, as in Francis and Gontier's account, but who 'accost her in the streets and in bars' and make her 'really frightened' (Crosland 1992: 63). And while Francis and Gontier suggest that this period of de Beauvoir's life is dominated by men (on her first evening out, for instance, she is accompanied by her cousin Jacques), in Crosland's biography de Beauvoir is surrounded by women (she first goes out with her sister Hélène). For Crosland, it is Stépha (her friend), rather than Jacques, who has 'sex appeal' (Crosland 1992: 63) and who 'undertook to educate the *oie blanche* in some of the harder facts of life' (Crosland 1992: 64).

Crosland's and Francis and Gontier's biographies demonstrate how the same events might produce two quite different representations of de Beauvoir, each corresponding to the overall narrative 'plot'. For Francis and Gontier, de Beauvoir is principally a daring lover who rejected the traditional monogamous rules of marriage in favour of a liberating and open relationship. Befitting the notion that de Beauvoir is afraid of nothing (which in its turn enables her to defy convention), she enters a man's world abruptly, and with brutal courage. Crosland's biography, leaning towards the feminist, links de Beauvoir's entrance into 'the adult world' to her emerging sexuality. If the birth of de Beauvoir's sexual consciousness is tentative and ambivalent, then this offers Crosland a further opportunity to demonstrate the support of her women friends: 'Sometimes she would feel depressed, but gradually, with help, especially from Stépha, she was entering the real, adult world' (Crosland 1992: 65–6). In short, the episodes in each biography are emplotted in such a way that the conclusion (in this example, the character of de Beauvoir's relationship with Sartre) is wholly acceptable to the reader.

The difference between Moi's and Fullbrook and Fullbrook's account of de Beauvoir and Sartre's relationship is not merely a question of colouring, but is rather written into the very structure of the narrative and, particularly, in the different ways that the narrative events are emplotted. In keeping with their efforts to establish de Beauvoir's intellectual and emotional superiority, Fullbrook and Fullbrook emphasise Sartre's dependence upon her throughout the biography, a dependence which is exemplified in his attempts to establish a relationship with her. One of the chief means by which an impression of 'effort', on Sartre's part, is created is through the biographers' emphasis on the length of time it took him to 'engineer' (Fullbrook and Fullbrook 1993: 58) his meeting with de Beauvoir and for their relationship subsequently to develop.

According to Fullbrook and Fullbrook, although Sartre first sees de Beauvoir in the university at 'the beginning of May', '[w]hen June ended, Sartre, the womanizer, had still not met the friendly fellow student he was so "dead set" on knowing' (Fullbrook and Fullbrook 1993: 55–6). Towards the end of July the couple eventually meet in a study group, an event which, for Sartre, 'was the realization of a desire that had lasted throughout the spring and into the summer' (Fullbrook and Fullbrook 1993: 57). Following their exams, de Beauvoir, who 'had yet to be won away from Maheu [Sartre's 'rival']' (Fullbrook and Fullbrook 1993: 61), travels to the country where she meant to spend the remaining summer. In an effort to spend more time with her, Sartre turns up unexpectedly. After only four days together, Sartre proposes to de Beauvoir. She refuses, but Sartre, 'feeling that it was the institution rather than himself that she was rejecting, argued for several days on behalf of marriage' (Fullbrook and Fullbrook 1993: 62). De Beauvoir's parents then force him to leave and the couple are 'separated for a month and a half' during which time Sartre was 'uncertain as to whether he had secured de Beauvoir's affections on any other than a temporary basis' (ibid.). It is not until mid-October that de Beauvoir decides that Sartre is her 'dream-companion' (de Beauvoir quoted in Fullbrook and Fullbrook 1993: 64).

In this account then, de Beauvoir and Sartre's relationship progresses at an agonisingly slow pace and the reader is constantly reminded of the time (and space) between meetings and events. This narrative technique enables the biographers to linger over Sartre's efforts as he strains to 'earn' de Beauvoir's affections. The representation of Sartre's dependence on de Beauvoir is persuasive not only because Fullbrook and Fullbrook emphasise the passing of time, but also because they portray the events from Sartre's, rather than de Beauvoir's, perspective. Moi, by contrast, not only collapses the time it takes between de Beauvoir and Sartre's meeting and the making of the pact, but also represents the affair, for the most part, from de Beauvoir's point of view.

According to Moi, de Beauvoir's stake in the relationship is overdetermined by her conflicting psychic needs:

Beauvoir's sense of duty and responsibility, the intellectual vocation instilled in her by her education, her own social image of herself as a promising young woman, her father's expectation that she might become a writer – every super-egoic structure in her, one might say – enters into violent conflict with her yearning for harmonious merger with the beloved.   (Moi 1994: 226)

As a consequence, de Beauvoir is forced to create a 'myth of unity between herself and Sartre' (Moi 1994: 221) which Moi believes was 'the cornerstone of a highly elaborate . . . defensive strategy' (Moi 1994: 227) against her warring super-ego. This representation of de Beauvoir is coupled with a portrait of an emotionally distanced Sartre. Commenting on an interview between Sartre and Olivier Todd, Moi writes:

If Todd is right [that Sartre lied as much, if not more, to de Beauvoir as he did to his other female lovers], Sartre never considered the famous 'pact' as more than a casual concession to yet another woman in love: in one light-hearted aside he deals de Beauvoir a devastating blow. For Beauvoir, on the other hand, their agreement had dramatic consequences.   (Moi 1994: 223)

Moi's account of Sartre's marriage proposal to de Beauvoir supports this representation and is, therefore, dramatically different to that of Fullbrook and Fullbrook's. According to Moi Sartre proposes to de Beauvoir only because he is 'upset by [her] emotional crises' (Moi 1994: 227). De Beauvoir refuses him not because she objects either to Sartre or to marriage (as in Fullbrook and Fullbrook's interpretation) but because she is '[d]istressed by what she saw as her own childish dependence upon Sartre' (ibid.). She subsequently decides to leave Sartre and teach in Marseilles in order to 'recuperate a sense of identity' (ibid.). De Beauvoir's emotional dependency is additionally confirmed by the narrative structure itself, which creates an impression that the pact was agreed almost immediately after the two had met. Devoid of Fullbrook and Fullbrook's extensive prologue to the agreement, Moi merely comments that: 'it did not take many weeks for Sartre to propose the two "pacts" that were to regulate their life for the next fifty years' (ibid.).

Not surprisingly, the two accounts of the pact itself differ remarkably (each corresponding to the preceding events). In Fullbrook and Fullbrook's biography, de Beauvoir 'obliges' Sartre with a two-year promise of fidelity and 'agrees' to end her relationship with Maheu (Fullbrook and Fullbrook 1993: 69). The tone here implies that it was de Beauvoir who deigned to bend to Sartre's emotional needs. This is further confirmed by the assertion that:

Sartre, in his self-reported melancholy, came to accept the fact that Beauvoir was not going to marry him and that the famous terms they laid down for their relationship were merely the best *he* could get.   (Fullbrook and Fullbrook 1993: 68)

In Moi's analysis however, Sartre:

was trading two years of monogamy for a lifetime of infidelity, [while] Beauvoir would seem to have been willing to pay just about any price for the promise of two years of immediate intimacy and absolute monogamy.   (Moi 1994: 220)

In short, for Moi, 'the two may well be one, but *he* is the one they are' (Moi 1994: 222) while for Fullbrook and Fullbrook '[a]s she [de Beauvoir] turned from Maheu to Sartre, she turned not to a protector but to an equal' (Fullbrook and Fullbrook 1993: 59).

In all four accounts, the events which lead up to the pact anticipate the perceived balance of power in de Beauvoir and Sartre's relationship. These 'contingencies' do not detract from the overall plot therefore, but rather, as Ricoeur argues, render the conclusion acceptable insofar as it appears to be the result of an inevitable and continuous progression of events.[19] Such is the configuring role of the plot. The implications of this assumed continuity between present (conclusion/s) and past (events) for the production of de Beauvoir's identity will be explored in the following section.

Individuality, responsibility and psychoanalytic 'truths'

Ricoeur calls the continuity between present and past, actual and potential, 'the highest form of narrative repetition' (Ricoeur 1980: 186). This, he argues, ensures that the hero not only 'becomes *who he is*', but is also shown to be 'who he *was*' (ibid.). The effect of narrative repetition then, significantly, is that the protagonist is seen to be *the same* in the present as s/he was in the past. Ricoeur also argues that by the end of the narrative the protagonist is (perceived to be) possessed of a story for which s/he may 'take charge of and consider to be constitutive of [his or her] *personal identity*' (Ricoeur 1991a: 30). The story itself therefore, confers individuality on the self in question insofar as it 'belongs' to the protagonist alone. The 'quest of personal identity', Ricoeur writes, 'assures the continuity between the potential or virtual story and the explicit story for which we assume responsibility' (ibid.). With this in mind it is clear why, even though Francis and Gontier's and Crosland's representations of de Beauvoir vary, by the end of each narrative de Beauvoir is seen to be not only who she is (the de Beauvoir of the initial representation), but also who she always already was. In other words, by the end of a story which is 'her' responsibility, de Beauvoir is also possessed of individuality, the identity of an individual, which, by definition (like her story), belongs only to her.

Francis and Gontier end their first chapter with de Beauvoir giving expression to what appears to be one of the 'deepest' aspects of her identity: 'The fact remains that I'm a writer . . . someone whose entire existence is ruled by writing' (de Beauvoir quoted in Francis and Gontier 1987: 4). The emphasis on writing produces a continuity in the narrative which begins before de Beauvoir meets Sartre and which is strengthened by her relationship with him: 'Sartre told her that she must at all costs preserve her taste for freedom, her love of life, her curiosity, and her determination to be a writer' (Francis and Gontier 1987: 92). The writing theme not only provides a continuity between de Beauvoir as a child and as an adult, but also represents a bridge between de Beauvoir and Sartre both during life – 'Any separation was compensated for with nearly daily correspondence' (Francis and Gontier 1987: 3) – as well as after his death – '[de Beauvoir] breath[es] youth back into their saga by returning to [publish] those spontaneous words scrawled for her [by Sartre] from day to day' (Francis and Gontier 1987: 3).[20]

Francis and Gontier ensure, significantly, that the relationship is seen to serve Sartre, and his writing, as well as it does de Beauvoir: 'In a certain way, if you like, I owe her everything . . . I put complete trust in her . . . You could say that I write for her' (Sartre quoted in Francis and Gontier 1987: 111). Writing therefore, both expresses and confirms the mutual reciprocity between de Beauvoir and Sartre – 'they were writers, and their works should benefit from their combined experiences' (Francis and Gontier 1987: 103) – and appears to provide a 'deeper' bond than sex ever could: 'their [writing] efforts united them more surely than an embrace' (Francis and Gontier 1987: 168). Hence writing, usually understood as a technique of the (one) self (a practice whereby the self works on itself to magnify the self) is now transformed into a technique of romance by which each individuality is achieved (a technique which is narrative, insofar as it draws disparate elements – writing, de Beauvoir, Sartre, as well as their relation – together to produce individuality). This does not *detract* from the individual identity conferred on de Beauvoir's self, so much as *intensify* it. Together, de Beauvoir and Sartre are *more* than the sum of their parts: 'they pooled their two free selves' (Francis and Gontier 1987: 353), Francis and Gontier write, and 'successfully accomplished the tour de force of living their two lives as if they were one dual life' (Francis and Gontier 1987: 111).

Francis and Gontier's narrative retrieves not only de Beauvoir's potential (her capacity for love and her ability to write), but also the potential of the couple. Together, de Beauvoir and Sartre represent completion: 'two human beings in absolute harmony' (Francis and Gontier 1987: 2); 'This alliance, dominating all, was total and sufficient' (Francis and Gontier 1987: 3). What is particularly interesting in Francis and Gontier's account is that the mutual reciprocity between de Beauvoir and Sartre is not only transcribed into a single, blazing, identity, but also into mutual responsibility. Insofar as de Beauvoir's identity is entwined with Sartre's (and vice versa), the responsibility for her story and their 'success' as a couple is shared, or rather doubled: 'if this splendor has always had a special allure, it is that there was a double brilliance, a twofold fame . . .The world was their prize, reflected in a double mirror' (Francis and Gontier 1987: 3). The relationship does not halve or dilute de Beauvoir's story, her personal responsibility for that story, or her individual identity then, so much as magnify them all into a 'double brilliance'.[21]

In Francis and Gontier's biography, writing and love appear to be constitutive elements in the construction of de Beauvoir's identity. What is distinctive about de Beauvoir is 'her (love) story', which in turn makes de Beauvoir a distinctive individual (both her story and her individual identity belong to nobody but her). In Crosland's biography, as noted above, it is feminism which marks de Beauvoir out as 'who she is'. At the same time however, it is de Beauvoir's individuality which inspires her feminism. Individuality itself is the vehicle for continuity, or, to put that another way, the defining feature of de Beauvoir's individual identity is individuality. Crosland writes:

The insistence that she was 'not a child', but her own individual self, a trait apparent so early, was to lead her down the road to her own individual radical beliefs, including feminism. The road was a long one, for she had far to travel, in metaphorical terms, from the safe hiding-place under [her father's] black pear-wood desk.   (Crosland 1992: 25)[22]

According to Crosland, individuality is inherent to de Beauvoir: it is with her as a child and stays with her throughout her life. It carries her away from the family (symbolised by the pear-wood desk) and into adulthood.[23] Notably, the 'road' along which de Beauvoir 'travels', is largely an internal one: in order that she may properly become 'who she is', de Beauvoir must not only leave her family, but also look into her self in order that she may retrieve the individuality which is constitutive of her individual identity:[24]

She was still an aspiring writer, making slow progress because, despite her self-discoveries . . . she was still searching for her own identity and for ways of relating to other people. Although she did not always relish her professional [teaching] work . . . it led her to an extension of her own personal life and later to an awareness of a world she had not thought about in any conscious way – the world of women, the problems of femininity.   (Crosland 1992: 117)

The journey into her self does not hinder de Beauvoir's 'progress' (even though it is 'slow'), so much as develop the self which *already* exists (in embryonic form). Thus her professional work serves to *extend* her personal life and her self-awareness is *enlarged* to include 'the world of women'.

In contrast to Francis and Gontier's account, it is de Beauvoir's separation from, rather than her union with, Sartre that is in part constitutive of her individual identity (and which serves as another expression of her individuality): 'Despite Sartre's constant presence the essential conquest of freedom within her own mind was achieved by Beauvoir on her own' (Crosland 1992: 259).[25] The division between Sartre and de Beauvoir (like the division between de Beauvoir and her family),[26] which Crosland goes out of her way to emphasise here, illustrates de Beauvoir's independence (an independence, particularly, of mind): freedom is achieved by de Beauvoir 'on her own'. Neither does de Beauvoir's writing develop alongside Sartre, as in Francis and Gontier's biography, but instead develops as she herself matures and evolves:[27]

Unconsciously, through her chaotic experiences and close observation, she laid the foundations for her own later work . . . she overcame her uncertainties and as a writer she learnt how to use both her problems and her solutions to advantage.

(Crosland 1992: 259)

During the course of this metamorphosis all the elements from which de Beauvoir's identity will be constructed are drawn from de Beauvoir herself. The main tool which de Beauvoir has at her disposal is her own life ('experiences', 'observation', 'uncertainties', 'problems', 'solutions') and she employs this resource in order to effect a transformation (an auto-pupation of sorts) which will enable her, on her own, to become her self. Crosland writes that de Beauvoir sets out from her 'self' – 'In her response to the outside world the young Beauvoir foreshadowed the woman' (Crosland 1992: 13) – and arrives back at the self: 'everything in her [de Beauvoir's] personal history destined her for existentialism and her own responsibility for every aspect of her personal life' (Crosland 1992: 311). Significantly, these two extracts (one drawn from the start of the biography, the other from the end) highlight how, by the end of the narrative, de Beauvoir has retrieved her potential (a potential embodied in the 'young Beauvoir') and accepted responsibility for 'every aspect of her personal life'. To the extent that de Beauvoir's potential identity is already within her, Crosland's biography demonstrates what Ricoeur describes as a distinguishing feature of narrative repetition: that is, the 'heritage of potentialities' which is 'transmitted from oneself to oneself' (Ricoeur 1980: 188).

The perception of de Beauvoir as a woman possessed of a driving and energetic individualism which sustains her throughout her life tallies neatly with (Crosland's conception of) existentialism, in which human beings are obliged to make choices and take responsibility for their actions and identities. De Beauvoir, Crosland writes, 'had trusted her own wishes and deliberately chosen the doctrines which encouraged her in that attitude' (Crosland 1992: 311). As with de Beauvoir's defiance of bourgeois morality in Francis and Gontier's biography, for Crosland, existential philosophy is a doctrine which compliments features which *already* exist within the self of de Beauvoir. It is not a departure from what de Beauvoir 'is', but rather serves to magnify and further develop what Ricoeur calls the 'heritage of potentialities'. The result: de Beauvoir becomes herself more fully. Like Ulysses, de Beauvoir is on 'a voyage toward the center . . . which is to say, toward [her]self' (Eliade quoted in Ricoeur 1980: 185).

Moi situates her own account of de Beauvoir's life and work against biographies such as Crosland's. She argues that because she has displaced the 'truth' of the subject, she is also rid of the obligation to follow the traditional structure of the biographical genre which, she argues, 'is narrative and linear, argues in terms of origins and finalities and seeks to disclose an original identity' (Moi 1994: 7). It is arguable however, that even though Moi rejects the notion of a 'true' self, it is nevertheless narrative which produces the truths on which the psychoanalytic interpretation rests. The remainder of this section will illustrate this, again with reference to Moi's reading of *L'Invitée*.

Moi argues that de Beauvoir had invested in a philosophy (existentialism) which, in its attempt to repress 'the very notion of repression', resurrects the unconscious 'with a vengeance in the concept of bad faith' (Moi 1994: 104). This analysis stands in direct contrast to the main tenets of existential philosophy. Existentialism begins from the premise that human beings are above all conscious beings who are entirely free to make choices (which define their identities).[28] This given, human beings are also able, are *obliged,* to take full responsibility for these choices. To deny choice or to suggest that in any given situation there was 'no choice' is to deny one's freedom (one's being) and to act in 'bad faith'. Hence Sartre's[29] philosophy is radically opposed to the notion of the unconscious which, by definition, precludes conscious control of one's self and therefore makes absolutely free choice an impossibility.[30] In Moi's analysis however, existentialism must be understood, like every other phenomenon, to be 'a text, that is to say as a complex network of signifying structures' (Moi 1994: 7) that will contribute to/constitute an aspect of de Beauvoir's psyche (itself a text).

Moi suggests, somewhat ironically, that it is the nature of existential philosophy *specifically* which produces a singularly profound effect on de Beauvoir's psyche. Although the murder scene at the end of *L'Invitée* for example, is by all accounts (including de Beauvoir's) something of a literary failure, Moi argues that de Beauvoir was nevertheless *impelled* to write it. This murder, of one of the leading protagonists, was for de Beauvoir a physical and psychological 'necessity' (Moi 1994: 96) since it represents the symbolic 'murder [of] her own unconscious . . . to kill Xavière is to deny that the repressed ever returns' (Moi 1994: 124). In other words, this psychoanalytic interpretation reinscribes psychoanalysis into a discourse which seeks to displace its significance: by suggesting that de Beauvoir was compelled symbolically to murder her own unconscious in order to deny its return, Moi constructs a scenario in which it is impossible to reject the unconscious without it returning, as above, with 'a vengeance'.

In order that Moi's reading of *L'Invitée* be meaningful, the reader must admit a causal relationship between the denial of the unconscious and its return. This given, catharsis is a 'necessary' outcome. However, this interpretation is intelligible only insofar as it is structured by a narrative which itself constructs a logical sequence of causes (the unconscious), effects (its return if repressed) and outcomes (catharsis). In other words, it is the narrativisation *itself* which renders Moi's psychoanalytic reading persuasive. Moi's account of *L'Invitée* displays two principal features of narrative. In the first place, it offers a relatively simple succession of discrete events (de Beauvoir invested in existentialism, de Beauvoir wrote *L'Invitée*) which Ricoeur characterises thus: 'and then? and then?' (Ricoeur 1991a: 22). Secondly, Moi's reading draws a configuration out of this succession (the investment in existentialism *led to* the repression of the unconscious which *led to* the writing of *L'Invitée*) and thereby renders otherwise random events meaningful (the novel was a literary disaster but a psychological necessity). This second synthesis of time is characterised by 'integration, culmination and closure' (ibid.): *because* random events are integrated and emplotted by the (psychoanalytic) narrative (if the repressed is denied it will return), they *must* subsequently be subject to culmination and closure (all will out – and the 'evidence' for this is witnessed in the aesthetic failure of the final scene of *L'Invitée*). Psychoanalytic theories, according to Ricoeur, 'serve as narrative forms that *must* be used in each case as an interpretive scheme for an individual's life history *in order* to find the original scene of his unmastered conflict' (Ricoeur quoted in Bernstein 1990: 56. My emphasis.)

Rather than posit a causal relationship, Ricoeur's analysis, as noted above, suggests that events in the plot are shaped teleologically (by the purpose that they serve). Moi looks *back* on de Beauvoir's investment in existentialism in order to explain the literary failure/necessary catharsis of *L'Invitée*. Hence the 'truths' on which psychoanalysis is based could not be expressed outside of the narrative form: the psychoanalytic interpretation itself produces the psychoanalytic necessity. In short, as in the biographies described above, it is emplotment which ensures that these (psychoanalytic) events appear to lead, inevitably, from one to another through to the final climax.

In each of the accounts described above, even in Moi's representation which seeks to deconstruct a coherent and integrated notion of the self, the identity of an individual is produced as a significant feature of meaningful selfhood. Narrative continuity, and the emplotment of otherwise random events, enable these commentators to construct acceptable, and even persuasive, representations of de Beauvoir (and her relationship with Sartre). The 'episodes' described above do not detract from the narrative identity ascribed to de Beauvoir but rather, as Ricoeur anticipates, are constitutive of a story for which she is assumed to take responsibility. Narrative closure, as well as the death of the 'actual individual' (Foucault 1979a: 23), as the final part of this chapter will show, may amplify this identity still further.

Narrative closure

It is significant that both Francis and Gontier's and Crosland's biographies tail off after de Beauvoir is perceived to have become 'herself' (in this respect, the narrative closure appears *before* the actual conclusion of the biography). Crosland's account of *The Second Sex*, for example, appears in chapter 17, three chapters prior to the end of the book but only just over half way through de Beauvoir's life. For Crosland, *The Second Sex* represents the apex of de Beauvoir's achievement. Not only had the thesis 'influenced her entire life so far' (Crosland 1992: 360), but it also captured all that de Beauvoir expected from life: 'Each individual woman must work her life out for herself, as she [de Beauvoir] had done' (Crosland 1992: 373). This suggests that by the time *The Second Sex* was written, de Beauvoir's own life was 'worked out'. Moreover, the comparatively abrupt ending suggests that the achievement of one's self is all that is interesting in life, after which there is nothing more to say. Moi appears to confirm this point insofar as she explicitly chooses not to deal with the later part of de Beauvoir's life:

by the end of 1949, the year in which she published *The Second Sex*, Simone de Beauvoir had truly become Simone de Beauvoir: personally as well as professionally, she was 'made'. Her later life adds little to the repertoire of themes and obsessions established by this time.   (Moi 1994: 6)[31]

The accent on how de Beauvoir 'arrives' at her self, coupled with the paucity of interest in the period after this self is achieved, suggests that the 'plots' of the biographies, like the 'territory of morality for psychotherapy' (N. Rose 1989: 241), are 'marked out by a limited set of terms: the need to [describe] work on the self to improve the quality of life, the achievement of autonomy, the release of potentiality, the opposition of a restricting dependency to a liberating freedom' (ibid.). Both Francis and Gontier's and Crosland's biographies, for example, clearly describe how de Beauvoir released her 'potentiality' (although her potential is different in each). In Crosland's account, de Beauvoir's 'work' on her 'self' (in order to achieve autonomy from her family and from Sartre) is emphasised, while in Francis and Gontier's de Beauvoir's imputed opposition to the restrictions of bourgeois marriage propel her into a liberating relationship with Sartre. In each case, de Beauvoir is 'presumed to be an agent, wishing to exercise informed, autonomous and secular responsibility in relation to . . . her own destiny' (N. Rose 1997: 145). Even Moi's reading of *L'Invitée* produces, albeit inadvertently, a representation of de Beauvoir who appears to be better equipped to deal with 'life'. Subsequent to writing the novel, where she 'killed the fantasmatic bad mother in the very act of writing' (Moi 1994: 124), de Beauvoir is able to represent herself; she 'always had something to say' (de Beauvoir quoted in Moi 1994: 124).

The desirability of features such as autonomy, identity and self-realisation, which define successful selfhood, are not unique to the biographical genre. It is precisely because de Beauvoir is perceived to have realised her 'self' that she is considered to be a 'heroine'/role model in a number of newspaper representations. The *Guardian* writes:

Her rebellion against her family and constrictive middleclass [*sic*] values, her existence as an independent woman, her famed lifelong liaison with the philosopher Jean-Paul Sartre . . . her judicious affiliation with radical causes and in old age with feminism, her devouring curiosity, her integrity and ceaseless energy – all provide fertile ground for identification. This is the very stuff of which exemplary lives are made and through the four volumes of her autobiography, de Beauvoir emerges as the only 'positive' heroine of her considerable oeuvre.

(*Guardian*, 6 December 1989)

De Beauvoir's 'rebellion' and 'independence' signify an active and autonomous responsibility for her own destiny. The narrative of self-realisation, which embraces judiciousness, integrity, curiosity and energy, all constitute the very stuff of her 'exemplary life' and exercises its influence on readers who are implicitly encouraged to identify with the protagonist/heroine. To this extent the narrative ascribed to de Beauvoir, whether it is represented in full length biographies or media sound bites, can be compared to 'the modern literature of psychotherapeutics' (N. Rose 1989: 219) and the narratives of early Christian spiritual pilgrimages (see chapter 1), which 'constitute manuals for the bringing of the self to happiness and perfection . . . their point of address is not to a few, but, at least in principle, to us all' (N. Rose 1989: 220). Insofar as others are enjoined to follow de Beauvoir's trajectory and to acquire for themselves an 'ideal' self, her story may be understood as one example of the way that, in Western society, the self is incited to monitor and improve itself, to establish a relation to its self and thereby to become an ethical self. The incitement to become an ethical being thus applies as well to those who identify *with* de Beauvoir as to de Beauvoir herself. Lisa Appignanesi, writing for the *Guardian*, argues: 'for a woman who was first and foremost an intellectual, de Beauvoir's personal trajectory has been as influential in shaping women's consciousness as anything she has written' (*Guardian*, 6 December 1989).

Appignanesi's review, written three years after de Beauvoir's death, also illustrates that it is not de Beauvoir's 'work', so much as her individual identity – what she is and what she has done – which ensures that the significance of her life extends beyond its own (mortal) boundaries. Indeed, de Beauvoir's death magnifies this individual identity more thoroughly than her life ever could. The 'finality' of de Beauvoir's death is immediately effaced by Crosland, for example, in an heraldic call to continue, indefinitely, the socialist feminist tradition with which de Beauvoir was engaged: 'There is no need for any nostalgic pictures of Beauvoir [as there are of Sartre] because the problems she addressed are still current, still unsolved' (Crosland 1992: 428). For Crosland, the significance of de Beauvoir's life is not confined to the past (as she says Sartre's is), but instead has a relevance which informs the present and, Crosland implies, will continue to inform the future. Thus de Beauvoir's narrative identity appears to achieve a depth which Sartre's lacks, insofar as it includes within it, and *surpasses*, the death of de Beauvoir herself:

Does not narrativity, by breaking away from the obsession of a struggle in the face of death, open any mediation of time to another horizon than that of death, to the problem of communication not just between living beings but between contemporaries, predecessors and successors? . . . Is it not part of the plot to include the death of each hero in a story that surpasses every individual fate?   (Ricoeur 1980: 188)

In suggesting that the urgency of the task which de Beauvoir inspired will last longer than the nostalgic interest in Sartre, Crosland writes de Beauvoir into a narrative which transcends death itself. Arguably however, this does not diminish de Beauvoir's individual identity, so much as transform it into, and preserve it as, 'history':

It is always a community, a people, or a group of protagonists which tries to take up the tradition – or traditions – of its origins. It is this communal act of repetition, which is at the same time a new founding act and a recommencement of what has already been inaugurated, that 'makes history' and that finally makes it possible to write history.   (Ricoeur 1980: 189)[32]

De Beauvoir's death not only amplifies her individual identity, but also, generously, magnifies the identity of *others* who acquire, in the shape of de Beauvoir, a 'history'. Thus just as de Beauvoir's death serves to extend the life-span of her narrative identity, so history ensures the continuing life of a collective identity. The significance of both individual identity and history then (or the retelling of de Beauvoir's story, as a part of, particularly feminist, history), can be compared to the motivation of the storytellers in *The Arabian Nights* who sought to defeat death by telling tales 'late into the night', 'to delay the inevitable moment when everyone must fall silent' (Foucault 1979a: 15). Foucault suggests that Scheherazade's story 'is a desperate inversion of murder; it is the effort, throughout all those nights, to exclude death from the circle of existence' (ibid.). Although this tale-telling represents an attempt to sustain life, paradoxically, it inscribes death at its very core.

4

Preclusion

At . . . moments of extreme exposure, the null response, far from declaring the question empty, returns to it and preserves it as a question. What cannot be effaced is the question itself: who am I?

Paul Ricoeur, 'Narrative Identity'

The analysis in chapter 3 illustrated that individuality, responsibility (taking responsibility for one's narrative identity) and continuity (being the 'same' throughout one's life) are central among the features which contribute to intelligible selfhood, which construct de Beauvoir as a coherent self. These are themes which I will take up again in this chapter, although here I will be concerned not only with those identities which *are* attributed to de Beauvoir – in particular, lesbian and heterosexual identities – but also with how it is that bisexuality is precluded from being a property of her self. Indeed, it is the *relation* between the ascription of heterosexuality or lesbianism to de Beauvoir and the preclusion of bisexuality – even though it is present in the biographical accounts of de Beauvoir's life and work (named as it is) – that is especially interesting.

The ascription of heterosexuality to de Beauvoir occurs in four main ways. In the first instance, in Francis and Gontier's, Crosland's and Moi's accounts, de Beauvoir is understood to have had no conscious 'choice' in her relationships with women and, hence, appears not to be personally responsible for them. The only stories that de Beauvoir *is* held responsible for (and the only ones which provide narrative closure) are stories of (usually) rewarding and reciprocal heterosexuality.[1] This is the second way that de Beauvoir's same-sex relationships are precluded from the sexual-narrative-identity conferred on her. The third method of preclusion is found in Crosland's biography. This is a particularly interesting representation of de Beauvoir's life and work because it foregrounds gender and

sexuality and suggests that they are in conflict. Despite this potentially productive tension however, the configuration of the narrative is such that
Crosland is able to dispel any suspicions surrounding both the sexuality
and the gender imputed to de Beauvoir: the former is brought back into the
fold of heterosexuality, the latter tied firmly to femininity. Finally, unlike
the other accounts, both Fullbrook and Fullbrook and Margaret Simons
construe de Beauvoir's relationships with women to be an active 'choice'
and a source of pleasure. As I will argue however, Fullbrook and
Fullbrook's representation configures this pleasure as part of a voyeuristic
heterosexuality, while in Simons' account it confirms de Beauvoir not as
bisexual, but as lesbian.

Drawing on Ricoeur's distinction between identity-as-sameness and
identity-as-selfhood (Ricoeur 1991b), I will be looking at why it is almost
impossible, in these texts, to gather de Beauvoir's relationships with men
and women together, such that they are constitutive of a bisexual-narrative-
identity. However, while the distinction between identity-as-sameness and
identity-as-selfhood offers much to the analysis of bisexuality, this analysis itself serves to reveal the presuppositions on which Ricoeur's theory of
narrative identity is based. For this reason I will be considering not only the
implications of Ricoeur's thesis for bisexuality, but also the implications *of*
bisexuality *for* Ricoeur's understanding of the relation between selfhood,
identity and individuality.

'There was no choice'

While most representations of de Beauvoir rest on an apparently secure
assumption that her gender is female, for Crosland the ambiguity of de
Beauvoir's sexuality calls her gender into question: to what degree is de
Beauvoir 'really' a woman?[2] This is a tension which troubles Crosland, in
different ways, throughout the biography. At the start of her book for
example, clearly wishing to anticipate the future feminist, Crosland
attempts to demonstrate de Beauvoir's rejection of 'orthodox' feminine
pursuits by arguing that she is more concerned to teach than to mother her
dolls (Crosland 1992: 23) and by pointing out that she chose role models
who were 'not interested in being "good" and "feminine" in the orthodox
way' (Crosland 1992: 38). The stress on 'orthodoxy' seems to be a
significant qualification: Crosland implies that while de Beauvoir may not
have been feminine in a 'conventional' way, she was nevertheless feminine
in her 'own way' (a representation which accords with her view of de
Beauvoir's individuality, outlined in chapter 3). She writes:

although she hated being classed as 'a child' along with other children, she had no objection to being classed as a girl . . . her early view of herself must not be forgotten: 'In my games and day-dreaming I never transformed myself into a man'.

(Crosland 1992: 30)

Despite this explicit signal to the reader that de Beauvoir did not imagine herself to be a man, Crosland's portrait of de Beauvoir's femininity is repeatedly disrupted by the perception that de Beauvoir's friends and family have of her. Crosland quotes Jacques-Laurent Bost (one of de Beauvoir's lovers), for example, saying to de Beauvoir 'Oh you! You're like a man!' (Bost quoted in Crosland 1992: 195) and Jean Genet too, is said to have thought that de Beauvoir 'was the man of the couple and Sartre was the woman' (Crosland 1992: 426). This particular comment, according to Crosland, 'renewed speculation about Beauvoir's bisexuality' (ibid.).

Crosland's reference to bisexuality, raised in the context of de Beauvoir's gender, indicates that she will confine bisexuality to androgyny, where androgyny denotes both masculine/male and feminine/female characteristics.[3] Indeed, Crosland quotes one of de Beauvoir's female admirers saying that she had loved de Beauvoir 'as passionately as if she were a man' (Crosland 1992: 233). This is significant because it implies that Crosland believes that women love de Beauvoir passionately *because* she is like a man. The initial implication of her definition of 'bisexuality' then, serves to recuperate heterosexuality: women are not in love with the 'woman' de Beauvoir, they love her as though she were a 'man'. Ironically, this is something of a queer move on sex/gender (see for example Däumer 1992; Zita 1992) without the radical political intentions: de Beauvoir's relationships with women are not lesbian (or even bisexual). Instead, these two women would potentially be engaged in a heterosexual relationship.

This singular attempt to reinstate heterosexuality is not enough to secure it however. The narrative of bisexuality-as-androgyny also enables Crosland to suggest that women are attracted to de Beauvoir because de Beauvoir is in some way inherently attractive to women: 'There was a magnetism about Beauvoir', she writes, 'that drew admiration and love from other women, and was to do so for the rest of her life' (Crosland 1992: 155). De Beauvoir's imputed 'magnetism' allows Crosland to qualify statements, such as Bost's (above), that de Beauvoir is 'like a man'. She suggests that this 'ambiguous remark' (Crosland 1992: 195) has its roots in Bost's awareness of de Beauvoir's 'bisexual nature, he knew how deeply Olga had been attracted to her and how later students had developed "crushes" on her' (ibid.). Thus it is de Beauvoir's 'magnetism', a magnetism born of 'bisexuality', that inspires women's admiration and love, significantly, whether de Beauvoir wants it or not. Indeed, Crosland makes it clear that these same-sex relationships are ultimately one-sided.[4] She argues, for example, that de Beauvoir worked whenever she could to 'escape from the young women she cared for but didn't care for enough' (Crosland 1992: 233).

Such nonchalance is most clearly manifest in her affairs with Nathalie Sokorine, Olga Kosakiewicz and Louise Védrine (three women who comprised part of a circle of friends and lovers called 'The Family' which surrounded de Beauvoir and Sartre). Sokorine is perceived to be the one who does all the 'work' in the relationship with de Beauvoir:

> [Sokorine] worked hard to win Beauvoir's interest, waiting for her as she left her hotel in the morning for the lycée, waiting for her when her lessons were over, refusing to leave her room at night, sleeping on the doormat. She . . . regularly gave Beauvoir little gifts . . . She was jealous of Beauvoir's women friends and particularly jealous of Sartre.
> (Crosland 1992: 223)

In response to Sokorine's 'need' – which 'did not stop at schoolgirl admiration; she wanted something more' (Crosland 1992: 224) – Crosland quotes de Beauvoir saying that Sokorine is 'very demanding and authoritarian, I'm rather upset about it' (de Beauvoir quoted in Crosland, ibid.). Védrine's 'passionate letters' (de Beauvoir quoted in Crosland 1992: 194) too, apparently inspire reactions which range from despair – de Beauvoir feels 'tense, knowing that she would soon have to abandon herself "to the frenzied hands of Védrine"' (Crosland 1992: 230) – to ennui: '[de Beauvoir] found it *drôle* that she was now going to spend two days with Védrine, who had fallen in love with her' (ibid.). In Crosland's interpretation, de Beauvoir 'felt sorry for Védrine, but could not offer her any love' (Crosland 1992: 220).

The narrative of bisexuality-as-androgyny then, enables Crosland to suggest persuasively that de Beauvoir, because of her 'magnetism', did nothing actively to encourage these women's affections. In this context, de Beauvoir's character is defined by a sexual and emotional passivity (which is, on occasion, transformed into a more active dislike of the women's attentions). This in its turn renders de Beauvoir's indifference to the women's 'passion' 'acceptable' (Ricoeur 1980: 174) to the reader: the configuration of the plot – whereby the conclusion (de Beauvoir's passive indifference) makes sense in the light of the preceding events (de Beauvoir's lack of choice in, or active encouragement of, the relationships) – is such that the reader does not question de Beauvoir's response but rather 'accepts' it as entirely intelligible. Indeed, the effect is to so disassociate de Beauvoir from these same-sex relationships that she does not appear to be *implicated* in them. This point is more clearly demonstrated with reference to Ricoeur's notion of selfhood. Distinguishing between identity-as-selfhood and identity-as-sameness, Ricoeur argues that:

We can begin to unfold the concept of selfhood by considering the nature of the question to which the self constitutes a response, or a range of responses. This question is the question *who*, distinct from the question *what*. It is the question we tend to ask in the field of action: looking for the agent, the author of the action, we ask: Who did this or that? Let us call *ascription* the assignation of an agent to an action. By this we certify that the action is the property of whoever committed it, that it is his, that it belongs to him personally.   (Ricoeur 1991b: 191)

Since de Beauvoir does nothing to encourage these women (her 'magnetism' is beyond conscious control), it is impossible for Crosland to ask the question 'who is responsible for these same-sex relationships?' and answer with de Beauvoir: acts of same-sex seduction cannot be ascribed to de Beauvoir, they do not 'belong' to her 'personally'. Instead, stories of passion and seduction belong to other women, women other than de Beauvoir, and are therefore constitutive of their, rather than de Beauvoir's, sexual identity.[5] Adding to his analysis of the role of ascription in the production of selfhood, Ricoeur writes:

Onto this as yet morally neutral act is grafted the act of *imputation* which takes an explicitly moral significance, in the sense that it implies accusation, excuse or acquittal, blame or praise, in short appraisal in terms of the 'good' or the 'just'.
                    (Ricoeur 1991b: 191)

If de Beauvoir has not consciously acted herself, then it is equally impossible for the biographers to appraise her behaviour.[6] In other words, without ascription there can be no imputation and, in this respect, de Beauvoir appears to be 'innocent' of same-sex desire.[7]

Before comparing these ultimately unsatisfactory same-sex relationships with the closure that de Beauvoir's heterosexual relationships are perceived to provide, I want briefly to consider the issue of choice as it is played out in Toril Moi's representation of de Beauvoir's relationships. Unlike in Crosland's biography, Moi's account of de Beauvoir does not rely on a narrative of bisexuality-as-androgyny, a narrative which serves to preclude the possibility that de Beauvoir's relationships with women were consciously instigated, or even encouraged, by her. Nevertheless, her psychoanalytic reading of de Beauvoir's 'bisexual period' (Moi 1994: 201) does explicitly raise the issue of 'choice' as an important factor to be addressed in this context. Emphasising that de Beauvoir 'claims not to enjoy her sexual relations with women very much' and that she considered sex with men to be 'invariably superior' (Moi 1994: 232), Moi goes on to ask 'why she regularly submitted to the female caresses in which she claimed to take so little pleasure' (ibid.).[8] 'Why', she asks, 'did Beauvoir want to live in this way? Did it make her happy? And did she feel free to choose otherwise?' (Moi 1994: 230).

Moi argues that de Beauvoir 'took up with a number of younger women' (Moi 1994: 230) only *after* she had confronted Sartre's 'passion' for another woman. By linking de Beauvoir's same-sex relationships to her relationship with Sartre – specifically, to her disillusionment with this relationship – Moi situates Sartre at the centre of de Beauvoir's emotional world: it is only in *response* to his behaviour that she embarks on affairs of her own. Moi argues that de Beauvoir 'needed her female lovers desperately' in order to keep at bay 'the emptiness hidden beneath her games of hide-and-seek' (Moi 1994: 234). Fearing the loss of Sartre's love (Moi 1994: 235), de Beauvoir's feelings of 'ferocious intensity' (Moi 1994: 232) for these women, which include feelings of hatred, are inspired by their (potential) ability to 'plug the gap': 'What truly mattered to Simone de Beauvoir is that *they were there*: filling the void, they were her very own anti-depressants' (Moi 1994: 236). Insofar as de Beauvoir's same-sex relationships are an attempted 'cure' for the void generated by Sartre's absence, it is hetero-sexual emptiness that lies at the heart of de Beauvoir's 'bisexual period' (Moi 1994: 201). Nevertheless, '[w]hether they are friends or lovers, women rarely manage to replace the sexual and emotional fulfilment provided by Bost, and they can only put up a futile struggle to fill the gap left by the absolute presence of Sartre' (Moi 1994: 236). In other words, these women cannot even replace the sexual and emotional fulfilment that Bost, a 'con-tingent' love, offers de Beauvoir. They too, then, signify absence: absence over absence constitutes de Beauvoir's 'bisexual period'.

The narrative of bisexuality-as-androgyny installed by Crosland, and de Beauvoir's inherent magnetism in this context, suggests that de Beauvoir had *no choice* in her same-sex relationships. And, since de Beauvoir does not 'choose' (to seduce or to flirt) with her women admirers, the questions 'who did this/who is responsible?' cannot be answered 'with de Beauvoir'. Similarly, Moi's own answer to the question of choice suggests that even though de Beauvoir *is* emotionally engaged with her women lovers, these relationships are founded on a fear of heterosexual emptiness which, rooted in her unconscious, is by definition beyond her conscious control. The implications in both accounts then, is that if de Beauvoir *had* been able to choose – if she had not been inherently attractive to women, or if she did not fear the heterosexual 'void' – she would not have been involved in these relationships with women at all. In this respect the 'truth' of de Beauvoir is perceived to be heterosexual and, as such, does not need to be 'explained' (away) as same-sex relationships do.

Heterosexual closure

As in Crosland's biography, Francis and Gontier suggest that de Beauvoir is for the most part emotionally and physically detached from women who are, by contrast, attracted to her 'to the point of virtual bewitchment' (Francis and Gontier 1987: 138). Yet both Crosland's and Francis and Gontier's accounts highlight her passionate engagement with a variety of men,[9] and particularly with the American writer Nelson Algren. This relationship, according to Francis and Gontier, is 'a fierce and passionate love, a true understanding on every level' (Francis and Gontier 1987: 236). In Crosland's biography, de Beauvoir is said to be able to enjoy 'the cerebral, theoretical Sartre and the emotional, physical Algren' (Crosland 1992: 353). Significantly, Algren returns these feelings, and it is this emotional and physical reciprocity which signals the second narrative technique by which the significance of de Beauvoir's same-sex relationships is displaced: heterosexual relationships offer closure in a way that same-sex relationships do not.

The romantic heterosexual narrative which characterises accounts of de Beauvoir's relationship with Algren climaxes in the writing of *The Second Sex*. Crosland claims that '[w]hile writing the book Beauvoir was celebrating the fact that she herself had found [the "Joy of Sex"]. The whole rapid emotional movement behind the book was probably the result of that unexpected meeting with Nelson Algren in 1947' (Crosland 1992: 371). *The Second Sex* appears as the apotheosis of de Beauvoir's newly discovered sexuality not only for Crosland, but also for Moi who claims that 'it is not hard to perceive the traces of Nelson Algren in Beauvoir's glowing praise of ideal [reciprocal] heterosexual sex [in *The Second Sex*]' (Moi 1994: 203).[10] Making this point somewhat more explicitly, Crosland writes: '[de Beauvoir] had obviously discovered true and satisfying sexuality for the first time in her life' (Crosland 1992: 355). Not only does this representation stand in stark contrast to her relationships with women, where she is emotionally and physically distant, but it also implies that de Beauvoir had not discovered the 'truth' of her sexuality prior to her affair with Algren. In other words, Crosland precludes the possibility that de Beauvoir's sexuality might at least in part be based around a desire for women.

That *The Second Sex*, in both Moi's and Crosland's representations, is linked to de Beauvoir's 'flowering' heterosexuality is significant: it attributes what Foucault calls a psychological motive to de Beauvoir's work, 'a "deep" motive, a "creative" power, or a "design"' (Foucault 1991d: 110) (see also chapter 3). Because (much of) *The Second Sex* is understood to be inspired by de Beauvoir's love-affair, she (and her (love-)story), specifically, are tied to the text such that both her individuality and her status as an author are confirmed. By the same token however, ironically, the very vehicle (sexuality) which enables de Beauvoir to be perceived as an author also undermines her authorial status. Crosland suggests that in her letters to Algren, de Beauvoir:

seemed as far away as possible from the author of *The Second Sex* who had tried to be scientific and objective about women: no wonder she had failed. Beauvoir was as emotional and prone to tears all her life as any heroine of romantic fiction, and when she wrote to Algren she might have been eighteen, not forty-two.

(Crosland 1992: 375)

The technique of romance, which transforms de Beauvoir into a 'heroine of romantic fiction', displaces her as an author since author and lover/sexual woman appear to be mutually exclusive in Crosland's narrative. The former signifies all that is conventionally characterised as 'masculine' (scientific objectivity), while the latter signifies femininity (emotional tearfulness, puppy love). Although Crosland clearly approves of de Beauvoir's failure as an author (Crosland 1992: 360), it is a failure nevertheless. Hence heterosexuality plays so important a role in producing *The Second Sex* that it appears to subsume both author and book as de Beauvoir is constituted exclusively as 'woman' – *more* woman, perhaps, than ever before. Tragically, this substitution of woman for author appears in the context of a book which cements de Beauvoir's authority as a feminist, philosopher and writer and which clearly marks the difference between her and Sartre's existentialism. The role attributed to Nelson Algren serves to qualify this author/ity and reduces de Beauvoir's position as an author into the less highly regarded, but more feminine, woman-in-love.

That de Beauvoir ultimately chooses Sartre over Algren does not disrupt the romantic narrative, so much as (re)affirm it. In the first instance, it enables Francis and Gontier to demonstrate the 'depth' of Algren's feeling for de Beauvoir, a depth which can be conceived of as a durable narrative property in that it is said to last throughout the course of his lifetime. Indeed, it is Algren's love of de Beauvoir which apparently kills him. Francis and Gontier suggest that the very memory of de Beauvoir's choice of Sartre over himself puts him in such a rage during an interview that he suffers a heart attack: 'Love had killed him. His final rage had been directed against Simone de Beauvoir, whom he had been unable to forget despite two marriages and divorces' (Francis and Gontier 1987: 237). If Algren's death signifies a narrative closure worthy of any 'romantic fiction', as Crosland would put it, de Beauvoir's love for Sartre is simultaneously reconfirmed: Sartre, Crosland claims, 'was still more important than anyone. He represented all she truly cared about' (Crosland 1992: 377).

What is common to all three representations is that de Beauvoir's heterosexual-narrative-identity is consolidated through narrative closure, 'the pole attraction of the entire development', the point from which a retrospective glance over the events occurs and which confers meaning on a story. Both Francis and Gontier and Crosland, while acknowledging the breakdown of de Beauvoir and Sartre's relationship towards the end of their lives, ensure that ultimately the relationship remains largely untarnished. Crosland ends her biography by suggesting that despite the variety of epitaphs read at de Beauvoir's funeral, the most fitting summary of her (heterosexual) life was one that defines de Beauvoir primarily by her 'passion, for life and for a man. A woman's destiny, in the end' (Crosland 1992: 424). She and Francis and Gontier also confer symbolic significance on de Beauvoir's final illness (which Sartre also died of) as well as on her burial (de Beauvoir was dressed in similar coloured clothes and was buried on the same day as Sartre) (see Francis and Gontier 1987: 362 and Crosland 1992: 423). In Moi's psychoanalytic narrative, although resolution is not achieved *directly* through Sartre, it is nevertheless inspired *by* him. The act of writing – letters and diaries which help her to 'produce a coherent image of herself' when 'Sartre is not there to "process" her experiences for her' (Moi 1994: 244) and the novel specifically, which 'becomes the very object that covers up for lack' (Moi 1994: 248) – stands in for Sartre when he is absent. Thus Sartre remains at the centre of de Beauvoir's psychic needs, again precluding the significance of same-sex relationships which, the reader must assume, did little to salvage, and may even have increased, her sense of *incoherency*. In each account then, de Beauvoir's 'contingent' relationships are ensconced within the larger Sartre/de Beauvoir story. Unlike those contingent affairs, this 'primary' relationship has a purpose within the plot (witnessed in the conclusion) not least because it contributes to the production of a credible heterosexual-narrative-identity.

This is the second way then, in which de Beauvoir's relationships with women are rendered insignificant (with respect to the sexual-narrative-identity ascribed to her). In Crosland's account (as in Moi's): 'only Sartre gave [de Beauvoir] any real satisfaction. Without him she felt "hollow" and "hungry"' (Crosland 1992: 221). Towards the end of the biography

Crosland acknowledges de Beauvoir's relationship with Sylvie Le Bon,[11] but at once effaces its significance by suggesting that after Sartre's death de Beauvoir was 'alone' for 'the first time' since 1929. Implying that Le Bon cannot – like de Beauvoir's female relationships before her – 'fill' the gap left by Sartre, Crosland affirms the common trope that women together (but without men) are seen to be women alone. Given that these (same-sex) relationships are not configured by the plot, they appear to be meaningless in the context of de Beauvoir's sexual-narrative-identity; random and unintelligible, they are described as 'fruitless' (Francis and Gontier 1987: 162). This in itself perhaps explains the frequency of the question 'why?' in accounts of de Beauvoir's relationships with women. In short, the Sartre/de Beauvoir couple is recuperated despite the number of relationships which occur on both sides. Indeed, representations of de Beauvoir and Sartre's relationship are cemented not *in spite of* but *by* their contingent liaisons.

I briefly drew attention, in the previous chapter, to Francis and Gontier's use of the mirror metaphor when describing de Beauvoir and Sartre's relationship. This notion of 'reflection' also plays a part, although a very different one, in accounts of de Beauvoir's relationships with women. Specifically, it serves to return de Beauvoir to a femininity which is perceived to be under threat. I will explore this representation in some detail in the following section because it is here that the same-sex relationships come to serve a purpose within the plot. This is not a purpose however, which contributes to a portrait of de Beauvoir as 'bisexual'.

Sex and gender[12]

Crosland's understanding of bisexuality-as-androgyny, as I have suggested, displaces (some of) the threat that de Beauvoir's relationships with women pose for heterosexuality in that it 'explains' how women come to be attracted to de Beauvoir without her active encouragement. Having 'no choice' in the matter, de Beauvoir appears not to be implicated in these relationships. A further way in which Crosland 'deals' with the ambiguity of the sexuality often imputed to de Beauvoir (even though, as the extract below indicates, she finds it disturbing to the point of 'abnormal') is by tying it to a 'quest of personal identity'. She writes:

[de Beauvoir was contending with] Sartre's polygamous life, her own bisexual adventures . . . When younger, both she and Sartre had been fascinated by the extremes of human behaviour, they had studied abnormal people because they believed this was one way of understanding human nature and all its potential. Perhaps they found these extremes, even this 'abnormality', in each other.

(Crosland 1992: 208)

Crosland turns this 'abnormality' to her advantage by linking 'bisexuality' to the notion of 'adventure', or the narrative quest for self-knowledge. And this quest, she suggests, is specifically anchored to de Beauvoir's femininity. Crosland quotes de Beauvoir musing on 'a point within myself which interests me . . . it's my "femininity", the way in which I am of my sex and not of it' (de Beauvoir quoted in Crosland 1992: 229). Immediately following this extract, Crosland herself comments:

> Her bisexual nature was confusing to her . . . 'In what way am I a woman and to what extent am I not one?' . . . It seems evident that this major study [*The Second Sex*] grew from her personal sexual problems, for she had to come to terms with her own elusive nature.
>   (ibid.)

Insofar as de Beauvoir's sexuality is perceived to lie at the heart of the self (such that to 'come to terms' with the truth of sexuality is to 'come to terms' with the truth of the self), it is 'bisexuality', de Beauvoir's 'bisexual nature', which prompts a journey of self discovery. And one of the ways that de Beauvoir acquires this 'truth' of the self is by exploring why it is that women are attracted to her:

> [de Beauvoir] was fascinated by her own attractiveness to girls and young women . . . She remarked to Sartre, with cynical irony, that if this sort of thing went on, then by the time she was sixty girls would be committing suicide in the classroom.
>   (Crosland 1992: 233)

Here again, de Beauvoir's interest in women is not driven by an active desire (sexual and/or emotional) for them, but is instead inspired by a will to know more about her self, a will that leads her to 'find' her self reflected in the women who surround her. Francis and Gontier write: 'Face to face with Olga, a very young Simone reawakened to find her reflection in a living mirror' (Francis and Gontier 1987: 138). Crosland too, argues that: 'Beauvoir saw in Olga some reflections of herself' (Crosland 1992: 155–6). As in Francis and Gontier's account of de Beauvoir's relationship with Sartre (see chapter 3), the self ascribed to de Beauvoir is in part constituted through her reflection in another. However, whereas in the latter instance the mirror metaphor creates a wholly positive impression of mutual reciprocity and responsibility, de Beauvoir's 'reflection' in and of other women, by contrast, is negatively portrayed. Although Crosland, for example, is generally approving of any, literally, 'self-seeking' goal, she claims in this instance that de Beauvoir's 'wish to know more about herself made her almost narcissistic' (Crosland 1992: 233). Hence although, in the context of heterosexuality, the mirror is allied to a portrait of reciprocity, where same-sex relationships are concerned, the metaphor positions de Beauvoir as narcissistic.[13]

That de Beauvoir is charged with narcissism is especially interesting in the light of Sandra Bartky's (1990) analysis of the relation between narcissism and femininity. Drawing on de Beauvoir's work, Bartky argues that 'the existentialist conception of "situation" . . . account[s] for the persistence of narcissism in the feminine personality [. . .] the pleasures of narcissism arise from a self-deceived effort to escape the anguish of freedom' (Bartky 1990: 38–9). Although narcissism is defined by Bartky (and de Beauvoir) as an effort to *escape* the anguish of freedom and being-for-itself, in Crosland's biography it is linked to de Beauvoir's efforts to *find* her self. That her relationships with women are tied both to a quest *for* self-knowledge and simultaneously denounced as narcissistic is ironic, particularly given de Beauvoir's own existential analysis of lesbianism. In *The Second Sex* de Beauvoir writes:

> Between women love is contemplative; caresses are intended less to gain possession of the other than gradually to re-create the self through her; separateness is abolished, there is no struggle, no victory, no defeat; in exact reciprocity each is at once subject and object, sovereign and slave; duality becomes mutuality.
>
> (de Beauvoir 1988: 436)

According to de Beauvoir, same-sex relationships may potentially offer an 'exact reciprocity' which heterosexual relationships, under patriarchy, cannot (Moi 1994: 203).[14] The distance between subject and object, self and other, is closed (these dualities are dissolved in favour of mutuality) as the other 're-creates' the self. Nevertheless, it is not this aspect of de Beauvoir's study which accounts of her life choose to emphasise. Indeed, the link de Beauvoir establishes between lesbianism and exact reciprocity is reversed (as in a mirror): Francis and Gontier find true reciprocity only in a heterosexual relationship (between de Beauvoir and Sartre) while Crosland, along with Moi, warns of the dangers of narcissism in same-sex relationships.[15] Moi writes: 'too much similarity reduces sexual interaction to a narcissistic mirroring of the other: it is not a coincidence that [de Beauvoir] speaks of the "miracle of the mirror" precisely in the context of lesbian sexuality' (Moi 1994: 203). In short, on the whole, biographical representations of reciprocity/heterosexuality and narcissism/same-sex relationships are both mediated by the mirror metaphor to strikingly different effect.[16]

Just as reciprocity is transformed into narcissism in relation to women, so the notion of 'responsibility', which is portrayed as *mutual* responsibility in de Beauvoir's relationship with Sartre, is also used differently, and to different narrative effect, in representations of her same-sex affairs. Here de Beauvoir is the *sole* bearer of responsibility, and this specific portrait serves to reinstate her femininity, as femininity and 'responsibility' are construed to be co-extensive. Crosland suggests, for example, that the friendship between de Beauvoir, Sartre and Kosakiewicz is saved because of de Beauvoir's 'responsible attitude' (Crosland 1992: 164):

She had never felt disadvantaged by her femininity, now it enabled her to understand those two complex characters, Sartre and Olga, and their equally complex relationship. No man, and Sartre least of all, could have resolved the situation, in which a basic friendship continued to exist. Beauvoir possessed the instinctive strength to deal with circumstances in which intellectual analysis and 'transparency' were useless.   (Crosland 1992: 165)

Crosland implies that Sartre's 'intellectual analysis' and his notion of 'transparency' are inappropriate to the occasion and that only de Beauvoir's 'femininity', and her 'instinctive strength', can resolve the 'complex' relationship. The opposition that Crosland establishes between (objective?) intellectual analysis and (subjective?) femininity resonates with the author/woman duality identified above. In each case, specifically feminine characteristics (such as 'instinctive strength') are attributed to de Beauvoir which appear to over-ride, and perhaps even exclude, her from being represented as 'intellectual' or 'objective'. De Beauvoir has to sacrifice some aspect of her self therefore, in order that she be perceived as feminine. This is perversely fitting, given that the sacrifices Crosland imposes on de Beauvoir are ultimately compatible with femininity, since to be feminine *is* to sacrifice one's self for others:

[Sartre] had once told her that she was 'too much loved'. Everyone wanted her. Sartre had more of her than anyone else but at thirty-two . . . she belonged surely to her fragmented self, even if she had not yet decided the true nature of that self, that woman, that femininity.   (Crosland 1992: 246)

Although de Beauvoir may not herself have decided about the 'true nature' of her self, Crosland apparently has: de Beauvoir is 'woman' and 'femininity'. And to be a woman and to be feminine is to be in a state of being 'wanted'. De Beauvoir is said to be 'too much loved'.

This representation of de Beauvoir as responsible (for others) ties her not merely to femininity, which is to be in a state of being 'wanted', but also to motherhood, which is portrayed as being 'needed'.[17] Describing de Beauvoir's 'near-motherly instinct' (Crosland 1992: 224), Crosland writes:

All these young women needed her dramatic individuality, her blend of aloofness, stability and controlling intelligence, for this was the figure she presented to her admirers. Sartre was probably the only person ever allowed to see any sign of anxiety or uncertainty within her.   (ibid.)

For Crosland, de Beauvoir's 'motherly instinct' signifies not merely *being* needed, but *needing* to be needed in order to be:

Beauvoir needed Olga. Through her, she said, she had discovered the pleasure of giving. It became usual, after the publication of *The Second Sex*, to say that Beauvoir knew nothing or understood nothing about motherhood, but through her relationship with Olga she experienced something very much like it: she admitted that she had known previously how moving it was to feel useful, how 'disturbing' it was to believe that she was 'necessary'.   (Crosland 1992: 163. *See also* 224)

There is a short and apparently 'natural' shift here then, from woman and femininity, which is to be 'wanted', to motherhood, which is both to be needed and to need to be needed. And if de Beauvoir, as a woman, *has* to 'give in to that near-motherly instinct' (Crosland 1992: 224) (*because* it is an instinct), then she cannot also, or can only with difficulty, be perceived as sexual in relation to the 'young women'. The way that Crosland emplots these relationships within the narrative resolves the 'problem' of de Beauvoir's imputed sexuality by transforming her lovers into 'young friends' who, resembling children, need to, and must, be cared for (specifically, by de Beauvoir).[18] And indeed, de Beauvoir assumes the reproductive role of motherhood, offering these women emotional, financial and also material support: 'Beauvoir did everything she could to minimise the problems of cold and hunger for her group of young friends. She now found herself entirely responsible for Nathalie' (Crosland 1992: 287–8). Insofar as de Beauvoir's same-sex sexual relationships are circumscribed through the mother/child dyad, Crosland is able to go some way to displace the perceived conflict between sexuality and gender that bisexuality-as-androgyny installed. De Beauvoir's previously 'ambiguous' sexuality is configured (by the plot) as motherhood and, through motherhood, her feminine/female gender is confirmed. Despite de Beauvoir's 'bisexuality' (Crosland 1992: 426) then, she is, after all, a woman. Sexuality and gender are composed.

There is a final point to be made here, and one which again raises the issue of choice in the context of de Beauvoir's same-sex relationships. Crosland's description of de Beauvoir's mothering activities portrays her as definitively older, and more knowledgeable, than her female lovers. Her 'indifference' towards the young women, which was noted above, may therefore (now, at the end of the narrative), be (re)viewed as an 'aloofness' (Crosland 1992: 224) which appears to be the pre-requisite feature of someone who has, and even requires, 'stability and controlling intelligence' (ibid.). But while on the one hand this represents an 'instinct' for mothering, on the other it is portrayed as something of a performance, since, as the above extract suggests, it is a figure that de Beauvoir '*presented* to her admirers' (Crosland 1992: 224. My emphasis.) In other words, there also exists an alternative de Beauvoir, a de Beauvoir who is 'anxious' and 'uncertain' (ibid.). Significantly, it is only Sartre, here representing the husband/father, who is *close enough* to the 'real' de Beauvoir to be 'allowed to see' (ibid.) what she hides from her admirers.[19] This is consistent with the representations I outlined in the first two sections of this chapter where de Beauvoir is understood to be close to her male lovers, but maintains a distance from her female ones. Now however, her relationships with women are refigured as a *choice* because, despite her anxious uncertainty and feeling that 'she had endless responsibilities towards [the women]' (Crosland 1992: 233), Crosland makes it clear that de Beauvoir continues to care for them. Choice does feature in de Beauvoir's same-sex relationships then (she is in some way implicated in them), but only after these relationships are emplotted within the 'safe' confines of a narrative of motherhood, a narrative which also situates the affairs in the context of a heterosexual nuclear family. De Beauvoir's 'bisexuality' therefore, once again, returns her to heterosexuality.[20]

Bisexuality-as-heterosexuality

What distinguishes Fullbrook and Fullbrook's account of de Beauvoir's same-sex relationships from those described so far is that here de Beauvoir *is* perceived to have, in some way, 'chosen' the relationships and, relatedly, appears to obtain some reward from her female lovers. This is possible however, only because bisexuality is configured as an aspect of de Beauvoir and Sartre's heterosexuality.

Fullbrook and Fullbrook's agenda is as clear in this context as it is elsewhere: de Beauvoir is equal, if not superior, to Sartre. Disputing the notion that de Beauvoir 'patiently tolerated his many affairs' (Fullbook and Fullbrook 1993: 93), the authors suggest instead that she 'joined him in vying for the honours in their mutually enjoyable and voyeuristic accounts of sexual athleticism' (ibid.):

Beauvoir's bisexuality, which she repeatedly and publicly had a good deal of fun denying during her lifetime (including during the 1970s when such tastes became politically fashionable and even politically advantageous in some parts of the feminist movement), was clearly a source of titillation to Sartre. His accounts of his sexual antics . . . were just as much a source of amusement to Beauvoir.   (ibid.)

Although, as in Moi's representation, Fullbrook and Fullbrook situate de Beauvoir's women lovers in the context of her 'primary' relationship with Sartre, where Moi's analysis is a weighty account of psychoanalytic lack, Fullbrook and Fullbrook's is distinguished by light-heartedness. Bisexuality is defined as a particular 'taste', and one that is 'fun' – too fun even to bear confession in the (by contrast) 'serious' feminist movement. While de Beauvoir is identified as bisexual then, 'bisexuality' is constituted as a part of *her and Sartre's* (hetero)sexuality: 'as the ardor of their own sexual attachment cooled, their intellectual and emotional bonds were tightened by the detailed accounts of their intimate activities' (Fullbrook and Fullbrook 1993: 94). Here, as above, de Beauvoir and Sartre's hetero-sexual relationship is confirmed because of, rather than in spite of, their contingent relationships. De Beauvoir's 'bisexuality' draws her all the closer to Sartre and to heterosexuality, albeit in an apparently non-physical (but nevertheless sexual) way.

To the extent that de Beauvoir's bisexuality is comparable to, and signifies no more or less than, Sartre's heterosexual antics, it 'belongs' to, and cannot be separated from, a vicarious and voyeuristic heterosexuality. Bisexuality is a *variation* on 'straight' and monogamous heterosexuality:

> Beauvoir's letters to Sartre in the late 1930s indicate a degree of sexual collusion and competition between the pair that shows them both as working out a highly ambiguous desire for joint sexual imperialism . . . [This was] justified in terms of working out a shared life in terms of authenticity which was to remain primary, no matter how many lovers they acquired. That Sartre and Beauvoir's 'confessions' robbed their contingent lovers of their sexual privacy, and thus of their potential power, was very much to the point.   (Fullbrook and Fullbrook 1993: 93–4)

This description of the power relations clearly establishes de Beauvoir's lovers in a secondary position to Sartre. De Beauvoir and Sartre may compete *against* each other but, more importantly, they are always in 'col-lusion' *with* each other. At no other point in Fullbrook and Fullbrook's representation are de Beauvoir and Sartre understood to be as 'equal' and as close to each other as they are in this description of de Beauvoir's rela-tionships with women. Voyeurism serves an important role in this context, since it ensures that de Beauvoir's relationships with women do not threaten Sartre as her affairs with men ultimately do. It is her relationships with Bost and with Algren for example, which are perceived to rival Sartre as essen-tial loves (Fullbrook and Fullbrook 1993: 114 and 164).

For Fullbrook and Fullbrook the significance of de Beauvoir's relation-ships with women lies not in their gender (which would by implication raise questions about de Beauvoir's sexuality thereby linking these relationships to the sexual-narrative-identity ascribed to her), but in the purpose they serve with respect to a broader narrative. De Beauvoir and Sartre's promis-cuity is seen to generate 'material for the production of some of their major writing', 'gossip, intimate scandal, and emotional thrills', an image of themselves as 'bohemian rebels rather than . . . bourgeois respectab[les]' and most significantly, it 'witness[ed] and validate[d] their own singular bond' (Fullbrook and Fullbrook 1993: 95). In other words, Fullbrook and Fullbrook do not consider de Beauvoir's relationships with women to be important *in themselves*. Instead, their value lies in their contribution to her work, her bohemianism and, significantly, her heterosexual relationship with Sartre.

So far, this chapter has been concerned with the different ways in which the significance of de Beauvoir's same-sex relationships is precluded in favour of an authoritative heterosexual-narrative-identity. I want now to consider the implications of this, and of the production of de Beauvoir's sexuality as lesbian, as they challenge Ricoeur's conceptualisation of narrative identity. In particular, the presence of bisexuality in these texts, combined with its preclusion as an identity housed in the self of de Beauvoir, challenges Ricoeur's claim that the question 'who am I?' is persistent and intractable.

Sameness and selfhood

I have drawn on Ricoeur's thesis, both here and in chapter 3, to illustrate how a narrative identity is conferred on de Beauvoir through the attribution of a story to her. This story is subsequently perceived to belong to her and, as such, she is assumed to take responsibility for it. The relevance of Ricoeur's theory, in this context, is perhaps unsurprising however, given that most biographies aim not to destabilise the self, but to produce a coherent portrait of the protagonist as a (usually) singular individual who *warrants* a biography (Stanley 1992).[21] But Ricoeur argues that his theory of narrative identity is compatible even with the 'modern novel', in which 'the *lack* of identity of a person is readily spoken of' (Ricoeur 1991b: 195. My emphasis.) In the modern novel, Ricoeur writes, the crisis of character is matched by a crisis in the identity of plot: 'To the loss of personal identity corresponds a loss of narrative configuration and in particular a crisis of its closure' (Ricoeur 1991b: 195–6). At the height of this disintegration: 'The unidentifiable becomes unnamable [*sic*]' (Ricoeur 1991b: 195).

For Ricoeur, this lack of narrative identity in the modern novel does not signify a loss of the self but rather a loss of identity-as-sameness. One of the ways in which identity-as-selfhood and identity-as-sameness may be distinguished, as noted above, is through the questions which are asked of them: of identity-as-selfhood, we ask the question 'who?': who are you? who did that? and also, particularly, who is responsible? Of identity-as-sameness we ask 'what?': what is that? These two features of identity are frequently confused and collapsed, Ricoeur argues, because they overlap.

Specifically, they overlap in '*permanence* in time' (Ricoeur 1991b: 190) since both identity-as-sameness (*idem*) – such as 'the identity of a thing, of a plant, of an animal' (ibid.) – and identity-as-selfhood (*ipse*) are perceived to be *the same* through time.[22]

Ricoeur's suggestion that a loss of sameness does not necessarily signify a loss of self implies that the self amounts to *more* than a permanence in time, more than identity-as-sameness. He argues that the difference between identity-as-sameness and identity-as-selfhood 'is not just grammatical, or even epistemological and logical, but frankly ontological' (Ricoeur 1991b: 191). This ontological break between *idem* and *ipse* is distinguished by the capacity of the self 'to question itself as to its own way of being and thus to relate itself to being *qua* being' (ibid.). Despite this ontological distinction, identity-as-sameness and identity-as-selfhood are often conflated because they may, and frequently do, share the characteristic of sameness. When we ask the question 'who?' we borrow from the problematic of the same and answer with 'what' (Ricoeur 1991b: 198). Hence: who is de Beauvoir? Answer: lesbian or heterosexual (that is what she is). The self of de Beauvoir is thus constituted, at least in part, through sameness – she is perceived to be lesbian or heterosexual throughout the course of her (life)story.

This narrative production of continuity, of 'sameness', is particularly clear in Margaret Simons' article because she seeks to replace what she calls the 'coherent heterosexual gender identity' (Simons 1992: 137) constructed by de Beauvoir's biographers (and her account is directed principally against Deirdre Bair's biography) with a portrait of de Beauvoir as an 'authentic lesbian'. In order to do so, Simons downplays the role of Sartre in de Beauvoir's life in favour of an emphasis on her same-sex relationships. In a reversal of the biographical representations of de Beauvoir's same-sex and heterosexual relationships described above, Simons argues that 'Sartre could not provide the emotional intimacy that characterised her [de Beauvoir's] closest relationships with women'. She argues that de Beauvoir rejected Sartre's marriage proposal in order that she might live alone and continue with her 'lesbian connections' (Simons 1992: 148), 'connections' which begin with what Simons describes as de Beauvoir's 'passionate adolescent friendship with Zaza' (Simons 1992: 139).

According to Simons, this 'passionate' attachment to Zaza is the first of many same-sex relationships which continue throughout de Beauvoir's life. The detailed description of de Beauvoir's relationships with seven women ensures that Simons' account of her final relationship, with Sylvie Le Bon, does not jar with the overall narrative. Le Bon is the 'acceptable conclusion', as Ricoeur might put it, to a series of events (de Beauvoir's other same-sex relationships) which are configured by the plot. In other words, the relationship with Le Bon signifies the closure in the narrative, it seals de Beauvoir's lesbian identity and ensures that her previous 'lesbian connections' are not perceived (retrospectively) to be random events, a temporary straying on de Beauvoir's part, but rather lead 'naturally' to what Simons describes as 'the most mature and autonomous of all of Beauvoir's relationships with women and . . . closest to what . . . has [been] defined as an authentically lesbian relationship' (Simons 1992: 156). Simons' narrative therefore stands in contrast to the narratives which I have outlined above, in which de Beauvoir's same-sex relationships are either recuperated into heterosexuality and/or are perceived to be so unfulfilling that they are almost unintelligible.

By the end of the narrative then, Simons has replaced the 'coherent' heterosexual identity ascribed to de Beauvoir by her biographers with an (almost) coherent lesbian narrative identity. Significantly, she argues that the 'most important relationship in the *last* two decades of Beauvoir's life' is 'rooted in the most important relationships of the *first* two decades' (Simons 1992: 139. My emphasis.) Insofar as Simons produces a clear continuity between the beginning and the end of de Beauvoir's life, de Beauvoir's sexual-narrative-identity is defined by what Ricoeur calls 'a certain constancy of . . . dispositions' and a 'kind of fidelity to the self' (Ricoeur 1991b: 192). Simons quotes de Beauvoir saying that Le Bon: 'draws me forward into her future, and there are times when the present recovers a dimension that it had lost' (de Beauvoir quoted in Simons 1992: 156). Through Le Bon, past, present and future are connected; de Beauvoir is possessed of an identity-of-sameness which remains permanent, or constant, through time. Indeed, Simons' construction of narrative continuity is persuasive enough to override her own acknowledgement that de Beauvoir 'does not identify her and Le Bon's relationship as lesbian' (Simons 1992: 156). Not only does the narrative itself displace the significance of this denial, but Simons also offers the reader *reasons* for it, 'reasonable' reasons such as fear of professional reprisal for Le Bon (Simons 1992: 138).[23] This suggests that were conditions more favourable, de Beauvoir *would have* identified herself as lesbian. As such, Simons' account bears comparison to Crosland's and Moi's, both of which imply that were there no extenuating circumstances (de Beauvoir's 'magnetic' attractiveness to women, her need to 'fill the void'), she *would have* been 'wholly' heterosexual. In each of these representations some aspect of de Beauvoir's sexuality requires explanation and, through that explanation, its significance is erased and its role in the sexual-narrative-identity ascribed to her precluded.

If we take Simons' word for it, that Deirdre Bair is able to construct a heterosexual identity for de Beauvoir (where the answer to the question 'who is de Beauvoir?' is that de Beauvoir is heterosexual), and if Simons, for her part, convincingly constitutes de Beauvoir as lesbian, then what of bisexuality? In the first instance, it appears that bisexuality, in Simons' article as well as in the representations outlined above, is not constituted as an identity-as-sameness. These narratives clearly do not direct the reader to see de Beauvoir as bisexual from the start to the finish of her life.[24] On the other hand, neither is it possible to 'explain' these interpretations by suggesting that bisexuality represents a crisis in the identity of the plot, a crisis of identity-as-sameness. Ricoeur argues, as noted above, that a crisis in the plot – such that one can no longer speak properly of identity-as-sameness – occurs when '[t]he unidentifiable becomes unnamable [*sic*]' (Ricoeur 1991b: 195). Bisexuality however, as I have illustrated, maintains a consistent presence in these texts. Simons, for example, makes a direct reference to the 'rather clinical label "bisexual"' (Simons 1992: 140), she *names* bisexuality. In other words, even though bisexuality is nameable, in none of these accounts is it one of the 'durable properties' which are constitutive of de Beauvoir's narrative identity. Instead, the question 'who is de Beauvoir?' is answered either by heterosexuality or by lesbianism.

This might suggest that bisexuality is an identity-as-selfhood, since Ricoeur argues that with or even without identity-as-sameness, the problematic of selfhood remains. He writes:

> it must be said that even in the most extreme case of the loss of sameness-identity of the hero, we do not escape the problematic of selfhood. A non-subject is not nothing, with respect to the category of the subject . . . Suppose someone asks the question: Who am I? Nothing, or almost nothing is the reply. But it is still a reply to the question *who.*   (Ricoeur 1991b: 196)[25]

To suggest that bisexuality is identity-as-selfhood would be to conflate the presence of bisexuality in the texts with a 'bisexual I' (or rather, a bisexual 'she').[26] According to Simons however, the 'rather clinical label "bisexual" leaves Bair's heterosexual interpretive framework intact' (Simons 1992: 140). Thus again, as in the biographies, 'bisexual' is not an identity which *of itself* authors the self of de Beauvoir; rather, it is subsumed under the broad umbrella of heterosexuality. Unlike lesbianism and heterosexuality, bisexuality (based on the gender of object choice) is perceived neither to inhere in, nor to be expressive of, the individual de Beauvoir.

Ricoeur's theory of narrative identity is useful to the analysis of bisexuality insofar as it demonstrates that, in these texts, bisexuality is not a durable property, constitutive of de Beauvoir's sexual-narrative-identity. In none of these accounts are de Beauvoir's relationships with women *and* men 'gathered together' and emplotted in such a way that they produce a specifically bisexual-narrative-identity. Indeed, the very existence of de

Beauvoir's relationships with men appears to preclude any relationship with women from being perceived as meaningful (in terms of the sexual-narrative-identity ascribed to her) – and vice versa. However, if Ricoeur's analysis of narrative identity illustrates why bisexuality is not identity-as-sameness, by the same token, because bisexuality does not signify a *breakdown* in identity-as-sameness, its position in these texts serves as a rejoinder to Ricoeur's theory. Specifically, it demonstrates the extent to which the privileging of narrative produces a self which is *itself* bound by the productions wrought by narrative.

Like Foucault, Ricoeur displaces the subject as the originary source of meaning-production, arguing that while we may 'learn to become the *narrator* and the hero *of our own story*', we are not able to become 'the *author of our own life*' (Ricoeur 1991a: 32). However, where Foucault's assertion that the self is produced through discourse allows for the possibility that discourse might not always produce the self in the shape that it currently does (or, indeed, that it might not produce it at all), Ricoeur's emphasis on narrative as *the* primary technique by which selfhood is established, although displacing the concept of an 'essential' self, nevertheless suggests that the self is essentially narrative. Narrative identity, he claims, bridges 'the apparent choice between sheer change and absolute identity'. It produces 'a *self* instructed by cultural symbols, the first among which are the narratives handed down in our literary tradition' (Ricoeur 1991a: 33). Thus narrative identity, as Ricoeur defines it, is that which mediates between a loss of self ('sheer change') and an essential self ('absolute identity'). In other words, narrative identity is itself based on an *a priori* conception both of the self and of identity. Ricoeur presupposes the intelligible self to be that which is possessed of an identity, while identity is presupposed to be that which is possessed by the self. Identity and selfhood then, are defined in terms of each other.

Yet the example of bisexuality indicates that the theorisation of identity does not necessarily invoke the problematic of selfhood. Bisexuality is present in these texts, but de Beauvoir is not bisexual. This suggests not merely that the question 'who is de Beauvoir?' is not answerable with a bisexual 'what', but also that bisexuality, as it is produced here, is precluded from being *intelligible* in terms of the question 'who?' In the case of bisexuality, identity and selfhood are separated, such that they are no longer defined in terms of each other.

Exceeding individuality

In chapter 3 I demonstrated the significance of individuality in the production of plausible selfhood and the role of responsibility and continuity (sameness) therein. In order to be perceived as a unique individual, I argued, de Beauvoir must be possessed of a story, a story which is productive of a 'fidelity to the self' throughout her life. In this chapter I have explored the different ways in which those stories which might have been constitutive of a bisexual-narrative-identity are precluded. In the first instance, only stories of heterosexuality are perceived to 'belong' to de Beauvoir and to be her responsibility. They alone provide narrative closure. Same-sex relationships, by contrast, play no role in the production of de Beauvoir's sexual-narrative-identity, particularly since she appears to have no 'choice' in them. Secondly, the 'adventure' or quest for self-knowledge, which is galvanised, in Crosland's account, by bisexuality-as-androgyny, ensures that the femininity ascribed to de Beauvoir is secured and, additionally, that stories of same-sex attraction are transformed into a story of mother and child (where Sartre represents the father/husband figure). In this biography, it is only in the context of a heterosexual nuclear family that de Beauvoir is perceived to have taken responsibility for, and to have chosen, her relationships with women. In Fullbrook and Fullbrook's account, where de Beauvoir is also understood to have 'chosen' bisexuality, bisexuality is configured as integral to (her and Sartre's) heterosexuality. In none of these representations therefore, nor in Simons' construction of de Beauvoir as lesbian, does bisexuality reside within the individual de Beauvoir where it might disclose the 'truth' of the self.

There is a double preclusion here then, since bisexuality can be understood neither as two stories, one of heterosexuality and the other of lesbianism (which could potentially be gathered together in order to constitute a bisexual-narrative-identity), nor as one story which has been erased. In short, although bisexuality is present (nameable) in these texts, no notion of bisexuality as an identity-as-sameness, or of a continuous story of bisexuality, is produced *to be* lost. Neither however, is bisexuality an identity-as-selfhood. Indeed, it is the very narrative techniques which constitute de Beauvoir as a self – individuality, femininity, sameness and authenticity for example – which *also* disallow bisexuality from being produced as that which inheres in the self of de Beauvoir. Bisexuality exceeds selfhood, specifically de Beauvoir's self, insofar as it is not constitutive of an individual sexual-narrative-identity.

I will return to the themes of responsibility and choice in chapter 6. What I want to pursue further now, is the issue of representation. I have already argued that bisexuality, although it is precluded from the sexual-narrative-identity ascribed to de Beauvoir, is nevertheless 'visible' in some sense: it maintains a 'presence' in the texts. What is especially significant about the newspaper portrayals of de Beauvoir, to which I will turn in the following chapter, is that they have the effect not merely of displacing bisexuality as an identity which is the 'property' of de Beauvoir, but of situating it entirely 'beyond the frame' of representation.

5

Displacement

This chapter is structured by a concept of the 'frame' which I have taken from Lynda Nead's study of the female nude (Nead 1993: 2).[1] Nead's understanding of the female nude is useful here, because it enables parallels to be drawn between the processes by which the naked female body is held within the frame of cultural acceptability and the ways that representations of de Beauvoir (and especially of 'her' sexuality) are aestheticised and situated within the confines of a predominantly heterosexual culture.[2] It is especially important to draw attention to the processes of aestheticisation in the context of press representations given that, as Susan Sontag argues in relation to professional photographers, journalists often claim that their work is characterised by a 'disavowal of empathy, a disdain for message-mongering, a claim to be invisible' (Sontag 1979: 77). As with the biographies, where the narrative appears to unfold 'naturally' and to be driven by the 'facts' themselves, journalistic deference to a 'professional code' (S. Hall 1993: 101) – which foregrounds 'neutrality' and which does not overtly signal the discursive paradigms within which it operates – seemingly displaces the role the media play in the active production of meaning.

The frame metaphor also situates techniques of the self firmly within the aesthetic domain and, as such, I will be including in this chapter some discussion of the debates around, and implications of, the aestheticisation of the self (and how this aestheticisation might be gendered). Similarly, Sontag's work *On Photography* (1979) allows me to highlight the way that the biography of de Beauvoir is portrayed, in newspaper representations, through a series of 'snapshot summaries'. These condensed images serve, in *spectacular* freeze-frame fashion, to halt the flow of broader narratives which circulate 'beyond' or 'outside' the frame. At the same time however, the nebulous presence of these narratives 'behind the scenes' endow the fleeting clips of de Beauvoir with an impression of substance. The images acquire their potency in part because the reader *already* knows the de Beauvoir and Sartre 'story'. As Sontag notes: 'Photographic images are pieces of evidence in an ongoing biography or history' (Sontag 1979: 166). To this extent the opaque presence of these narratives inform, but is not directly present, in the texts.

My analysis of the ways in which the newspapers constitute de Beauvoir's self will proceed by way of three frames, all of which displace bisexuality from the field of visibility. Taken together, these frames do not form a coherent or unified vision of sexuality and, in some respects, are even mutually exclusive. What they do share however, is a resistance to producing bisexuality as a subject of representation. This ensures that de Beauvoir emerges (almost) 'fit for art' (Nead 1993: 77), an aesthetic self whose sexual biography is purged of contention and held within the frame of cultural 'respectability'. Unlike in chapter 4 however, where bisexuality is explicitly raised as an issue in the texts, these newspaper representations make no direct reference to bisexuality at all. Bisexuality is therefore not merely not produced as a property of the self of de Beauvoir, it is entirely displaced from view.

I will also, during the course of the following analysis, be considering the issue of boundaries (of all sorts): the boundaries between public and private, author and audience, and between high and popular culture. In particular, and in order to illustrate that the frames within which de Beauvoir is contained are far from secure, the final part of the chapter will consider the art/obscenity coupling, and those moments when the boundaries of the frames are pulled out of shape, or threatened. What I want to do first however, is to consider the relevance of Nead's work as it contributes to an understanding both of representations of de Beauvoir and to the production (or not) of bisexuality.

An 'ethics of seeing'

Nead argues that in Western metaphysics:

form (the male) is preferred over matter (the female); mind and spirit are privileged over the body and substance and the only way to give meaning and order to the body in nature is through the imposition of technique and style – to give it a defining frame.

(Nead 1993: 23)

For Nead, the frame suggests 'a metaphor for the "staging" of art, both in terms of surrounding the body with style and of marking the limit between art and non-art, that is, obscenity' (Nead 1993: 25).[3] The naked female body then, in its 'raw' state, is perceived as 'matter'. Through the imposition of (male) 'artistic' techniques, this matter is tamed, literally framed, and delivered from obscenity: stylisation and aestheticisation transform the naked female body into 'the female nude'. This nude conforms to the Aristotelian definition of 'beauty' to the extent that it embodies 'order and symmetry and definiteness' (Nead 1993: 7).

Like the naked female body, de Beauvoir is subject to processes of stylisation that serve to ascribe to her a specific social identity. She is often photographed, for example, in the act of writing.[4] Pen and paper – the tools of her trade – are on her lap, in her hands or on the table.[5] Usually, these portraits of de Beauvoir 'at work' capture her in a straight-backed and upright position, modestly dressed, with her hair held in a neat bun. Such images reveal a calm and *composed* de Beauvoir – an ordered, orderly and overwhelmingly well-*maintained* woman. Written representations support this kind of visual image – journalistic reportage chooses to constitute even de Beauvoir's psychic happiness in terms of her passion for writing:

> All her life she regarded them [herself and Sartre] as primarily a writing couple. Her image of happiness was a sunny room, with two people in it, both of them writing. And in cafés, bars and hotels, chiefly in and around Saint-Germain-de-Prés [*sic*], this was the pattern of their life together. She was, and acknowledged herself to be, a happy woman.   (*Independent on Sunday* 10 June 1990)

The order of mental exercise, the assumed 'symmetry' of heterosexuality and the concrete assurance that an intellectual secures happiness through writing each corresponds to Aristotle's definition of beauty. This is de Beauvoir framed: in a photograph, in a room, in a description. A further parallel with the female nude – and a further result of the process of containment – is that de Beauvoir is situated within the realm of 'high culture'. Her life and work furnish an academic industry and her books and biographies are reviewed in 'quality' broadsheet papers.[6] This 'high' cultural interest in de Beauvoir is partnered by a mode of visual representation which positions de Beauvoir at three-quarter angles (as opposed to full frontal) – a representation which conforms to the conventions of Western art and which, echoing the genre of (White upper class) family portraits, establishes de Beauvoir in a specific social setting (Berger 1972; Tagg 1988).

Sontag's analysis of photography offers a bridge to cross from Nead's 'visual' analysis to an analysis of written material. She writes: 'Photography is commonly regarded as an instrument for knowing things. When Thoreau said, "You can't say more than you see", he took for granted that sight had pride of place among the senses' (Sontag 1979: 93). Sontag's thesis, that the ubiquity of photography in Western society has led to an 'aestheticising of reality' (Sontag 1979: 176), is confirmed in journalese – a style that defers to an assumed 'photographic imagination'. The written texts not only encourage a static, unchanging perception of de Beauvoir (as in a freeze frame), but are also frequently even literal descriptions of photographs themselves:

> The photograph on the back jacket [of the book *Letters to Sartre*] stays in the reader's mind. Here is the great philosopher [Sartre], in his knitted shirt buttoned up to the neck: his dear little shirt, as Beauvoir would say. Here is the author of the letters [de Beauvoir], looking frayed, hair knotted in a cleaning lady's scarf. Her glass is empty, Sartre's is half full. So many years of hard thinking, hard loving: so sad they look like an old janitor and his wife, out on a (very modified) spree.
>
> (*Independent on Sunday*, 2 February 1992b)

Despite this author's long review of de Beauvoir's letters to Sartre, which highlights her relationships with women as well as men, it is *the photograph* that ultimately 'speaks the truth' of de Beauvoir and tells the reader what there is to 'know' about her. When all is said and done, the ambiguity of the past is dissolved in favour of a representation which (re)figures de Beauvoir as no more than one half of a parochial, heterosexual, 'married' couple. Like the privileging of de Beauvoir's unpublished and unedited letters in the biographies (see chapter 3), photographs (as well as written descriptions of them) have come to acquire the status of a 'raw record' (Sontag 1979: 74).[7] Photographs teach us 'a new visual code, [they] alter and enlarge our notions of what is worth looking at and what we have a right to observe. They are a grammar and, even more importantly, an ethics of seeing' (Sontag 1979: 3). Thus when de Beauvoir's turban – something of a trademark[8] – came undone at Sartre's funeral, newspaper coverage emphasised that the 'symbolic' moment (de Beauvoir herself is coming undone/falling to pieces) was 'not missed by photographers' (*Independent on Sunday*, 2 February 1992a). Sontag's suggestion that the 'whole of a life may be summed up in a momentary appearance' (Sontag 1979: 159) is demonstrated in a flash (of the camera's eye): captured on film, the potent heterosexual image was not merely encapsulated, but dramatically magnified.

The style of writing which dominates press reports bears witness to the privileging of photo-journalism in an increasingly spectacular society. The reader is frequently encouraged to 'visualise' the written description: '[de Beauvoir] looked to me frailer and less tall than one might have expected. In her trouser suit and its matching purple turban she was still essentially feminine. Her voice was dry and rapid, her red-nailed hands impatient and restless' (Margaret Crosland quoted in *Independent on Sunday*, 2 February 1992a). This 'portrait' of de Beauvoir ('a verbal picture; a graphic description' according to the OED) lends itself to the imagination. The reader is prompted 'to image' the frail, slight and (therefore?) 'essentially feminine' de Beauvoir. The interchangeability of literary and visual terms – a photographic *grammar,* a literary *portrait* – indicates how thin a line divides the visual from the written: all of the examples above, whatever their medium of expression, indicate to the reader 'what is worth looking at' and 'what we have a right to observe'. In the written representation of de Beauvoir and Sartre in 'a sunny room', in the description of a photograph of de Beauvoir and Sartre in a café and of de Beauvoir at Sartre's funeral, the reader is directed to observe de Beauvoir's heterosexuality. And when the *Independent on Sunday* describes de Beauvoir's 'frailty', her clothes and her nails, it is her femininity which is signalled.

Like the distinction between the naked female body and the nude, an 'ethics of seeing' constitutes what can and cannot be consumed, what is figured, and what is excluded, from the frame: 'the policing of the boundaries of cultural acceptability is, quite blatantly, a policing of the boundaries of sexual acceptability' (Nead 1993: 95). The very maintenance of frames and boundaries presupposes – constitutes – a threatening 'exterior'. Thus the female nude marks not only 'the internal limit of art', but also 'the external limit of obscenity' (Nead 1993: 25). The 'obscenity' of bisexuality will be the focus of the final part of this chapter. First, three frames explore precisely how it is that contention is displaced.

The paint and oil of existentialism

This frame explores how the link forged by the press between de Beauvoir and (representations of) 'existentialism' effaces bisexuality. Existentialism has two (related) functions here. Firstly, it is perceived to be the *raison d'être* behind de Beauvoir's many relationships. As such, her 'motive' lies not in sexual desire for both men and women but rather in her infamous intellectual 'pact' with Sartre (that they should have 'contingent' affairs while maintaining their 'essential' relationship). Secondly, existentialism serves as the vehicle through which a certain 'masculinity' is ascribed to de Beauvoir. This is not to suggest that de Beauvoir plays the 'man' in her relationships with women, as implied in Crosland's account (see chapter 4), but rather that she is assumed to possess characteristics which are conventionally designated 'masculine' (voyeurism, lack of emotion) which consequently position her 'outside' the affairs. Nevertheless, while not identical to Crosland's, this representation does have similar effects: 'distanced' from her 'contingent' affairs, both de Beauvoir's perceived investment in her female lovers and their role in her sexual biography are diminished.

A number of newspaper representations of de Beauvoir's sexual relationships confirm Nead's contention that: 'The evocation of blanket terms such as "love" and "human relations" can . . . work to hide a range of cultural, sexual and moral norms in a hazy mist of universal consensus' (Nead 1993: 106). De Beauvoir's 'pact' with Sartre robs her 'contingent' relationships of those features traditionally associated with affairs: spontaneity, romance and love. Nelson Algren encapsulates the majority of press opinion in the question: 'How can love be contingent? . . . Contingent upon what?' (Algren quoted in the *Financial Times*, 15 August 1987). The virtually legal terminology in which the pact with Sartre is often represented suggests that it is the 'dry' flavour of the arrangement that warrants disapproval. Thus: 'the terms of de Beauvoir's contract with the existential maestro do not seem to have been negotiable' (ibid.). What the press must negotiate therefore, is an expression of sexuality unescorted by 'love'. To this end, Algren comes to represent the figural enactment of all that is 'normal', all that is 'not French' and all that is heterosexual: 'Algren was so un-French as to be distraught . . . [he] thought in his naive American way that two people who loved as they did ought to get married and be faithful to one another' (*Financial Times*, 19 January 1991).[9] His belief in marriage and fidelity constitutes 'a breath of fresh air amongst the welter of self-justification in the Sartre-Beauvoir circle' (*Financial Times*, 15 August 1987).

If de Beauvoir's pact with Sartre deprives the press of a traditional heterosexual love story, they in turn use this 'contract' to deprive her of sexual pleasure. De Beauvoir is perceived to have affairs because she 'want[s] experience more than pleasure' (*Independent on Sunday*, 2 February 1992b); she 'had several lovers at once – though curiously not always with much pleasure' (*Sunday Telegraph,* 8 December 1991). The 'existential experiment which was their [de Beauvoir and Sartre's] long, open "morganatic" marriage' (ibid.) thus comes to play a significant role in de Beauvoir's (a)sexual biography and, in particular, in the occlusion of sexual pleasure. As in biographical representations of de Beauvoir's relationships with women – which are understood to be inspired by extenuating circumstances (her inadvertent attractiveness to women (Crosland 1992) or her psychic needs (Moi 1994) for example) – such an occlusion, contrived by the press, implicitly suggests that while heterosexual pleasure is absolute, any other form of sexual expression requires a motive other than pleasure itself. *The Sunday Times*, for example, suggests that de Beauvoir's 'relations with women were tortured, rarely erotic' (*The Sunday Times*, 2 August 1987). Although directly acknowledging de Beauvoir's relationships with women, the paper dismisses the 'erotic' in favour of the 'tortuous' (and figures these as mutually exclusive). Within this context it seems inconceivable that Olga Kosakiewicz, say (as opposed to Algren), should question the philosophy behind de Beauvoir's contingent affairs or should ask how it is possible for love to be contingent.

'Existentialism' therefore, in this first instance, bears comparison with the 'paint and oil' of artistic representation which, by foregrounding its technique, 'inhibits or blocks the immediate sexual gratification' (Nead 1993: 97). Wrought as the motivation behind de Beauvoir's relationships, existentialism 'clothes' an otherwise wayward sexuality and transforms de Beauvoir into the equivalent of a nude. Since sexual pleasure alone cannot explain (or justify) de Beauvoir's behaviour, it must be entirely forfeited. Without this, the unspeakable issue of 'sexual gratification', in a same-sex affair, might bear articulation.

A-sexuality also features in de Beauvoir's relationship with Sartre, once again as a consequence of existentialism. The relationship is perceived, by the *Sunday Telegraph*, to be 'as much cerebral as sexual', and de Beauvoir is quoted saying that she and Sartre 'went to bed, blissfully happy, our heads full of words' (*Sunday Telegraph*, 26 January 1992). In short: 'Words were what they [de Beauvoir and Sartre] both lived for until quite late in life. True to their doctrine of "transparency", they kept few secrets from each other' (ibid.). De Beauvoir's pleasure is based in the academy, her 'marriage' 'a marriage of true minds' (*Guardian*, 16 April 1986). This sexual inflection situates de Beauvoir firmly within the hierarchy of Western metaphysics: her 'mind' dominates and takes precedence over (and is, by implication, separable from) her 'body'. An aesthetic stylisation which employs existentialism as the medium of expression thus signifies 'form' as opposed to 'matter' and 'order' over the abyss of chaotic substance. Like the representation of de Beauvoir writing, the woman here is contained within a scaffold of scholarship.

The representations of de Beauvoir and of sexuality outlined above are aesthetic insofar as they are literally 'purified of pleasure'. To this extent they can be distinguished from venal sensuality:

Legitimate, or high, culture is . . . constituted through the denial of lower, vulgar or venal enjoyment and the assertion of the sublimated, refined and disinterested pleasure . . . Bourdieu provides us with an example of cultural distinction based on the separation of the aesthetic ('pleasure purified of pleasure') and the venal ('pleasure reduced to the pleasure of the senses').
(Nead 1993: 84)

The qualities that existentialism defines in this context not only situate de Beauvoir within 'high' culture but are also, relatedly, the very same as those which constitute the sublimated pleasure of the aesthetic: voyeuristic distance, 'objectivity' and intellectualism. These features, conventionally dubbed 'masculine', harness the female nude and produce it as 'an extension of the elevated male attributes associated with the mind' (Nead 1993: 14). Thus de Beauvoir 'looks' with 'masculine' eyes: 'She and Sartre were incurable voyeurs who specialised in emotional threesomes' (*The Sunday Times*, 2 August 1987). The voyeurism which is perceived to motivate these relationships finds resonance with the disinterested pleasure of the aesthetic and, in this respect, implies that there is a distance between de Beauvoir and her (women) lovers: 'Certainly there is something cold, exploitative in her attitude . . . we cannot know how the experimental subjects feel, for theirs are merely contingent lives' (*Independent on Sunday*, 2 February 1992b). That it is the *lives* of the 'experimental subjects' which are contingent (as opposed, simply, to their relationship with de Beauvoir), indicates that love-story and life-story are collapsed here: life is (all about) love/sex relationships. This complete contingency additionally situates de Beauvoir in a still more powerful position over her lovers. If her lovers are objects in a cold and exploitative experimental research project, by extension de Beauvoir must be the objective researcher, a rational self who 'acts on' others. In short, de Beauvoir, like the masculine spectator, is situated 'outside' her relationships: she looks *at*, but does not partake *in* (as in Crosland's representation of de Beauvoir, where she appears to be indifferent to, and aloof from, her same-sex partners).

This then, is the second way in which existentialism is employed to frame the figure of de Beauvoir within the boundaries of cultural acceptability. Positioned as the masculine artist/dry philosopher, she is figured as power 'in, as well as under, control' (Nead 1993: 17). The metaphorical gender switch enables not only de Beauvoir's own, now masculinised, body to be 'mastered' but also, *through* this body, those of her female lovers as well. Again, existentialism ties her sexuality not to pleasure, but to intellectualism. In the following extract, the roots of de Beauvoir's 'cold' attitude are perceived to lie in the existential concept of 'inauthenticity':

De Beauvoir has a very chilling habit of describing other people's emotions of jealousy and resentment against herself as 'inauthentic', even lecturing one girl about it: in existentialist philosophy 'inauthentic' means self-deceiving, or being in bad faith, and that seems to me to describe exactly de Beauvoir's own behaviour in using the term to deny other people's feelings.   (*Sunday Telegraph*, 8 December 1991)

De Beauvoir, appearing to value 'authenticity' (a notably *intellectual* authenticity) over and above 'other people's feelings', sacrifices her own 'humanity' in the process. Her behaviour is 'inauthentic' insofar as 'inauthenticity' is constituted as a denial of 'other people's feelings'. That this criticism is rarely levelled at men (indeed, sensitivity to others may be regarded as *e*masculating), suggests that the masculinisation of de

Beauvoir cannot be sustained at any great length. In the final analysis, de Beauvoir 'is' a woman and the cost of effacing her femininity in order to account for her sexuality is too high to maintain. The preferred strategy in this example then, is to constitute intellectualism and emotional responsibility as mutually exclusive: de Beauvoir's femininity, albeit somewhat wayward, is ultimately recuperated and subsequently her (feminine) behaviour is condemned as inauthentic.

In sum, 'existentialism' serves as a two-pronged strategy of containment through which the representations of sexuality ascribed to de Beauvoir are aestheticised (anaesthetised) and purified (sterilised) of sexual pleasure. Firstly, like the application of 'art' (on) to the naked female body, de Beauvoir is restrained and styled through the technics of an asexual biography. Like the nude, she is confined to the unemotional, controlled and intellectually reflective arena. Secondly, representing the 'masculine' artist/painter herself, de Beauvoir controls not only her own female body (insofar as it is denied an energetic sexuality) but also the bodies of her female lovers as well (they are her 'objects').

A further implication is that de Beauvoir's relationships with women are perceived to be not only specifically *not* pleasurable and *not* erotic, but are also orchestrated from within the frame of heterosexuality: the relationship with Sartre, itself bound by the intellect (Sartre is inevitably found at the heart of all things existential), circumscribes her liaisons with women. This is demonstrated by the *Independent Weekend* headline which reads: 'Letters from a radical lover – in which Simone tells her beloved Jean-Paul what she gets up to while he's away' (*Independent Weekend*, 23 November 1991). The effect here is to render de Beauvoir's relationships with women second to Sartre: they occur only when he is 'away'. On Sartre's return (the return of the primary relationship), their importance will presumably be diminished. Constituted as additional (extra-curricular even?), rather than central, the affairs qualify for neither serious nor independent consideration. As in the biographies, they have no 'inherent' value because they are inspired by something other than themselves. In the first instance they derive from existentialism, in the second, Sartre. These representations of de Beauvoir therefore not only displace bisexuality, but also ensure that heterosexuality is in no way threatened.

Being bohemian

The second frame explores the consequences for bisexuality of the reputation of de Beauvoir and Sartre, in Britain, as 'universal Parisians' (*The Times*, 19 April 1986).[10] In this context, representations of de Beauvoir are housed in three adjoining rooms: 'French', 'intellectual' and 'bohemian'. This triad exerts such magnificent force over de Beauvoir that bisexuality becomes subsumed within it. Hence bisexuality is not perceived to be constitutive of the self (as other sexualities, particularly heterosexuality, are); instead, de Beauvoir's sexual behaviour is informed by her bohemian milieu. If it were possible to 'separate' this lifestyle from de Beauvoir, the press imply that her capricious sexual behaviour might also (by her own preference even) have been circumvented. This is confirmed in the final frame.

Representations of de Beauvoir/Paris (for they are often collapsed) appear as no more than snapshots in the album of a collective popular imagination. Like a tourist visiting France, the images collected here repeatedly confirm British images of French national identity:[11]

Resemblance is a conformity, but to what? to an identity. Now this identity is imprecise, even imaginary, to the point where I can continue to speak of 'likeness' without ever having seen the model . . . I spontaneously call them 'likenesses' because they conform to what I expect of them.   (Barthes 1981: 101–2)

The cumulative effect of these images, found also on book covers and posters, in films, journals, novels and in the academy, is that history, 'past and present', represents only 'a set of anecdotes' (Sontag 1979: 23). Replicated thousands of times over, these images do not emerge, but rather remain static and motionless, even 'naturalised' (things could never be different), like a photographic 'still'. This second frame thus uses a 'postcard device' in order to capture the flavour of the stylised and aestheticised 'souvenirs' – 'featherweight portable museums' (Sontag 1979: 68) – offered by British newspapers, and from which the reader is free to consume and purchase a history.[12]

Postcards from France

The first postcard finds de Beauvoir collapsed with 'France'. It is the postwar period, and French society is ripe for radical change: 'the reader is taken through a story which, however plainly told, cannot fail to fascinate, for it is woven into important aspects of France's twentieth-century history, above all with the often tumultuous post-war resettlement of French society' (*Financial Times*, 1 February 1992). The historic moment is dominated by a changing political climate – rebellion is possible and romantic. A sleight of hand positions de Beauvoir both inside and outside this self-reflective period. She offers 'insider' information on the events – 'Simone de Beauvoir's most successful novel was *Les Mandarins* (1954) a roman à clef about Sartre, Camus, herself and other luminaries of the French left-wing after the liberation' (*The Times*, 15 April 1986) – and yet she is also central to those events herself:

the prize-winning novel, *Les Mandarins*, explores the postwar Parisian cultural world where they were the joint dominant force . . . They were closely involved in attempts to start a Left Bank resistance movement during the war, and were at the centre of leftwing postwar political protest.   (*Guardian*, 15 April 1986a)

De Beauvoir is not only imbricated *in* and *with* post-war France, but also *creates* post-war France.

A large, front-page photograph in the *Independent Weekend* (23 November 1991) shows de Beauvoir in a typical French boulevard – her youthful face is set against a predictably opaque background, complete with tall 'French' buildings and traditional streetlights. The photograph – playing on the tension between the naive and the risqué which so frequently represents 'the French' to 'the British' – is as much of France as it is of de Beauvoir: each defines the other to the extent that they are inseparable. Like written representations, this visual chronicle does not 'reflect' so much as constitute both de Beauvoir *and* France.[13] The impenetrable link ensures that when de Beauvoir dies, a part of France is perceived to be buried with her: 'Vive la difference/Simone de Beauvoir and the death of Parisian Left Bank Culture' (*The Times*, 19 April 1986). The demure satisfaction surrounding de Beauvoir's death implies an ambivalent combination of fear of, and hope for, the demise of French national identity on the part of much of the British press: 'It was one of those times when France stops to look at itself and at the rich literary tradition which its current writers seem unable to top up' (*The Economist*, 19 April 1986).

Three years later, France's national literary archive acquired the rights to de Beauvoir's and Sartre's letters which enabled the British press to confirm again that de Beauvoir is an established part of France's national cultural heritage. In this context, Gilbert Joseph's 'wild, vitriolic attack on their [de Beauvoir and Sartre's] Second World War Resistance record' (*Sunday Telegraph*, 26 January 1992) was interpreted in the British newspapers to be an attack on French national identity. The British coverage of the 'Parisian response' to the incident not only affirmed that the reporters' perception had been justified (a curiously circular exercise), but also occasioned further nationalistic stereotypes and a trace of badinage on the part of the press: 'Paris literary papers have divided over the issue, and few are content to dismiss the matter, as one new year reveller in a Boul' Mich' café did, with a Gallic shrug' (*Financial Times*, 1 February 1992). Gallic shrugs in Gallic cafés proved, to the British, that de Beauvoir and Sartre not only 'arouse fierce passions in France' (*Sunday Telegraph*, 26 January 1992), but also, in some measure, define France.

Notably, the British newspapers' production of de Beauvoir and Sartre as an integral part of the French cultural heritage serves to tie them all the more closely to each other. Echoing Francis and Gontier's claim that de Beauvoir and Sartre lived 'their two lives as if they were one dual life' (Francis and Gontier 1987: 111) (see chapter 3), the *Guardian* writes: 'Now that they are both dead, they again seem to be one person, a two-sided manifestation of French social, political and cultural history' (*Guardian*, 15 April 1986b). Physical death breathes new life and a new dimension into the de Beauvoir/Sartre relationship: confirming the cultural significance of heterosexual unity, the couple acquire an immortalised and mythic position in memory and history.

Post-cards from intellectual Paris[14]

De Beauvoir's French national identity is further collapsed with an 'intellectualism' that is perceived to reside in Paris: 'In their prime', *The Times* writes, 'Sartre and de Beauvoir were Paris' (*The Times*, 19 April 1986). 'Parisian intellectualism' provides a forceful vehicle through which to construct and confirm the difference between the *'English'* (notably) and the 'French':

Simone de Beauvoir has no parallel in English life. Brains have never replaced blood as a means of procuring social eminence here. . . . If you want to see importance attached to grown-up authors, you had better see how they order these things in France.   (*The Sunday Times*, 2 August 1987)

'Earnest' French seriousness is positioned against a somewhat scornful English anti-intellectualism, a scornfulness which appears to validate the acquisition of social eminence via blood ties. *The Times* suggests, somewhat nostalgically, that those were 'happy days', days of blood ties perhaps, and certainly the days when there were no 'professional intellectuals':[15] 'You could scour London, look in every café in Soho and never find their like . . . professional intellectuals who lived on and off their ideas – Britain in those years had none. Happy days' (*The Times*, 19 April 1986). This 'seriousness about the life of the mind' is understood to be a 'prized' 'Gallic trait' (ibid.) which extends as far back as the Revolution:

When the ancien regime was overthrown, new heads had to be supplied to replace those that had rolled. The *philosophes* and provincial lawyers who had inspired the revolution thought it natural that those with *bonnes notes* – the highest marks – should go to the top of the classes. Intelligence maintains a centrality in Paris which, in London, is reserved for sportsmen, princesses and the dead.

(*The Sunday Times*, 2 August 1987)

Despite the ironic tone, de Beauvoir's lifestyle is constituted with the full force of French history behind it. No surprise then, that the press dramatically highlighted de Gaulle's response to requests that he should arrest Sartre (for his role in inciting French workers to rebellion): 'On n'arrête pas Voltaire' (*Independent on Sunday*, 10 June 1990). Seemingly above even law and order, this perceived lifestyle, hewn of immense proportions, gives rise to conclusions like that of *The Times* that: 'Sartre and de Beauvoir begin to appear in retrospect famous for their membership of a celebrated menage as much as for their philosophy and novels. They had achieved, in this age of mass culture, star status on account of their lifestyle' (*The Times*, 19 April 1986).[16] The media machine's production of de Beauvoir and Sartre as 'stars' distances them from the public at large. Because de Beauvoir is unlike 'ordinary' folk, her perceived sexual difference (from the unspoken 'norm' of heterosexuality) can be attributed not to individual preference, but to her celebrated lifestyle – a lifestyle, notably, that acquires legitimisation in Paris/France in particular.

Post-cards from bohemian cafés

French intellectual identity is also an 'inherently' bohemian identity. Indeed, existentialism is constituted as the *consequence of* 'bohemianism', an 'expression of Sartre's deeply rooted café complex' (*Guardian*, 22 December 1992), a ruse with which to justify the lifestyle: 'there is certainly something enviable in so much free-loving, free-loading and free-wheeling. François Mauriac, appalled and fascinated, conceded that unless God existed there was no reason not to want to live their way' (*Sunday Times*, 2 August 1987). In short: 'What a winning trick to turn doing what you want into a revolutionary morality!' (ibid.). The marriage of intellectualism and bohemianism, neatly packaged in historical tradition, enables a comparison to be wrought between de Beauvoir and Sartre and the protagonists of *Les Liaisons Dangereuses*. The extract is critical: de Beauvoir's and Sartre's work and sexuality are judged elitist (and therefore hypocritical), malicious (and therefore unoriginal). The analogy enables both French tradition and high culture to be turned against themselves:

Simone de Beauvoir devoted herself to didactic sedition. She and Jean-Paul Sartre spent their lives sawing high-mindedly at the lofty branch on which their talents had entitled them to sit. It is hardly news that the two of them had an unusual relationship. In fact, it was less 'unique' than a variation on the one to be found in *Les Liaisons Dangereuses*, where a pact binds the 'essential' lovers to disclose to each other the details of their 'contingent' affairs. The existential mandarins were left-wing aristos: Laclos Deux, you might say.   (*The Sunday Times*, 2 August 1987)

That a viable juxtaposition can be sustained between two fictional characters and de Beauvoir and Sartre confirms the suspicion that they too are no
more than fantasy. The shift from French intellectual tradition to bourgeois
bohemianism easily slides further into soap opera: 'what seemed to be a
daring challenge to convention was also viewed as the lifestyle of a village
spinster who provided the world with intimate gossip about the famous and
ended up living in a flat overlooking her companion's graveyard where she
will soon be buried' (*Guardian*, 15 April 1986b). Neither a significant thinker
nor a celebrity, de Beauvoir is here 'reduced' to the status of a gossip-mon-
gering spinster in a global village. The implicit tension here between individual author and mass public, as well as between high and popular culture,
is played out in a specifically gendered caricature. Gender is again the vehicle
through which de Beauvoir's status as an author is called into question.

It is around the ubiquitous café that this lifestyle is centred. Photographs
frequently show de Beauvoir in a typically Parisian café, replete with brass
bar running around the walls and the paraphernalia of café snacks. De
Beauvoir and Sartre are also often pictured with the inevitable glass of red
wine that accompanies representations of so many café lifestyles. *The
Economist*, in an article entitled 'Life is a Café', dispels any doubts the reader
might be harbouring about the map of Parisian culture: 'For France, read
Paris: for Paris, the Left Bank . . . for the Left Bank . . . read Saint-Germaine-
des-Prés, and for this bare square mile, read the Café de Flore' (*The
Economist*, 20 October 1984). De Beauvoir herself is portrayed as much concerned with the trappings of this café culture. The *Sunday Telegraph* draws
attention to the 'list of cafés, titles of films and books, names of people at
parties, food, cocktails, money and pretty clothes' in de Beauvoir's letters to
Sartre, and wryly concludes that 'existential woman seems to be material
woman too' (*Sunday Telegraph*, 8 December 1991).[17] The cumulative effect
of this soap opera-cum-fairy tale, however ambivalently presented, is that de
Beauvoir's relationships with women are rarely highlighted and are usually
passed over without comment. Typically: 'They [de Beauvoir and Sartre] are
often sleeping with the same woman' (*Independent on Sunday*, 2 February
1992b). The emphasis lies instead on de Beauvoir and Sartre's 'literary reputation, the glorious days of the liberation, existentialism and Saint-
Germaine-des-Prés, de Beauvoir's *The Second Sex* and her Prix Goncourt'
and finally 'their many complex affairs' (*Independent*, 9 June 1990).

It is this reduction to an equivalence, of historical and personal events
alike, which is the crux of this postcard.[18] De Beauvoir's 'many complex
affairs' merit no individual attention since they are just one of any number
of 'glorious events' that took place during her lifetime. Her 'rebellion' is
additionally perceived to be well past its sell-by date: 'if her antics now

sometimes seem an adolescent rebellion, only those who remember France in the Thirties can really measure how necessary that rebellion was' (*Sunday Telegraph*, 26 January 1992). Although necessary *then*, de Beauvoir's frolicking 'adolescent antics' now represent no more than growing pains on history's 'progressive' road to full 'adult' maturity. De Beauvoir's writings (about her sexual partners) 'seem dated, quaint, or innocently self-conscious, "her emotional navete" [*sic*], as Margaret Crosland says, "was nothing short of endearing"' (ibid.). 'Endearing' but not threatening, de Beauvoir's 'rebellion' speaks of the past rather than the future. As such, both de Beauvoir and 'her' history appear to suffer from 'a strange stasis, the stasis of an *arrest*' (Barthes 1981: 91). As Sontag notes: 'Images transfix. Images anesthetise' (Sontag 1979: 20). So anaesthetised are these images that the possibility of an alternative is almost impossible to imagine. The central pleasure here then, lies in expectations confirmed. In this respect, pleasure 'passes through the image' (Barthes 1981: 118).

These representations of de Beauvoir create the impression that bisexuality is more a product of history and culture than an example of a sexuality which is perceived *of itself* to contribute to the production of the self. Bisexuality is not an expression of de Beauvoir *specifically*, so much as an indication of the flavour of the period and ambiance of the setting in which she happened to be situated. Not merely inspired by this specific time and context, bisexuality is also confined to it. If it *has* a history, bisexuality is equally imprisoned *in* and *by* that history.

Heterosexual scandal

The suspicion that bisexuality is born of, and confined to, Parisian bohemianism is confirmed in the media responses to de Beauvoir's letters to Sartre:

readers may have felt there was little more light to be shed on this very public pair, but it seems they were wrong; in the year of her death, de Beauvoir's letters to Sartre were found in the back of a cupboard and when they were published in French last year they caused a sensation . . . her letters revealed how partial the disclosures of the past had been.   (*Sunday Telegraph*, 8 December 1991)

The letters may have come out of the cupboard, but de Beauvoir remained in the closet. Although they documented once and for all de Beauvoir's relationships with women as well as men, the coverage these letters received emphasised instead the author's 'guilt' regarding her sexual behaviour. It was de Beauvoir's *anxiety* that ultimately proved 'the scandal': 'the horrid truth that emerges from these accounts is that de Beauvoir is at some level sorry. She understands the jealousy she and Sartre have caused; she

describes it page after page. She feels remorse . . . she feels jealousy herself'
(ibid.). The 'truth' of de Beauvoir which emerges from the annals of historical myth is heterosexual: 'For those who have not suspected it already
. . . Simone de Beauvoir is not Existential Woman, heroine of Bohemia.
Not only does she have feet of clay; she has the ruthless and sentimental
heart of a bourgeois housewife' (ibid.).

The effect of representing de Beauvoir as 'emotional' returns her first to
femininity and then to heterosexuality. The shift of frame from 'heroine of
Bohemia' to 'bourgeois housewife' also erases all notion of bisexuality.[19]
Even though de Beauvoir was not physically heterosexual, or monogamous, she was still emotionally chaste to Sartre: 'through all these [her
affairs] and other, briefer "flings" she remained loyal to Sartre, an unmar-
ried cuckold, a submissive non-wife' (*Sunday Telegraph*, 26 January 1992).
Although the marital imagery in this extract is somewhat ambivalent (it is
both recalled and dismissed at once), as in the first frame identified,
bisexuality is again perceived to stem from de Beauvoir's 'primary' relationship and her pact with Sartre.[20] In both instances, the emphasis on the role
of Sartre in de Beauvoir's sexual biography serves to deny her her own
agency. This final frame however, moves the figure of de Beauvoir one step
nearer coherent heterosexuality: that her emotions are predominantly
those of 'guilt' and 'remorse' suggests that were an alternative available, de
Beauvoir might have taken it. She was not 'happy', but she nevertheless 'did
it' to keep Sartre: 'she [de Beauvoir] is constantly trying to manipulate
Sartre, and keep her position as number one wife. Significantly, at one particularly threatening time for her, she addresses him as husband' (*Sunday
Telegraph*, 8 December 1991).

Using the letters then, commentators inscribe onto de Beauvoir a sexuality that inheres in her *self*, as opposed to in existentialism or bohemianism.
Imbued with the authoritative weight of autobiographical narrative, this
final framing ensures that it is de Beauvoir herself (as opposed to either a
philosophy or a lifestyle) who is in 'possession' of 'her' sexuality. It is de
Beauvoir who bears sole emotional responsibility for – as well as,
significantly, the ensuing 'remorse' over – her actions.[21] The constitution of
de Beauvoir as a sexual protagonist *only* in relation to a heterosexual narrative suggests that she 'is' heterosexual.

Disclosure and revelation

Hell, love-letters should be private. I've been in whorehouses all over the world and
the woman always closes the door.

(Algren quoted in the *Independent on Sunday*, 2 February 1992a)

In the above extract, the much cited Nelson Algren is once again the vehicle through which press disapprobation with de Beauvoir is played out. Here, de Beauvoir is perceived to be 'worse' than a whore because 'even' a whore 'closes the door'. The metaphor of condemnation, which is both gendered and derogatory, bears comparison with the charges brought against porno-graphic obscenity:

> The crime of pornography is . . . the reintroduction of sex into the public sphere. Pornography makes sex visible; it takes what has become the most profound and private aspect of individual being and transforms it into a public commodity, exposed to the public gaze.   (Nead 1993: 100)

The exposure of the letters, as in the pornographic scenario, reduces 'love' (the love letters) to 'sex' (the whore metaphor). As private intrigue becomes public 'common' knowledge, 'high' culture (de Beauvoir) is trans-formed into 'low' culture (a whore).

The incident with Nelson Algren indicates that the 'obscene' is unwel-come within the frame of the aesthetic. (Attempted) censure is a pre-requisite to the maintenance of order: 'Desirable femininity has been constructed specifically in terms of both health and beauty – to be fit for life is to be fit for art' (Nead 1993: 77). In order that de Beauvoir be ren-dered fit for life and art, her relationships with both men and women, as I have illustrated above, must be 'framed'. In this respect, these frames repre-sent 'rituals of purification' which 'clothe' the figure of de Beauvoir in art and halt the 'filth and pollution' (Mary Douglas in Nead 1993: 7) that this body would otherwise issue. However, since the art/obscenity pairing con-stitutes an (almost) complete system of meaning, de Beauvoir, like the nude, although frequently conforming to the conventions of art, also threatens risk and instability: 'all margins are dangerous. If they are pulled this way or that the shape of fundamental experience is altered' (Douglas quoted in Nead 1993: 33). What I want to emphasise in this final section, particularly given that my own interpretations of the newspapers may have imposed a coherence of their own, is that these representations of de Beauvoir are not absolutely secure and that the 'framing' of de Beauvoir requires considerable work if she is to sustain cultural respectability.

Although, as the analysis of the biographical representations in chapters 3 and 4 shows, the impulse to expose and disclose 'the truth' of de Beauvoir is not unique to the newspapers, in this context it is no doubt also related to the British press's more general investment in the notion of the public's 'right to know'. Sontag suggests the ability to see and the expectation to know are so deeply imbricated as to have become almost conceptually inseparable (Sontag 1979: 176). Hence those spaces which were once considered 'private' are now *expected* to be open to public scrutiny. In order to expose the 'truth' of de Beauvoir however, newspapers are dependent upon *actively* creating, maintaining and exploiting the boundaries between public and private spheres. Indeed, Barthes argues that the rise of photography 'corresponds precisely to the explosion of the private into the public, or rather into the creation of a new social value, which is the publicity of the private: the private is consumed as such, publicly' (Barthes 1981: 98).

This battle for 'the publicity of the private' is complicated when the figure of de Beauvoir is herself reputedly engaged in an attempt to take control of the boundaries within which she is displayed. Chapter 3 has already illustrated how any perceived self-promotion on the part of de Beauvoir is greeted with suspicion by the biographers. Newspaper journalists also charge de Beauvoir with attempting to stage-manage the 'truth' and to 'fiddle history' (*Guardian*, 15 April 1986b). The *Financial Times* goes so far as to suggest that 'one of the chief aims of de Beauvoir's intellectual efforts seems to have been the construction, with an eye to posterity, of a carefully managed self-portrait' (*Financial Times*, 1 February 1992). Reviewing Francis and Gontier's biography, the *Guardian* argues that the account is 'an unsatisfactory compromise between her [de Beauvoir's] need, still, to justify and explain herself, and their search for the truth behind "the carefully designed public image"' (*Guardian*, 24 July 1987). The question at stake here, as Jacqueline Rose clearly illustrates in her study of Sylvia Plath, is '[i]n whose interests is this book being written – or rather, in whom does [the] truth-claim finally reside?' (J. Rose 1992: 94).

The tension between the individual figure of de Beauvoir and the press, as well as between author and critic, is amply demonstrated in the above examples: each appears to be attempting to control the processes of representation.[22] That this tension frequently coheres around issues of sexuality is hardly surprising given, as Foucault argues, that sexuality is profoundly entangled with notions of censure and disclosure. For Foucault, sexuality is 'related in a strange and complex way both to verbal prohibition and to the obligation to tell the truth, of hiding what one does, and of deciphering who one is' (Foucault 1988b: 16. See also Sedgwick 1991). It is not so much de Beauvoir's affairs themselves which are scandalous for example, but their *exposé*: 'Traditional morality would have it that, if affairs are to be permitted, they must be discreet. Simone de Beauvoir's decision to tell the world . . . set a record for public intimacy' (*Independent on Sunday*, 10 June 1990). Although this particular journalist is praising de Beauvoir for her 'honesty', to 'break' such records may also situate de Beauvoir in the 'low culture' atmosphere of sexual intrigue. Playing on tabloid headlines, as well as on the madonna/whore dichotomy, the *Sunday Telegraph* announces that: 'Nice girls didn't – de Beauvoir did' (*Sunday Telegraph*, 26 January 1992).[23] In a similar vein, *The Economist* suggests that the subject matter of de Beauvoir's book on Jean-Paul Sartre is 'personal and one feels a shocked intruder, who has no business to know these private things' (*The Economist*, 20 October 1984). Such press anxiety over de Beauvoir's perceived self-exposure points to a desire both to uncover but *also* to contain the figure of de Beauvoir; to have de Beauvoir exposed, but *also* to control the process of exposure as such.[24]

Hence although rarely censoring their own revelations (instead, these revelations constitute part of the professional journalistic code), where de Beauvoir is seen to 'exceed' herself, the press step in as guardians of public morality.[25] In doing so, they (re)define the boundaries which divide decent and indecent public exposure. The *Financial Times* for example writes: 'It is a commonplace that writers should plunder themselves for their materials, but de Beauvoir did much more: she indulged in self-justifying self-recreation, motivated by powerful vanity' (*Financial Times*, 1 February 1992). The notion that writers 'plunder themselves for their materials' indicates that an 'acceptable' line has already been drawn. The *Financial Times* is clearly not applauding de Beauvoir for experimenting with the limits of traditional autobiography. Instead, de Beauvoir's 'tampering' with the boundaries of what is seen to be acceptable constitutes her as narcissistic. Indeed, her imputed desire to 'manage' her own image situates her within what Featherstone calls 'the culture of narcissism' (Featherstone 1982: 27);[26] de Beauvoir is accused of displaying or staging herself with vainglorious intention. This in itself suggests that the 'author' is specifically gendered and that the degree to which a writer may decently 'plunder' him or herself for material is different for men and for women. Women's autobiography rarely achieves the classic status of their male counterparts (Rousseau's *Confessions*, for example) and while a male author's reflections on himself are perceived to benefit society as a whole, women's reflections are more frequently seen to relate only to themselves. Interestingly, a photograph of de Beauvoir in the *Independent* – whose caption reads: 'Simone de Beauvoir: the greater and most valuable part of her work is autobiographical' (*Independent*, 9 June 1990) – has her seated in front of a mirror. In short, de Beauvoir's insistence on a 'carefully managed self-portrait' (*Financial Times*, 1 February 1992), the presentation of her self with an audience in mind, is usually described by the press in metaphors of excess. Like the unrestrained naked female body, de Beauvoir is obscene because she is 'more' than what is acceptable, and in being so, spills out of the frame that should contain her.

The censure of the figure of de Beauvoir in the above examples, and the concomitant 'reframing' of the boundaries between public and private, recalls Andrew Wernick's analysis of promotional culture. Here, Wernick argues that an object becomes devalued through its very association with the process of promotion. One effect of promotional culture therefore, is a 'cheapening of the symbolic currency' (Wernick 1991: 189).[27] Such cheapening might be off-set however, as Richard Dyer shows, through the media's continuous (re)creation of 'authentic' celebrities, which is itself dependent upon a particular relation between public and private. The process of authentication, Dyer argues, is achieved through 'an infinite regress by means of which one more authentic [or more 'private'] image displaces another [. . .] Hence the growth of scandal magazines, unauthorized biographies, candid camera photo-journalism and so on' (Dyer 1991: 136). Seen from this perspective, de Beauvoir's letters to Sartre are a windfall because, although the representation of de Beauvoir as 'heroine of Bohemia' is displaced, it is *replaced* by a 'newer', more 'authentic' image of de Beauvoir (as 'bourgeois housewife'). This alternative representation is significant in part because the letters marshal the markers of authenticity that Dyer identifies: found in a cupboard (hidden from the public eye), the letters appear to be unpremeditated (suggesting unpremeditated feelings), private (which implies that promotion was not what was in mind), sincere, immediate, spontaneous and direct (Dyer 1991: 133).[28] Thus furnished with a new truth the press, as well as biographers and academics, are able to read (back) into old texts interpretations based on the latest revelation (a different 'conclusion', as Ricoeur would put it, which subsequently (re)configures the events in the plot). If de Beauvoir is in one respect 'de-authenticated' then, she is also 'reauthenticated' with an eye fixed on (future) promotion. This befits the contemporary 'attitude' that, Sontag argues, 'treats everything as the object for some present or future use' (Sontag 1979: 176).

Journalistic voyeurism also keeps a sharp eye on the nuances of disclosure, and the battle over and for the 'truth', as it is played out between de Beauvoir and Sartre. Participating in and facilitating further intrigue, Sartre and de Beauvoir's 'doctrine of transparency' and, more specifically, its failure, is documented: 'True to their doctrine of "transparency", they kept few secrets from each other . . . But near the end of his life he [Sartre] did conceal from de Beauvoir his decision to adopt as a daughter his last and youngest mistress' (*Sunday Telegraph*, 26 January 1992). If Sartre betrayed de Beauvoir by *concealing* a decision from her, she seeks her revenge (according to the *Sunday Telegraph*) through *revelation*. De Beauvoir apparently publishes Sartre's letters to her 'not merely as a contribution to the world's knowledge of the great philosopher, but also as a gambit in her bitter feud with Sartre's adopted daughter (who was also, in a humiliating gesture towards de Beauvoir, appointed his literary executor)' (*Sunday Telegraph*, 20 December 1992). The status of Sartre's letters can be profitably compared to the status of Sylvia Plath's work. Jacqueline Rose asks: 'What is the status of these manuscripts? Are they personal or cultural property? Or is the problem precisely that they are hybrids which sit on the boundary, or expose the delicacy, the artificiality, of the boundary, between the two?' (J. Rose 1992: 77). Perceived both to offer the public knowledge of the 'great philosopher' and to be a weapon in de Beauvoir's 'private' battle, the letters are situated on the thin line between public and private spheres. Indeed, they are the very means by which the lines or boundaries, as both Nead and Rose argue, are artificially maintained and exploited in the struggle to control representation.

Although, as I have illustrated, the framing of de Beauvoir is not absolutely secure, the joint force of the three frames does ensure that only heterosexuality is portrayed as though it were an integral part of de Beauvoir's *self*. In the first frame, de Beauvoir's relationships with women as well as men are acknowledged, but her experience is perceived to occlude sexual pleasure. The 'motive' for de Beauvoir's same-sex relationships instead appears to be grounded in existential experimentation, which is further bound to Sartre and (therefore) to heterosexuality. In the second frame, de Beauvoir's sexuality is seen to be the result of, and to have its roots in, the lifestyle that she lived and the historical period into which she was born. It is the specific combination of a French/intellectual/bohemian identity which produces, but ultimately confines, bisexuality to 'history'. In the final frame, bisexuality is displaced in favour of a representation of de Beauvoir as guilty and regretful of her 'other' (i.e. non-heterosexual) experiences. Here again her relationships with women are seen not only to be contingent upon, but also even inspired by, Sartre. A portrait of de Beauvoir as self-recriminating serves to contain her 'other' liaisons firmly within the confines of heterosexuality.

What is significant here is that, firstly, only heterosexuality inheres in de Beauvoir such that she is perceived to be both possessed of it (it belongs to her) and possessed by it (she belongs to it). This in itself is not unrelated to the concept of the frame. Nead identifies the Aristotelian definition of 'beauty' to be part of a larger discourse, where the issue at stake 'is the production of rational coherent subject. In other words, the notion of a unified form [exemplified by the female nude] is integrally bound up with the perception of self, and the construction of individual identity' (Nead 1993: 7). In these representations it is heterosexuality which expresses the 'truth' of de Beauvoir, and which is, as such, linked to her individual identity (insofar as de Beauvoir, *specifically*, 'is' heterosexual). Bisexuality, by contrast – and this is the second, related, point – is entirely displaced from the field of visibility, from the frames of representation. It does not contribute to the production of de Beauvoir's self because its 'roots' are perceived to be *external* to the self. The 'source' of bisexuality lies in existential philosophy, bohemianism or unhappy heterosexuality. And because bisexuality resides outside of the self (of de Beauvoir), the notion of 'bisexuality' as a property of the self is, in this context, inconceivable. It is not just the excesses ascribed to de Beauvoir then, which pull at the margins of these frames. (Bi)sexuality too, signifies an obscene feature which shatters the integrity of the unified self – what Nead identifies as the 'rational coherent subject' – because it implicitly indicates that not all sexual identities necessarily reside *within* an individual self (bisexuality does not cohere in the *unified form* of de Beauvoir's material body). Situated 'beyond' the frame, unconstituted bisexuality is inarticulable in terms of the self as well as in terms of visible representation.[29]

6

Erasure

> Heterosexuality does not have a monopoly on exclusionary logics. Indeed, they can characterize and sustain gay and lesbian identity positions . . . this logic is reiterated in the failure to recognize bisexuality as well as in the normativizing interpretation of bisexuality as a kind of failure of loyalty or lack of commitment – two cruel strategies of erasure.
>
> Judith Butler, *Bodies That Matter: On the Discursive Limits of 'Sex'*

The heart of this chapter is based on three related academic papers, written by Ann Ferguson, Claudia Card and Marilyn Frye, taken from a special issue of *Hypatia/Women's Studies International Forum* (1985) on the contemporary relevance of *The Second Sex* to (lesbian) feminist politics. This special edition of *Hypatia* is edited by Margaret Simons, whose paper 'Lesbian connections: Simone de Beauvoir and feminism' (1992), I touched on in chapters 3 and 4. I will be drawing on Simons' text briefly again in this chapter, insofar as she employs Card's thesis to frame her account of de Beauvoir's life. The articles are united by a shared commitment to explore and develop a feminist and lesbian identity politics. Published in a major feminist academic journal in the middle of the 1980s, they may be seen as indicative of a particular kind of politics and theorising born of the women's and gay liberation movements of the 1970s. Their focus lies especially on the role of responsibility and choice in the construction of individual and collective identities and the relation of these to a radical politics of change.

More specifically, Ferguson's, Card's and Frye's analyses are concerned with the relation between individual choice, responsibility, agency and the role of 'history' in determining (or not) the 'freedom' of the individual (to choose, to take responsibility, to act). All three employ *The Second Sex* as the springboard from which to discuss these issues, although each paper adopts a specific angle on it. These different emphases may be briefly summarised thus: for Ferguson, it is de Beauvoir's 'individualistic and ahistorical approach' which is of central concern and which, she argues, takes little or no account of the historical conditions which enabled a lesbian identity, as distinct from lesbian practices, to develop. During the course of her analysis, Ferguson outlines the historical changes which she perceives to have 'made all women's sexual choices more free' (Ferguson 1985: 208). In highlighting these historical changes, Ferguson implicitly develops a relation between individual choice and responsibility which is mediated by 'history'. This same relation may be identified in other academic texts which are concerned less with the arguments put forward in *The Second Sex* and more with de Beauvoir's own life choices. In other words, the presuppositions which govern Ferguson's evaluation of *The Second Sex* is elsewhere applied to de Beauvoir's life itself. Although Ferguson does not explore the implications of the relation between choice, responsibility and sexual identity which she implicitly assumes, her paper provides a general introduction to this paradigm which is subsequently developed by both Card and Frye.

Card's paper is based on a critique of de Beauvoir's analysis of heterosexuality: because de Beauvoir fails to perceive heterosexuality as a choice (as lesbianism is seen to be), Card argues that she is unable to evaluate it. In order to address this perceived omission in de Beauvoir's work, Card articulates a more detailed analysis of the relation between sexual identity, choice and responsibility. In the course of this analysis, she refers to what she calls 'a good example of inauthenticity in lesbian behavior' (Card 1985: 213). The woman in Card's example, as she puts it, 'would probably say she is "bisexual"' (ibid.). Margaret Simons applies Card's analysis of authentic and inauthentic lesbianism to de Beauvoir's own sexual relationships. This illustrates, again, that the charges brought against de Beauvoir's analysis of 'The Lesbian' in *The Second Sex* may equally be applied to her own life: the inauthenticity of the 'bisexual' woman identified by Card and the construction, by Simons, of de Beauvoir's own relationships as 'inauthentic' rest on the same logic. Finally, Frye's paper draws together some of the threads of both Ferguson's and Card's arguments in order to theorise (more generally) the relation between individual responsibility and choice, the role of historical circumstances in determining this relation, and a collective lesbian feminist politics. In the course of this discussion Frye explicitly lays out the expectations that a lesbian feminist politics might be founded on.

My intention here is to explore the presuppositions which create a ground for the politics put forward in these papers and in particular to consider the implications of these presuppositions for the 'bisexual' woman that Card identifies. I will argue that the specific figuration of choice and responsibility (and pleasure) as techniques of identity disallows bisexuality from being perceived as an identity which pertains to the self.[1] Again, as in chapter 4, I will be referring to sexuality as one of the techniques which constitutes selfhood textually, in terms of plausible narratives which configure particular events in a particular order so as to construct a sexual identity. And indeed, the paradox of bisexuality in this chapter is similar to the paradox of bisexuality in the biographical accounts of de Beauvoir's life. In each case, bisexuality is 'visible' but does not constitute a sexual-narrative-identity which could be ascribed to a self. Given that some notion of 'bisexuality' is identified in Card's text, it cannot – even though it is not produced as a property of the self – be understood as an absence. These issues will be explored in more detail in the following chapter in relation to the issue of 'resemblance' that Card raises (Card 1985: 213). Hence the analysis here also serves as an introduction to the final chapter which will draw together themes which have been implicit throughout the argument so far.

Choice, responsibility and history

Ferguson critiques de Beauvoir's chapter 'The lesbian' in *The Second Sex* on the grounds that her 'theory does not make the historical distinction between lesbian practices and a lesbian identity' (Ferguson 1985: 207). The reason for de Beauvoir's failure to make this distinction, she argues, may be found in her 'individualist and ahistorical approach' (Ferguson 1985: 206) to sexuality and choice. Specifically, de Beauvoir evaluates the (sexual) choices that individual lesbians make without taking into account the historical circumstances that shape women's choices more generally. Thus de Beauvoir, according to Ferguson, 'suggests the key problem for women is "bad faith" or inauthenticity (taking oneself to be an Object not a Subject)' (Ferguson 1985: 204). By focusing on *individual* women's 'inauthenticity', de Beauvoir gives 'us no historical understanding of how important the development of the modern notion of lesbian identity has been for broadening the sexual and value options open to women' (Ferguson 1985: 206).[2] In outlining what she perceives to be the significance of this development, Ferguson implicitly assumes a particular relation between choice, sexual identity and history.

Taking issue with de Beauvoir's assertion in *The Second Sex* that lesbianism is no more than an individual and isolated response to patriarchy, Ferguson maps out two particular historical events which enabled homosexuality to be perceived as an identity.[3] In the first instance, Ferguson suggests that it was only after late nineteenth-century sexologist discourses on 'sexual perversion' were developed that 'a social identity [could be] organized around homosexual object choice which had not existed earlier' (Ferguson 1985: 206). Thus although for Ferguson lesbian practices have always existed, the symbolic significance of these practices changed with the creation of the homosexual as a specific *species*.[4]

Ferguson's second point is that the changing material conditions of women in Western industrial societies (at approximately the same time) provided them with the opportunity of adopting this newly created identity. She writes:

increasing wage labor opportunities for women, urbanization, cheap mass pro- duced birth control devices, the liberalization of divorce, the development of mass media sexual advertising – all place more weight on the individual to consider the options which allow separating sexuality from marriage, from childrearing, indeed from heterosexuality altogether.   (Ferguson 1985: 206–7)

The grounds for criticising de Beauvoir's analysis of 'The Lesbian' then, rest not only on exposing what she perceives to be de Beauvoir's individu- alistic approach, but also challenging her (related) assumption that the individual makes 'free' choices which are undetermined by the contingency of historical conditions. Ferguson seeks to correct this analysis by demon- strating that: 'A lesbian lifestyle as we understand it today is an individual choice made possible only by the economic and social changes connected to capitalism' (Ferguson 1985: 206).[5]

Ferguson's understanding of the relation between choice, responsibility and history emerges only implicitly. It is clear however, that she believes that women's choices are not (always) entirely free (this constitutes the basis of her critique of de Beauvoir's individualistic approach) and therefore that they can only be evaluated in view of the specific historical circumstances in which they are situated (this is the counter to de Beauvoir's ahistoricism). In short, women may only be held responsible for their choices to the extent that these choices are (historically) available to them. Thus history itself mediates between individual choice and responsibility. This logic informs not only Ferguson's critique of de Beauvoir's work, but also, in other aca- demic articles, de Beauvoir's own personal life as well.

The severity of Mary Felstiner's (1980) evaluation of *The Second Sex* for example, is more or less tempered by the amount of information she per- ceives de Beauvoir, as an author, to have had available to her at any partic- ular historical moment. In other words, de Beauvoir cannot be held to be responsible for what she could not have 'known' in the 1940s: 'before the 1970s . . . hardly any published works spoke positively about lesbians . . . When Simone de Beauvoir wrote *The Second Sex*, she could find in lesbian- ism at best a private refusal to submit to men' (Felstiner 1980: 260).

Felstiner implies that because de Beauvoir did not have positive images of lesbians available to her in 1949, she had *no choice* but to find in lesbianism, 'at best', only 'a private refusal to submit to men'. Hence although Felstiner criticises *The Second Sex* on similar grounds to Ferguson, her evaluation is more generous largely because she perceives history, in this instance, to have had more of a role in determining de Beauvoir's choices as an author. Because of the sheer length of de Beauvoir's life however (during which time a number of changes are witnessed) Felstiner holds de Beauvoir accountable on issues where once she was not. 'These days', Felstiner reminds the reader, de Beauvoir 'works with lesbian feminists in France' (ibid.). This suggests that de Beauvoir now recognises the importance of the development of a collective lesbian identity and that she has moved on *with* history, rather than remaining behind *in* history.[6] In a sense, Felstiner confers authorial responsibility on de Beauvoir only if she had enough information, or 'facts', available to her. Information then, and knowledge (both of which are more or less available depending on the historical situation) mediate the relationship between choice and responsibility. Where de Beauvoir does not have information, and therefore does not have choice, the burden of personal responsibility shifts onto history – which, in its turn, indirectly assumes the role of the author.

Margaret Simons' (1992) explanation of de Beauvoir's persistent rejection of a lesbian identity during her life is governed by similar assumptions. The reasons Simons gives for this denial are based on the historical context in which de Beauvoir was situated. Thus:

another reason Beauvoir rejected a public lesbian identity was her fear that such an identity might be dangerous for her adopted daughter [Sylvie Le Bon, with whom de Beauvoir was said to be having a relationship]. This reading is supported by evidence in the journals of Beauvoir's own experience of being fired from a teaching position during the Nazi occupation of France for allegedly 'corrupting the morals' of a young woman student . . . Beauvoir 'feared personal embarrassment and possible political reprisal for Sylvie' if she proclaimed a lesbian identity . . . This concern might have been why Beauvoir left it to Le Bon to decide – after Beauvoir's death – whether to publish the journals and letters.   (Simons 1992: 141)

According to Simons, de Beauvoir denied her lesbian identity because she was unable to proclaim it with confidence: her earlier experiences of France under Nazi occupation had led her to believe that if Le Bon's lesbian identity was known, then Le Bon herself would suffer from the kind of personal and professional reprisal that she had endured. While this suggests that Ferguson's invitation to consider lesbianism as an option available to *all* women in Western societies in the twentieth century is not as assured as she implies, it does support her contention that the (open) adoption of a lesbian identity is determined by historical circumstance. In this respect, Simons' representation of de Beauvoir's sexuality is justified according to the same logic of responsibility and choice, mediated by historical conditions, that Ferguson and Felstiner employ.

The implication in all three texts is that more freedom to choose is desirable. This position accords with the focus of these articles, which are for the most part preoccupied either with lesbian feminist politics specifically, or with women's liberation more generally. One of the key aims of both movements has been to increase women's 'right to choose' across a range of issues from reproductive rights to equal rights at work. Felstiner illustrates this point – that more freedom to choose is politically desirable – by favourably comparing the historical situation of women today to the women of de Beauvoir's generation. Putting a clear distance between *The Second Sex* and contemporary feminists, she writes:

The generation now in women's studies classes can look at earlier analyses of women's condition from a particular vantage point – an enthusiasm and judgment learned by living through the women's movement and by drawing on a feminist literature in full flower [. . .] What can such a book [*The Second Sex*] do for us now – for the generation and the movement which Shulamith Firestone called the 'second wave of the most important revolution in history?'   (Felstiner 1980: 247–8)

Lived experience – the crucial experience of living through history and the women's movement – is the authority on which Felstiner draws to judge (Felstiner 1980: 271) *The Second Sex*. Her 'particular vantage point', which is the present day, enables her to look *back* on history and evaluate it. This suggests that history is progressive and that it confers an advantage on the present which the past, by definition, could not have had.[7] Ferguson also makes this point, more explicitly, when she notes approvingly that 'the development of the modern lesbian identity' has 'made all women's sexual choices more free' (Ferguson 1985: 208). The political intention of increasing women's freedom to choose is based on a presupposition that choice and freedom are intimately connected, that the more choices a woman has available to her, the more free she will be. This particular link between 'freedom' and 'choice' also belies an assumption that women can potentially, and should, be as 'free' a 'free agent' or voluntary subject as possible. As in existentialism, the 'liberty of the agent is the foundation and indispensable condition of all action' (Blackham 1978: 127). In this respect, this discourse of choice and responsibility hypostatises 'free will', charging it with ethical value (Sedgwick 1992: 586). My intention here is not to suggest that Ferguson's or Felstiner's texts are themselves informed by existentialism, but that there are striking, if unintentional, parallels to be drawn. In each, not only liberty, but the notion of the subject as an active agent capable of expressing free will, is assumed.

That the freedom of the individual to choose is politically desirable (that it is the basis of 'all action') is illustrated in Ferguson's analysis of the implications for women of women's increased sexual choices. Marking the political difference between individual lesbian practices (lesbianism) and a collective lesbian identity, Ferguson writes:

It is the *social bonding* of women into an oppositional subculture economically and socially independent of men . . . that makes possible the contemporary concept of a lesbian *identity* . . . And it is this *collective* and *social* lesbian identity (an identity not possible until the contemporary period), and not merely the courageous defiance of heterosexist assumptions about sexuality by *individual* women who love women, which constitutes the radical nature of contemporary lesbian-feminism.

(Ferguson 1985: 206)

Ferguson's point here is that the development of a collective lesbian identity introduces political implications that individual lesbian practices do not. More choice for individual women, she assumes, may lead more women to choose to live independently, both 'economically and socially', of men. Individual lesbian practices may thus potentially be transformed into a collective lesbian identity. Because de Beauvoir's approach to 'the lesbian' is based *solely* around individual choices (as illustrated in the title of her chapter), Ferguson argues that she is unable to evaluate the significance of these choices in the light of their potential political implications (the *social* bonding of women into an oppositional subculture). By emphasising the 'radical' and collective 'nature of contemporary lesbian-feminism' Ferguson illustrates how this in itself affects the way that individual lesbian choices may be evaluated. I will be returning to this difference between individual lesbian practices and a collective lesbian identity, and the implications of this difference for the 'bisexual' woman, again below. Because if, as Ferguson implies, individual women's lesbian practices may now be evaluated in the light of their contribution to a collective lesbian identity (and the implication here is that given this collective identity individual women's choices may more frequently be evaluated as 'authentic'), then it is also the case that individual women who do *not* identify with a collective lesbian identity might also be differently evaluated.

In order to illustrate how the existence of a lesbian collective identity might alter the way that individual lesbian practices are evaluated, it is worth considering why it is that the perceived increase in the number of (sexual) choices available to women in Western societies allows a more intense relationship between choice, responsibility and sexual identity to be forged. In all three of the accounts of de Beauvoir's life and work considered so far (Ferguson's, Felstiner's and Simons'), de Beauvoir *is* held responsible for choices, but only when those choices are seen to be (historically) available to her. Where de Beauvoir is not perceived to have a choice – either because of a lack of information (or knowledge) or because she has knowledge of the negative effects of a particular action (both of which are determined by her historical circumstances) – then she is not held responsible. Instead, history sweeps in as the author of de Beauvoir's choices in both life and work (history itself takes responsibility).[8] In other words, the relationship between choice and responsibility considered above implicitly rests on the *awareness* of having options and, as a consequence, is relatively clear cut. Because Card distinguishes between different types of choices, and because she identifies choice in circumstances where the subject may not be aware of having actively chosen, she develops a more complex notion of the choice/responsibility/identity paradigm.

Choice, responsibility and attitude

Card's principal objection to *The Second Sex* is that although de Beauvoir acknowledges that homosexuality is a choice,[9] she fails 'to draw the appropriately analogous conclusions about heterosexuality' (Card 1985: 209).[10] The importance, for Card, of acknowledging both homosexuality *and* heterosexuality as a choice is that it enables them to be evaluated on an equal basis.[11] Evaluated, that is, as either '"a mode of flight" from one's situation [inauthentic] or "a way of assuming it" [authentic]' (Card 1985: 209). De Beauvoir's failure to evaluate heterosexuality on the same basis as homosexuality, Card argues, is due to her failure to distinguish between choice 'as an *option* (of which one may or may not be aware) and "choice" as the *act* of choosing from among options (which presupposes one's awareness of them)' (Card 1985: 211).

While it is more likely, she argues, that lesbian women have *actually exercised* choice, since it is impossible to be 'ignorant of heterosexuality' (ibid.) as an option, this does not mean that heterosexual women have *not* made choices (or that there are no options). Rather, according to Card, it is simply that they are not necessarily *aware* of the choices they have made.[12] In other words, Card argues that we make choices whether we are aware of our options *or not*:

Is she free or is she not? The lesbian may appear to be free just because her choice is a defiance of convention; the heterosexual woman not free because hers appears to be determined by it. The compulsoriness of heterosexuality does not, however, imply that women are forced to choose it [. . .] The truth may be that lesbians are *choosing to be free* of convention . . . whereas heterosexual women are *choosing to be determined* by convention.

(Card 1985: 211)

Only because lesbians are more likely to have been *aware* of the choice that they have made, Card argues, are they more frequently called to account for their sexual choice.[13]

In order to consider whether a woman should be responsible for (sexual) choices which she may not be aware of having made, Card goes on to explore de Beauvoir's notion of sexuality as an attitude in more detail. For Card, de Beauvoir's analysis of sexuality as 'an attitude *chosen in a certain situation* – that is, at once motivated and freely adopted' (Card 1985: 209) raises the question as to whether sexuality *is* actually chosen or not: 'One may be able to take various attitudes *toward* one's sexual orientation – for example, be proud of it or ashamed of it – but can one choose the orientation itself?' (Card 1985: 211). Putting the question more directly she writes: 'What is an attitude? [. . .] Can an attitude be chosen?' (Card 1985: 212). It is the link that Card establishes between these two themes in de Beauvoir's work – choice and attitude – which has particular ramifications for the 'bisexual' woman that she identifies.

Card does not collapse 'attitude' with 'sexual orientation'. She writes, for example, that 'heterosexual women frequently manage not to let their lesbian attitudes determine their sexual orientation in any major way' (Card 1985: 210). This suggests that a woman may (appear to) be heterosexually oriented and at the same time might harbour lesbian attitudes. In this instance then, an attitude might be a 'disposition' (Card 1985: 212) which does not have to be openly or actively adopted. This is not all that an attitude is however. Card writes:

An attitude . . . has come to be a psychological term referring to a complex of behavior and valuation. Attitudes, like emotions, have objects . . . They also tend to have valences . . . attitudes are often modifiable through insight and understanding . . . attitudes like habits, can outlive the judgments upon which they were originally based.

(Card 1985: 212)

By comparing attitudes to habits Card is able to argue that while we may not be aware of having chosen our attitudes we nevertheless generally consider them to be open to change: 'If attitudes are not themselves directly the objects of choice, choices are among their causes, including such choices as the choice to acquire certain attitudes' (Card 1985: 212). Thus it is that attitudes are 'modifiable'.

Card's conclusion, that an attitude may not necessarily have been consciously chosen but is nevertheless open to change, is central to her analysis of sexuality. Referring to Aristotle, she argues that 'not everything that is voluntary is chosen, and not everything that is not voluntary is *in*voluntary' (ibid.). Hence something which is not chosen might nevertheless be voluntary. An attitude – and sexuality, if it is an attitude – falls into this category. Given that attitudes may be voluntary, Card argues that we could (indeed, we should expect to) be held responsible for them:

> We expect people to take responsibility for their attitudes. If sexual orientation is an attitude, then the idea of taking responsibility for one's sexuality belongs to that general expectation. Taking such responsibility requires developing habits of noticing things about oneself, identifying one's attitudes and determining whether they are well-founded or not.
> (Card 1985: 212)

This extract suggests that not only is having attitudes a technique of the self, but taking responsibility for them is also a technique which contributes to the production of the self. Card invites us to develop a 'habit' of 'noticing things' about our attitudes (as opposed to maintaining our attitudes out of habit). Much like Foucault's analysis of early Christian techniques of the self then, the contemporary self, according to Card, should be engaged in a process of systematic and regular self-inspection and self-monitoring. In this context, neither responsibility for one's attitude/sexuality, nor the attitude/sexuality itself, can be considered (entirely) inherent or innate, since both are able to be 'developed'.[14]

Card's analysis of attitudes – which may not be chosen but which are nevertheless voluntary – suggests that the crucial factor, for her, is that the *ability* to take responsibility for one's attitude/sexuality (whether it is chosen or not) is co-extensive with a *responsibility* to do so. This position displaces the relevance of the essentialist/social constructionist debate as it relates to the relation between choice and responsibility. Card argues that although researchers have always been, and continue to be, concerned with whether 'homosexuality has an inherited basis or is entirely acquired' (Card 1985: 209) (with whether it is or is not a choice for which one should/could take responsibility), the '"gay is good" slogan of the late 1960s paved the way for embracing responsibility' (Card 1985: 209) for one's sexuality whether it is chosen or not. Marilyn Frye makes the implications of such a responsibility clear, in relation to women's liberation. She writes:

> we cannot simply trust to random and disorganized stubbornness, sabotage, explosions of rage and so on, but must organize politically to pull *together* . . . it seems right to require or demand of each other changes of values and characters . . . In particular, it has seemed that we must require of each other the most fundamental change, namely, a shift of our primary loyalty from its attachment to the masters and their institutions to an attachment to our sisters and our liberation.
> (Frye 1985: 216)

What is significant here is that the shift of loyalty from masters to sisters requires, for Frye, not just that individual women be involved *with* each other, but also that they be responsible *for* each other (and it is this which signals the shift from individual lesbian practices to a collective lesbian identity).[15] Based on the assumption that the ability to assume responsibility is co-extensive with an obligation to do so, loyalty to the collective is itself figured as an obligation. This is an additional implication of increased choice then, that Ferguson neglects to explore when she celebrates the notion of choice *per se*. Because although on the one hand, as Ferguson implies and Frye confirms, the individual choice of lesbian practices may today be perceived to be authentic insofar as they are transformed into 'collective strategies for resistance', on the other hand shifting one's loyalty to this collective is rendered a constitutive feature of lesbian identity. Thus it is not only the case that individual lesbian practices may be more frequently evaluated as authentic (given the potential political implications of a collective lesbian identity), but also that individual women who are not perceived to be 'loyal' might not be evaluated as authentic lesbians. In other words, Ferguson's and Frye's analyses rest on the welcomed assumption that in order to claim an authentic lesbian identity for oneself one is obligated to confirm one's loyalty to other women by taking responsibility for them. Frye makes this assumption explicit when she writes: 'Loyalty and identity are so closely connected as to be almost just two aspects of the one phenomenon' (Frye 1985: 216). Card's analysis confirms and develops this presupposition still further.

Card argues that as well as habitually scrutinising our attitudes, we should also evaluate them. She writes: 'Even if attitudes are not chosen, they can still be evaluated as either authentic or inauthentic. They can be honest or dishonest, responsible or not responsible' (Card 1985: 212). In weighing up the authenticity or inauthenticity, honesty or dishonesty of its attitudes, the self casts the light of its objectifying gaze onto its self. However, this self-surveillance is figured by Card as part of a process whereby an individual may achieve a *greater* sense of self(-awareness).[16] In this respect, Card outlines an ethics of the self since both knowledge and experience of the self are organised by the self itself. This ethos is clearly at work in Frye's brief autobiographical account of the development of her own sexuality:

In my own case, being lesbian is an attitude evolved over perhaps fifteen years – from my earliest awareness of aptitude for passionate connection with women to a way of being which actualizes that possibility . . . It would have been 'inauthentic' to act the lesbian in certain ways too early in that process. It now would be inauthentic *not* to, in certain ways and certain situations. I assume responsibility for that choice, as I do for the choice I made of lifework, and for my continuing choice not

to revise such choices. I think it is not logically, morally or politically wrong to
assume others are responsible in the same way for making such choices about how
to be, even in the midst of circumstances of oppression, and against historical odds.
(Frye 1985: 217)[17]

It is possible to identify in Frye's account a process of strict but nevertheless welcome self-surveillance and disciplining. Accepting that her sexuality is a choice, Frye assumes responsibility for it. For her, there is no
question that the ability to take responsibility is co-extensive with an
obligation to do so. This obligation is witnessed both in her own evaluation
of her act(ion)s as either authentic or inauthentic (she continually scrutin-
ises her choices to ensure that they are, and continue to be, responsible
ones) as well as in her call to other women not only to make choices and to
assume responsibility for them, but also to assume a responsibility for
making choices. Although it is unclear whether Frye believes that *lesbianism* itself is a choice (the extract suggests that she does not, given that she
refers not to the choice of lesbianism itself, but rather to the choice of 'actualising' a (pre-existing?) potential), she does believe that it is possible to
choose (to develop) a lesbian *identity*.[18] Indeed, she compares her own
choice of a lesbian identity to the choices she made with respect to her 'lifework'.[19]

The ability to make choices and to take responsibility is important to
Ferguson, Frye and Card because it opens up a space to address the
possibility of political change. Much contemporary feminist work, including my own, is indebted to debates such as this. Frye is especially committed to considering how women's situation may be improved. She writes:

being responsible can simply mean one does not passively and unconsciously
submit to the winds of time and culture; it means primarily that one is living
throughout one's life, as an *agent* in the matter of who and how one is and the matrix
of circumstances that conditions that; and it means recognizing and caring about
the fact that who and how one is has consequences for others. That kind of
responsibility one can live with.   (Frye 1985: 217)

Frye's suggestion that we are not passive in the face of 'time and culture'
(that we are not wholly determined by time and culture) is an invitation to
consider how we might change our 'circumstances'. Nevertheless, despite
the intention to alter radically women's position in society, there are a
number of problems with her, Ferguson's and Card's analyses. In the first
instance, the significance of individual choices in contemporary notions of
agency, as well as the apparently strict opposition between 'agency' and
'passivity', has now been challenged. Both Judith Butler and Rosi
Braidotti, for example, address these issues (see chapter 2). Within the

context of their own framework however, the privileging of choice and responsibility suggests that they remain unconvinced by arguments which suggest that individual choice (and relatedly responsibility) is not universally available or even necessarily desirable.[20]

If Ferguson and Frye privilege choice and responsibility, Card appears to apotheosise them. As noted above, she argues that individuals should take responsibility for their choices whether they are aware of having made them or not. Further, the ability to take responsibility is seen by Card to be co-extensive with an obligation to do so and thus every choice can be evaluated as either authentic or inauthentic. What I want to consider now, are the implications of these presuppositions for the woman who Card suggests 'would probably say she is "bisexual"' (Card 1985: 213).

Bisexuality: choice, responsibility and pleasure

The constitutive roles that choice, responsibility and pleasure play in the production of the sexuality ascribed to de Beauvoir has already been raised as an issue in chapters 4 and 5. One of the ways that the significance of de Beauvoir's same-sex relationships is either precluded or displaced in biographical and newspaper representations for example, is through the suggestion that de Beauvoir did not choose these relationships for what they offered 'in themselves', and therefore that the pleasure she might have gained from them is not the direct result of the relationship but rather proceeds from sources which are external to it. Some of the press portrayals, for instance, figure existential experimentation and/or de Beauvoir's glamorous and bohemian lifestyle as the motives that inspire her relationships with women. In Crosland's biography, de Beauvoir is understood to have no choice in these relationships at all (she passively endured them rather than actively encouraged them) and, thus, is not perceived to be responsible for them. Attributed to women other than herself, de Beauvoir's same-sex relationships do not contribute the production of her sexual-narrative-identity. In other words, where same-sex relationships are concerned, only actively choosing the relationship *for* itself, or for what it offers *in* itself (and obtaining pleasure from it on this basis) qualifies it to be a constitutive feature of sexual identity. In Card's account too, the erasure of bisexuality is made possible through a specific, although different, configuration of the roles of pleasure, choice and responsibility in the production of sexual identity.

Card describes the 'bisexual' woman in some detail (quoting de Beauvoir):

'Disappointed in a man', [de Beauvoir] tells us, a woman 'may seek in woman a lover to replace the man who has betrayed her. Collette [*sic*] indicated in her *Vagabonde* this consoling role that forbidden pleasures may frequently play in woman's existence; some women spend . . . their whole lives in being thus consoled'. Others use women lovers for regeneration until they are able to deal with men again.

(Card 1985: 213)

Like Ferguson, Card understands de Beauvoir's notion of in/authenticity to be focused solely on the individual. And based on this definition, she speculates that de Beauvoir would not consider this woman to be acting inauthentically (she would not suggest that the 'bisexual' woman was engaged in a 'flight from reality') because she *does* take responsibility for herself. Indeed, Card dryly comments that: 'It seems . . . likely that the woman in these cases . . . has her situation very well in hand, from the point of view of taking charge of her own life' (Card 1985: 213). For Card however, the 'bisexual' woman's sexuality *is* inauthentic because she takes account only of her *own* pleasure. Drawing on Aristotle, Card argues that the 'bisexual' woman is engaged in a friendship of utility and pleasure rather than a 'true friendship' (Card 1985: 213). In the latter, the object of love is the friend, in the former, it is utility or pleasure. The 'bisexual' woman, according to Card, is less concerned for the woman with whom she is involved and more with what she may gain out of the 'friendship' for herself (for her own use and/or pleasure). Thus, in the first instance, it is the 'bisexual' woman's choice of pleasure – which is gained at the expense of the other woman – that renders her behaviour inauthentic.[21]

Margaret Simons (1992) applies Card's analysis of de Beauvoir's work and of the 'bisexual' woman to de Beauvoir's life. She argues that: 'Beauvoir's relationships with her young students – especially where Sartre is also involved – seem vulnerable to the charge of inauthenticity in both Card's sense and in Aristotle's broader sense as well' (Simons 1992: 149). Although one of the key issues for Simons is that neither de Beauvoir nor her women lovers were 'in an exclusive relationship' (Simons 1992: 150) (which suggests that monogamy is also central to authenticity), the thrust of her argument rests on the kind of pleasure that de Beauvoir obtains from her same-sex relationships. Jealous of Louise Védrine's attempts to win Sartre's time and attention for example, Simons suggests that: 'Anger transforms Beauvoir's attitude from one of authentic friendship, in which she was concerned about helping Védrine achieve her independence from her family, to one of mere pleasure' (Simons 1992: 152). Instead of taking responsibility for Védrine then, and helping her to leave her family, de Beauvoir exploits Védrine for 'mere pleasure'. And because she is concerned only with what she may gain from the relationship for herself, de Beauvoir's behaviour is perceived by Simons to be an example of inauthenticity.

It is the choice of their own pleasure over and above responsibility for others which renders the behaviour of both de Beauvoir, and the 'bisexual' woman that Card identifies, inauthentic. Card writes in her footnotes: 'See, e.g. Ulmshneider, "Bisexuality" for discussion of this combination of exploitation and failure to take responsibility' (Card 1985: 213*n*). Hence whereas in most of the biographical and press representations de Beauvoir's relationships with women are discounted on the basis that the pleasure she gained from them was not the result of the relationship *per se,* in these examples it is the *nature* of de Beauvoir's pleasure in the relationship – for there is pleasure here – which is problematic. The *lack* of the 'right' kind of pleasure in biographical and newspaper representations is replaced by an *excess* of the 'wrong' kind of pleasure in Card's and Simons' analyses. In all these cases though, specific presuppositions about pleasure (and specifically, about its source and character) are rendered a constitutive feature of sexual identities. What distinguishes Card's and Simons' texts is that they explicitly link the issue of pleasure to responsibility and choice.[22] Not only does the 'bisexual' woman and de Beauvoir exploit other women for their own pleasure (failing to take responsibility for them), this 'choice' doubly implicates their behaviour as inauthentic since both fail to take responsibility when they *could* have done. The reason for this two-pronged failure, as noted above, rests on the assumption that the ability to take responsibility is co-extensive with an obligation to do so.

To take pleasure at the expense of other women suggests that the 'bisexual' woman is loyal to no one but herself. And if, as Frye argues, 'Loyalty [to others] and identity are so closely connected as to be almost just two aspects of the one phenomenon' (Frye 1985: 216), then she cannot be possessed of identity. This lack of identity is confirmed by Card who suggests that although the *woman* 'would probably say she was "bisexual"' (Card 1985: 213) she herself, in this case at least, does not concede to this description. For Card, the very notion of 'bisexuality' is a misnomer. Instead, the woman's behaviour is 'a good *example* of inauthenticity in lesbian behaviour' (Card 1985: 213. My emphasis.). As an example of something else, bisexuality cannot be considered an autonomous sexual identity in its own right (as Ferguson, Card and Frye perceive a lesbian identity to be). 'Lesbian' is the subject here, such that even inauthentic lesbianism may be considered to 'belong' to the self. Bisexuality, by contrast, is merely an *example* of inauthenticity in lesbian behaviour. This suggests that there are, presumably, other kinds of lesbian behaviour which are also inauthentic, as well as authentic lesbian behaviours. However, since inauthenticity itself constitutes the *whole* of bisexuality, bisexuality is *nothing but* inauthenticity. In other words, given that bisexuality is not defined in any other way throughout the course of Card's article (that inauthenticity appears to be all there is to it) and that Card erases the notion of a 'bisexual' woman on this basis, the definition of bisexuality as inauthenticity, in this context, disqualifies it from being perceived as a sexual identity which expresses the self.[23]

Clearly, presuppositions about the roles of responsibility, choice and pleasure in the production of individual and collective sexual identities can serve to erase bisexuality as an identity which can be ascribed to a self such that that self might claim to be 'bisexual'. I began this discussion by exploring several different, but related, accounts of the relation between choice and responsibility and argued that, on closer examination, what might simply be perceived as a welcome increase in the number of choices available to women can have unexpected ramifications. In particular, the link established between choice, responsibility (for others) and a collective, political, lesbian identity has implications for how individual sexual 'choices' may be evaluated. Card's and Frye's arguments both suggest that loyalty to other women, and taking responsibility for others as well as for oneself, is an obligatory feature of a lesbian identity. Conversely, in order to claim an authentic lesbian identity for oneself, one must be loyal to, and responsible for, others.

Nikolas Rose argues that notions of '[a]utonomy, freedom, choice, authenticity' (N. Rose 1997: 145) are contemporary techniques of the self, ways of conducting conduct, which presume an active agent who wishes to exercise responsibility. This, he argues, 'forms a grid of regulatory ideals' which divides selves into those who *will* exercise responsibility, and 'the excluded or marginalized who through wilfulness, incapacity or ignorance cannot or will not exercise such responsibility' (ibid.). Similarly, as the epigraph at the start of this chapter indicates, the common perception of bisexuality as 'a kind of failure of loyalty or lack of commitment' (Butler 1993: 112) serves to erase it as an authentic identity. However, both Rose and Butler presuppose a self who is *able* wilfully or ignorantly to refuse responsibility, while Card's formulation of bisexuality as wholly inauthentic suggests that it is not anchored to a 'bisexual' self who would be *in a position* to make such a decision. As in chapter 4 therefore, bisexuality maintains a presence in the text, but this does not guarantee either that it will be produced out of a narrativisation of events (a narrative which constitutes the subject as a bisexual subject), nor anchored to an individual who 'is' bisexual.

The notion that an authentic lesbian identity is constituted through loyalty to and responsibility for others erases bisexuality as an autonomous source of selfhood (as lesbian identity is perceived to be). The impossibility, in this context, of constructing bisexuality as an identity which 'belongs' to the self is witnessed in Card's conclusion that although the woman in question calls herself 'bisexual' she is in fact an inauthentic lesbian.[24] This is an interesting move on Card's part, because it suggests that even if one were *not* loyal or *not* responsible for others, one could still claim a sexual identity as one's own. Card writes: 'it is not just that the *woman* is being inauthentic: her *lesbianism* is inauthentic' (Card 1985: 213). Notably, the woman remains in possession of *her* lesbianism (it is perceived as an identity in the conventional sense, that is, it refers to/belongs to the self) even though it is inauthentic. That inauthentic lesbianism *is* a property of the self where bisexuality is not, may have something to do with Card's claim that the woman who calls herself 'bisexual' '*resemble[s]*' (Card 1985: 213, my emphasis) an authentic lesbian. Card argues that while on the surface this woman may *appear* to be lesbian, and is able to adopt a 'pose' or 'stance' (Card 1985: 212) which *looks like* a lesbian attitude, this resemblance cannot be taken at face-value. Posturing and posing in this context does not represent a 'radical gesture', an act of plagiarism which subverts the spectacle (Plant 1992), nor does it signify a strategy to engender the new through mimesis (as in the performativity which has come to be associated with queer). Instead, according to Card, resemblance signifies inauthenticity.

It is impossible to ignore the significance of Card's comments about resemblance because it suggests that the paradox of bisexuality – as present but nevertheless not inhering in the self – may be linked to issues of representation, and to the cultural politics of 'looking like what you are'.[25] Drawing together the themes of the analysis so far, I want now to explore the implications of and for bisexuality in relation to theories of selfhood which are based on a specific relation between representation and identity. In doing so, I will be returning to the issue of 'difference', which I raised at the end of chapter 2, and to the 'difference' between bisexuality, as it is produced in various guises throughout the texts I have analysed here, and lesbianism and heterosexuality as they are conventionally conceived.

7

Lose your face

[N]o one knows ahead of time the affects one is capable of . . . you do not know beforehand what a body . . . can do, in a given encounter, a given arrangement, a given combination

Gilles Deleuze, 'Ethology: Spinoza and us'

Towards the end of her paper, Marilyn Frye marks a difference between 'being' and 'acting' lesbian, a difference which also distinguishes authentic and inauthentic lesbians. What I want to do in this chapter, firstly, is to examine the relation between acting and being that Frye raises and, secondly, to consider the implications of this relation for her notion of 'communication and community'. Central to this twofold exploration, and to almost all of the constructions of bisexuality analysed throughout the book so far, are the themes of representation and identity. Not only Frye and Card, but a number of other theorists of identity too, as I will illustrate, presuppose that the relation between representation and identity is mimetic. Yet the ability of the 'bisexual' woman in Card's analysis to *pass* as an authentic lesbian calls attention to the fragility of this relation and, in so doing, disrupts the assumptions on which the community that Frye describes is based. I will be examining how, in order to reinscribe the assumed relation between representation and identity, the role of the other (who is required to recognise and confirm identity) is privileged, which in its turn produces a tendency to negate difference in favour of a narcissistic model of identity based on sameness. Deleuze and Guattari's notion of facialisation aids in an understanding of the ways in which just such a negation transforms the 'bisexual' woman into an 'inauthentic lesbian'.[1]

At this point, rather than agree with Card and claim that the 'bisexual' woman is no more than inauthentic lesbian, I will turn to Deleuze and Guattari to consider the notion of a Body without Organs of bisexuality.

The Body without Organs offers a way of understanding bisexuality not only as it is produced in the texts that I analyse in this chapter, but in those that I have explored throughout this book. It offers a way of accounting for the possible implications of the preclusion, displacement and erasure of bisexuality as an identity which is possessed of and by the self of Simone de Beauvoir – a self which is produced, in part, *through* these strategies of erasure. Importantly, a Body without Organs of bisexuality enables me to explore the implications not only of theories of selfhood and identity *for* bisexuality, but also *of* bisexuality as it impacts, disrupts or confirms the presuppositions which often underpin such theories. As Deleuze argues, it is impossible to know beforehand the affective capacity of a body in any given encounter (Deleuze 1992: 627). I will begin an analysis of the Body without Organs of bisexuality here, in anticipation of the final chapter and conclusion.

Representation, identity and passing

Frye writes:

being lesbian or being heterosexual are not simply matters of sexual preference or bodily behaviors. They are complex matters of attachment, orientation in the world, vision, habits or communication and community . . . In my own case, being lesbian is an attitude evolved over perhaps fifteen years . . . It would have been 'inauthentic' to act the lesbian in certain ways too early in that process. It now would be inauthentic *not* to, in certain ways and certain situations.   (Frye 1985: 217)

By drawing a distinction between being lesbian and acting lesbian, Frye appears to suggest that they are profoundly different expressions of identity: the former is authentic, the latter inauthentic. However, in arguing that '[i]t would have been "inauthentic" to act the lesbian in certain ways too early' in the process of actualising her lesbian identity and that '[i]t now would be inauthentic *not* to, in certain ways and certain situations', Frye also implies that there might perhaps, after all, be only a shadowy difference between the two.

That 'being' lesbian remains a question of 'acting' like one recalls Joan Riviere's (1986) analysis of womanliness as a masquerade. Stephen Heath writes of Riviere's womanliness: 'The masquerade says that the woman exists at the same time that, as masquerade, it says she does not' (Heath 1986: 54). The same might be said of Frye's lesbian identity, on the basis of her own analysis, since she appears never to be able to 'be' a lesbian, except insofar as 'being' is about acting.[2] Peggy Phelan makes a similar point, using slightly different terms, about White women and gender identity:

White women like myself have been encouraged to mistake performance for ontology – to believe that the role is real, and thus sufficient to constitute an identity, a
sense of purpose, a reason for being.   (Phelan 1993: 105)

Although the parallels between masquerade/performance and ontology are
strikingly similar to Frye's analysis of acting and being, it is unlikely that
this is what Frye has in mind when she writes of 'acting'. Instead, it seems
that she is inviting us to believe in the act as a sign of the 'truth' of a lesbian
identity. This wish to 'close the gap' between performance and ontology or
acting and being suggests, as Carole-Anne Tyler puts it, a 'desire to be self-
present' both to oneself and to others. Tyler writes:

As signifiers of our selves with which we are deeply identified, we wish our name
and image to transparently reflect our being, like an iconic sign, and to be existen-
tially or naturally bound to it, like an index. Such signs are supposed to be 'motivated' rather than 'arbitrary' . . . and therefore less susceptible to the disarticulations
of signifier and signified, sign and referent, which make communication confusing.
                                                                          (Tyler 1994: 216)

Frye's analysis rests on the implicit assumption that the signifiers of the self
('name and image', the act) and being, are indeed coincidental or 'naturally
bound' to each other. Ideally, for Frye, acting like a lesbian *should* be a guarantee of being a lesbian (this is authentic behaviour): she herself attempts
to ensure that there is no gap between the performance of the (lesbian)
identity (the act) and the ontological status of 'being' lesbian by only acting
the lesbian when she believes she can claim that identity as her own. Indeed,
she is compelled to act in this way – as she says, 'it would now be inauthentic
not to'. In short, Frye is urging us to believe that we may, in good faith,
recognise and identify (and perhaps identify with) what it is that we see. If
this were guaranteed 'communication', as Tyler puts it, would not be confusing. In terms of a philosophy of representation, it is arguable that while
'being' lesbian (if this were possible) would be defined by self-identity or
self-presence,[3] 'acting' the lesbian – although a likeness or copy – would
'participate' in the original. Thus even though one could never actually 'be'
a lesbian, acting like one would express 'a special kind of internal resemblance to the original' (Patton 1994: 147). Perhaps one, as Tyler says, which
is 'motivated' rather than arbitrary.

Card's and Frye's conception of identity belies an implicit assumption
(which Phelan argues informs most theories of representation) that the
'relationship between representation and identity is linear and smoothly
mimetic. What one sees is who one is' (Phelan 1993: 7). Believing that the
field of the visible may be mastered, what one sees is not only who one is but
also what one knows: the visible constitutes the subject both ontologically

and epistemologically. And indeed, the inauthenticity of the 'bisexual' woman in Card's analysis (see chapter 6) appears in large part to rest on her ability to 'pass' as an authentic lesbian and, in so doing, to disrupt the mimetic relation between representation and identity (inauthentic behaviour is produced out of a discrepancy between acting and being). Outlining Aristotle's notion of a 'family resemblance', Card argues that the term 'resemblance' may be applied to anything which is called by the same name but which does not 'possess any one characteristic in common' (Card 1985: 213). This, she argues, is true in the case of the woman who calls herself 'bisexual', a woman whose attitudes 'are "lesbian" insofar as they resemble genuine lesbian attitudes, which also normally include receptivity to regeneration [*sic*] and nurturance from women' (ibid.).

It is precisely because the 'bisexual' woman's attitudes *resemble* 'genuine lesbian attitudes' that she may be misrecognised as an authentic lesbian and is therefore able to exploit, as Card puts it, 'other women's conditioning to service and nurturance' (Card 1985: 209). In short, it is the 'bisexual' woman's 'theft' (Tyler 1994: 241) of the signs of an authentic lesbian identity that constitutes her inauthenticity. While she and Frye might both be acting, Frye's act is authentic while that of the 'bisexual' woman is not. In this context, the 'problem is not the mask but its assumption or not, its fit or misfit, with the latter pointing to it as mask' (Heath 1986: 50). Because the woman who calls herself 'bisexual' *fails* to pass, the 'misfit' – the discrepancy between acting and being, between what we may see and what we may know – is revealed. And in this misfit, the 'bisexual' woman illustrates that acting and being are not after all the same or 'naturally' bound. Thus however much she desires it – and the 'bisexual' woman bears witness to this – Frye will not be able to 'close the gap between performance and utterance, performative and constative, subject and T-shirt, the one who is "outing" and the one who is out' (Tyler 1994: 221).

The issues of passing then, and resemblance (as its implications are understood by Card), raise a number of problems for theories of identity based on a belief that representation and identity are mimetic. It also reveals the extent to which these theories assume not only that the visible signifiers of identity, the representation, will correspond to the identity itself, but also, and this second presupposition in fact creates a ground for the first, that an identity will be produced as visible at all. Lisa Walker, in her article 'How to recognize a lesbian: The cultural politics of looking like what you are' (1993), demonstrates how the privileging of visible signifiers of difference in Donna Haraway's, Sue-Ellen Case's and Judith Butler's work results in the elision of identities which are not constructed as visible. Too often, Walker argues, it is assumed that the 'visibility' of ethnicity, for example, is closer to 'authenticity' (Walker 1993: 877) than the 'invisibility' of Whiteness. Analysing Haraway's description of Cherríe Moraga's relationship to writing, she says:

> By indicating that Moraga's writing marks her (light) body and keeps her from passing into the unmarked category of the Anglo father (Moraga's father was white), Haraway appears to be absolving Moraga from the guilt she harbors for being able to pass . . . This exculpating gesture draws Haraway into the discourses that establish a hierarchy of oppressions according to paradigms of visibility.
>
> (Walker 1993: 872)

While Walker agrees that the celebration of visible difference is an effective strategy for reclaiming signifiers of difference which have been negatively portrayed,[4] she also suggests that this may in its turn replicate the same 'dominant ideologies' (Walker 1993: 888) which have employed visibility 'to create social categories on the basis of exclusion' (ibid.). Where visibility and authenticity are conjoined, 'members of a given population who do not bear that signifier of difference or who bear visible signs of another identity are rendered invisible and are marginalised within an already marginalised community (ibid.).

Phelan's account of the artist Adrian Piper's 'calling cards', given to those who might mistake her light skin for 'White', demonstrates one way of resisting the 'invisibilisation' of those who are passed against their will. Piper hands out her cards, stating her racial identity, to those who would attempt to 'pass her [as White] without her consent' (Phelan 1993: 98). The cards serve to establish both 'the failure of racial difference to appear within the narrow range of the visible', as well as Piper's 'refusal to let the visual field *fail* to secure it. The card itself ruptures the given to be seen and exposes the normative force of everyday blindness: if no one looks black, everyone is white' (Phelan 1993: 98).

Piper's experience of the ways in which (racial) identities are established through the trope of the visible illustrates Walker's point that 'subjects who can "pass" exceed the categories of visibility that establish identity' (Walker 1993: 868). It also reveals how those identities which are rendered invisible might be absorbed into the dominant 'norm' (if no one looks Black, everyone is White).[5] Richard Dyer's (1988) analysis of Whiteness contributes to this debate insofar as he illustrates precisely how the 'invisibility' of Whiteness as an identity serves to secure its dominance. The power of Whiteness, he argues, is anchored not so much in its representation as superiority, but rather as 'normality'. However, where Piper insists on the value of (re)marking her difference – refusing, as Phelan says, to let the field of the visible fail to secure it – Dyer argues that the contemporary academic focus on images of those 'defined as oppressed, marginal or subordinate' serves to reproduce the 'sense of the oddness' of these groups, while meanwhile 'the norm has carried on as if it is the natural, inevitable, ordinary way of being human' (Dyer 1988: 44). Dyer's own solution is not to erase all marks of difference, but to ensure that Whiteness itself is also recognised as a visible identity: 'It is . . . important to try to make some headway with grasping whiteness as a culturally constructed category' (ibid.).

Where Piper and Dyer seek to make identities 'seeable', other theorists, for example Sara Ahmed, prefer to exploit the 'uncertain' colour of skin to destabilise the relations (and the assumed autonomy) between self and other, colour and race and White and Black femininities. Ahmed argues that the reduction of race to skin colour ('chromotism') involves *investing* skin colour 'with the meaning of racial difference', a difference which 'may fix the object of the gaze into a logic of inclusion (you are white like me) or exclusion (you are black like them)' (Ahmed 1996: 10). The colours Black and White thus become the vehicles through which subject and object, self and other, are established. However, these boundaries are not always transparent. Ahmed has herself been identified by White policemen, within the space of seconds, as first Aboriginal (Black like them) and then sun tanned (White like me). Passing as tanned, her body also passes as 'safe' (as opposed to 'criminal') because its colour is temporary, 'literally a detachable signifier, a "mask" that can be put on and taken off, inessential to the subject, and hence acceptable' (Ahmed 1996: 17). This split between 'natural' or 'essential' Black and 'inessential' tan also, Ahmed argues, shapes the differences between Black and White femininities. The Black woman's skin is perceived to be 'not pliable' (it is 'given' for all time) and, as such, is a sign of racial otherness, an always already sexualised femininity (Pettman in Ahmed 1996: 18). The White woman's tan, by contrast, is not only a sign of class privilege, but also demonstrates a proper 'care for the self', an adornment, which 'appropriates and domesticates the hyper-sexuality which is signified by Black skin, rendering the presence of colour a temporary aberration which confirms the proper sexual order based on her protection from Black men by white men' (Ahmed 1996: 18). Identifying herself as *both* Black *and* tanned, Ahmed will 'question [her reader's] construction of either' (Ahmed 1996: 21). She argues that it is the transformability of skin (Black as well as White) which illustrates that skin is not a secure boundary that demarcates subject from object, but rather 'represents the constant danger of our mingling in social encounters with the other' (Ahmed 1996: 19).

Walker, Piper, Dyer and Ahmed reveal, in their different ways, the political complexities surrounding issues of passing and the production of identity through visible signifiers. As Phelan's discussion of the male models[6] in Jenny Livingston's film *Paris is Burning* makes explicit, neither visibility nor invisibility can be held up as the inherently desirable political strategy. Phelan points out that while being passed against one's consent may be problematic, it is also the case that some might wish to pass. The male models who walked the stage of Harlem clubs in the late 1980s for example, often employed the accoutrements of femininity in order 'to be passed over, not vulnerable to the hostile gaze of heterosexual culture' (Phelan 1993: 104). In this instance, the security conferred by invisibility, its power, is actively sought. Beverley Skeggs' analysis of passing in the context of White working-class women also suggests that the problem with passing is not that one may be passed against one's will, but that 'someone may catch you out' (Skeggs 1997: 86). Skeggs argues that White working-class women's attempt to pass as middle class 'does not involve ironic mimicry . . . because it wants to be taken seriously; because it speaks from a position of powerlessness and insecurity' (Skeggs 1997: 87). In this context, attempting to pass is not actively to destabilise the visible/invisible binary nor does it expose the subject's inability to master the field of the visible; rather, it 'engenders anxiety and insecurity' (ibid.). This is because passing, Skeggs argues, usually presupposes the existence of an authoritative 'norm' to which the 'passer' attempts to conform: 'Passing . . . assumes a fit between the reality of one group and the naturalizing of its definition' (Skeggs 1997: 91). Thus, for example: 'The middle class do not need to pass' (ibid. See also Lawler 1997).[7] Card's and Frye's (and to a less explicit extent Ferguson's) definition of a lesbian is also naturalised – it includes the ability to make choices, to assume responsibility for others and to be loyal to a lesbian community (see chapter 6). Failing on at least two of these counts (the latter two), the 'bisexual' woman fails to pass and is exposed as an inauthentic lesbian. She is 'caught out'.

The role of the other

What all these analyses share, whatever their position on the desirability (or not) of passing, is an emphasis (either explicit or implicit) on the role of the other in the construction of the self. Phelan argues that the trope of visibility in the production of identities, both individual and collective, ties the subject to others since we cannot see ourselves, and are therefore dependent upon a detour through the eyes of the other to recognise and confirm our identities. It is this inability to see oneself, the failure of 'self-seeing', that Phelan calls the 'trap of the visual field' (Phelan 1993: 24). She argues that the gaze 'promise[s] to show all, even while it fails to show the subject who looks, *and* thus fails to show what the looker most wants to see' (ibid.). For example: although the symmetrical relation between the vanishing point and the viewpoint, on which the Western concept of perspective rests, gives the impression of a single perception and unified looker, in fact the subject is unable to see him or herself. Indeed, the 'annihilation of the subject as center is a condition of the very moment of the look' (Bryson quoted in Phelan 1993: 25. See also Foucault 1994, chapter 1). Equally, in relation to identity, Phelan argues that the moment of looking is about blindness and loss: unable to see itself, the subject is dependent upon the other to recognise and reflect its identity back to it.[8] Theories of identity based on representation then, are frequently premised upon the fear of loss or failure.

Given this fear of the failure of 'self-seeing', it remains that while we might wish to be 'self-present' to ourselves and to others, the other might not always 'provide a reassuring image of the self' (Tyler 1994: 225). Piper is passed off as White against her will, Ahmed passes as tanned. Card refuses to accept the name 'bisexual', and instead prefers to identify the woman in her example as an inauthentic lesbian. If it is the case that identity does not reside simply in the 'name you can say or the body you can see' but additionally requires 'a relation to an other' (Phelan 1993: 13), then one of the consequences of the gaze – whether real or imaginary[9] – is that it may be productive of an insidious anxiety. Thomas Cooley's notion of the looking-glass self is relevant here. He writes:

The thing that moves us to *pride or shame* is not mere mechanical reflection of ourselves [in another], but an imputed sentiment, the imagined effect of this reflection upon another's mind . . . We always imagine, and in imagining share, the judgments of the other mind.
(Cooley quoted in Scheff 1994: 285)[10]

As noted in chapters 3 and 4, the use, in some of the biographies, of the mirror as a metaphor to describe de Beauvoir and Sartre's association produces, on the whole, a positive portrayal of the relationship. De Beauvoir and Sartre's reflection of each other in each other is seen to 'double' their 'brilliance' (Francis and Gontier 1987: 3). However, while recognition that others are like oneself, that they are the same (as de Beauvoir and Sartre are perceived to be), and the subsequent identification with them may lead to pride (which perhaps accounts, for example, for the symbolic importance of the 'Gay Pride' slogan), as Cooley points out, it may also be the case that how others see us leads to feelings of shame:

The fundamental problem in the contact of peoples is the preservation of the individual's moral worth in his own eyes . . . It is difficult to develop self-respect if one is not respected by others . . . Without it [self-respect] they [human beings] can neither look themselves in the face nor stand before their children without a sense of shame.
(Shibutani-Kwan quoted in Scheff 1994: 284)

Although shaming, if it is effective, can serve to push an individual *out* of a community, it may also bring the individual *back* 'into line'. Nietzsche suggests that: 'Punishment . . . is valuable because it awakens a sense of guilt in the culprit; we should therefore view it as the true instrument of the psychological reaction called "remorse", "pangs of conscience"' (Nietzsche 1956: 214). Following the publication of de Beauvoir's *Letters to Sartre* for example, a number of the newspapers suggest that it was guilt over her treatment of her women lovers that led de Beauvoir to regret her relationships with them (see chapter 5). Margaret Simons too, in her account of de Beauvoir's relationship with Louise Védrine, argues that de Beauvoir eventually felt 'remorse' about 'her own exploitation of Védrine for sexual pleasure and lack of true tenderness' (Simons 1992: 154). Both these representations imply that it is the gaze of the other turned inward (a self-surveillance[11] which inspires de Beauvoir to feel shame and remorse) that marks the start of her perceived transformation to authentic hetero-sexuality (in the press representations) or authentic lesbianism (in Simons' analysis). Apparently nothing in de Beauvoir's relationship with Sylvie Le Bon, for example, gives her cause for shame. De Beauvoir 'reveals a genuine respect for Le Bon, concern for her well-being, and delight in watching her personality flower' (Simons 1992: 156). Not only is this relationship 'shame-free' but, significantly, Simons suggests that de Beauvoir's own account of it is also 'free of references to her heterosexual relationships' (ibid.).

For the major part of this analysis I have been concerned with tracing the implications *of* the presuppositions on which selfhood is understood to rest *for* the production (or not) of 'bisexuality'. In the above examples for instance, the feelings of shame imputed to de Beauvoir are understood to promote self-recognition, self-revelation and self-punishment on her part. As such, shame is rendered a technique of identity which plays a key role in the construction of de Beauvoir as either lesbian or heterosexual. As Eve Sedgwick says:

the forms taken by shame are not distinct 'toxic' parts of an identity that can be excised; they are instead integral to and residual in the processes by which identity itself is formed. They are available for the work of metamorphosis, reframing, refiguration, *trans*figuration . . .   (Sedgwick 1996: 142)

It is also the case however, that the position of bisexuality in the texts I have analysed have resonance for more than bisexuality alone. For example: the 'bisexual' woman identified by Card is herself an other to which the authen-tic lesbian might look to see her identity reflected. By passing through the lesbian community, the 'bisexual' woman introduces the possibility that

that community, and the authenticity of lesbian identities, are not after all secure. The 'bisexual' woman illustrates that not everyone in the 'community' shares the same identity and will therefore not necessarily recognise or reflect the authentic lesbian back to herself in the way that she might like. As Tyler notes: 'The community of signifying clones whose identities are clear, communications transparent, and desires identical is . . . a fantasy based on the repression of differences within both the self and the community' (Tyler 1994: 233).[12] The 'communication' on which community is founded cannot be guaranteed since, as the relation (of both similarity/her resemblance and difference/her inauthenticity) between the 'bisexual' woman and the authentic lesbian in Card's analysis indicates, there is a 'two-way traffic in signs whose inevitable doubleness can secure no identity – or identity politics – on a permanent basis' (Tyler 1994: 227).

This inevitable 'doubleness' introduces the issue of difference not only between self and other but also within the self. Tyler argues that the subject is an effect of mimicry:

which results from and expresses an alienating identification with something outside it . . . The subject is only retroactively the cause of what it brings into being, an imitation of a reflection or copy of which it 'will have been' the original (so that there can be a copy at all).   (Tyler 1994: 218–19)

In other words, as Frye's own analysis of her lesbian identity inadvertently reveals, 'being' lesbian is a question of acting or imitating an image of what a lesbian is supposed to be like. Thus the subject is an effect of the imitation of the image, an image whose source lies outside the self and, according to Phelan, in the other. From this perspective, Frye 'is' a lesbian only to the extent that others recognise her performance of (a lesbian) identity as authentic. It is the success (figured here as recognition) of the performance itself, the copy or imitation, which *subsequently* enables Frye to claim a lesbian identity as 'her own'. Representation and identity then, because of this detour through the image which is confirmed (or not) by the other, cannot be the identical:

Our representations appear to belong to us as sovereign subjects although they come to us from the Other. This is so especially for 'our' representations, the signifiers which represent us, with which we are deeply identified, and which in fact constitute us in the first place.   (Tyler 1994: 218)

If it is the case that identity is produced retroactively – through the imitation which is only subsequently claimed as an 'original' identity – then the imitation cannot be the same as the original identity. As Paul Patton, writing about theories of representation in art, points out: 'a perfect imitation is no longer an imitation at all but another instance of the same thing.

In other words, the detour through the eyes of the other ensures that imitation or copying depends upon the maintenance of a difference between the copy and the thing imitated' (Patton 1994: 149). In other words, the imitation or copy and the original are necessarily different for the individual to come into being, because otherwise there would be nothing with which to tell them apart.

Tyler argues that such differences must be erased or repressed if the 'desire to be self-present' (Tyler 1994: 216) both to oneself and to others, to be self-identical (the 'same' as oneself), is to be fulfilled. To this end the subject narcissistically perceives 'similarity where there is only difference' (Tyler 1994: 219). The following section will explore the way in which Card recuperates the 'bisexual' woman into a model of identity based not on difference but sameness.

Sameness

As chapter 6 illustrated, Card's argument rests on the presupposition that all identities may, and should, be evaluated according to the same criteria. Heterosexuality, Card argues, must be seen as a choice in order that heterosexuality and lesbianism (which, she argues, is usually perceived to be a choice) can be evaluated on an equal basis (Card 1985: 209). And just as heterosexuality and lesbianism are perceived to be comparable, so are the 'bisexual' woman and the authentic lesbian. Significantly, on the basis that the 'bisexual' woman's attitudes 'resemble genuine lesbian attitudes' (Card 1985: 213), Card concludes that even though they do not share any characteristics in common, the 'bisexual' woman is an inauthentic lesbian.[13] Hence the potential difference between the 'bisexual' woman and the authentic lesbian is erased (from now on there is no such thing as bisexuality, only inauthentic lesbianism) as the woman is defined as a lesser version of the same identity (lesbian). In other words, Card redefines the 'bisexual' woman on the basis of resemblance gone awry. Foucault writes:

The meeting point of the axes is the point of perfect resemblance, and from this arises the scale of differences as so many lesser resemblances, marked identities . . . For a thing to be different, it must first no longer be the same; and it is on this negative basis . . . that contrary predicates are then articulated.(Foucault 1977: 183–4)

Assuming that in Card's analysis the authentic lesbian is, ideally, 'the point of perfect resemblance', where the gap between representation and identity, copy and original, is (perceived to be as) closed (as possible), the inauthentic lesbian signifies a 'lesser resemblance' or imitation. And insofar as the inauthentic lesbian is different to the authentic lesbian only because she is not the same as her, the nature of the difference between the two is constructed as 'a difference *from* or *within* something . . . Difference is transformed into that which must be specified within a concept, without overstepping its bounds' (Foucault 1977: 181–2). In short, it is the resemblance between the authentic and inauthentic lesbian that enables Card to assume that they are in essential respects the same and therefore that their difference is no more than a 'difference within resemblance, so to speak' (Patton 1994: 153). The difference between the two then, according to Card, is secondary. Sameness remains primary.

By evaluating the 'bisexual' woman on the same basis as the authentic lesbian, Card achieves 'sameness of outcome' (Diprose 1993: 13). According to Card, it is not the 'bisexual' woman who passes as, or resembles, an authentic lesbian, but rather an inauthentic lesbian who passes as an authentic one. And because, by definition, the inauthentic lesbian has failed to pass (it is her having been 'caught out', as Skeggs puts it, that reveals her inauthenticity), she may be contained within the arena of visible representation, among 'marked identities'. A yoke is laid upon the potential difference between the 'bisexual' woman and the authentic lesbian and, constructed as an inauthentic lesbian, the woman becomes 'facialised' as Deleuze and Guattari would have it.

For Deleuze and Guattari abstract machines[14] of faciality, the white wall/black hole system, engender a face which ensures 'the almightiness of the signifier as well as the autonomy of the subject' (Deleuze and Guattari 1988: 181). The white wall on which signs are inscribed, the black hole in which consciousness and passion are lodged,[15] the face delimits anything other than 'appropriate significations' and any subjectivity that does not 'conform in advance to a dominant reality' (Deleuze and Guattari 1988:168). The abstract machine of faciality functions in two ways, both of which are based on binary relations. Firstly, it constitutes the dichotomies out of which concrete faces are produced (recognised and identified): 'it is a man *or* a woman, a rich person or a poor one, an adult or a child, a leader or a subject, "an x *or* a y"' (Deleuze and Guattari 1988: 177). And as Card's account suggests, such dichotomies might include and produce the concrete faces of an authentic and an inauthentic lesbian. Secondly, given a concrete face, the machine judges: 'whether it passes or not . . . This time, the binary relation is of the "yes-no" type . . . At every moment, the machine rejects faces that do not conform, or seem suspicious' (Deleuze and Guattari 1988: 177).

In relation to racism, Deleuze and Guattari suggest that there is no 'outside' of the face (no 'other'); instead, there are only degrees of deviance (established in relation to the White-Man face).[16] In other words, they illustrate the way that the face – 'a deviance detector' (Deleuze and Guattari 1988: 177–8) – is based on a model of identity which rests on sameness rather than difference and that, as such, it is able to recuperate deviance into sameness. Hence: 'There are only people who should be like us and whose crime it is not to be . . . Racism never detects the particles of the other; it propagates waves of sameness until those who resist identification have been wiped out' (Deleuze and Guattari 1988: 178). Card's redefinition of the 'bisexual' woman as an inauthentic lesbian has a similar effect. Because she is defined through a degree (or even degrees) of deviance (a lesser version of the identity produced by the face), she remains contained within the face. Even deviance, according to Deleuze and Guattari, is facialised: 'At any rate, you've been recognised, the abstract machine has you inscribed in its overall grid' (Deleuze and Guattari 1988: 177). It is a wave of sameness that erases the 'bisexual' woman and washes up in her place an inauthentic lesbian that is *able* to be recognised and identified: facialised. Thus, where Card is concerned, there is no 'bisexual' woman to (mis)recognise, there is no invisible 'bisexual' woman. Instead, there is only an inauthentic lesbian. It is on this basis that the example of bisexuality differs from the accounts of passing described so far.

Walker and Phelan share the presupposition that even those identities which are not 'marked', or immediately visible, may be produced in some form. Walker writes for example, that:

while a butch woman of color might not be recognized as a lesbian because she is not white, she might be perceived as a lesbian because her sexual style is considered 'blatant'. A femme woman of color, on the other hand, will probably not be recognized as lesbian, first because she is not white and then because she is not butch.

(Walker 1993: 886)

Although the femme in this example is not *recognised* as lesbian (firstly because she is Black and secondly because she is a femme), she remains a lesbian nevertheless (if she did not, Walker herself would not be able to identify her).[17] What Walker assumes then, is that even those identities which are not visible may in some way cohere in the self. In this respect, Walker's analysis is based on what we are and are not able to see, rather than on the issue of visibility in the production (or not) of identity *per se*. Indeed, Walker's analysis confirms the centrality *of* the visible as a technique of identity. She writes: 'it is my argument that we should continue to complicate our ideas about what counts as radical self-presentation for minority identities' (Walker 1993: 888).

For Phelan expanding – or even 'complicating our ideas about' – what we are able to see is not the solution to the tricky issue of representation and identity. The visible is itself problematic, she argues, since it usually introduces notions of 'surveillance, fetishism, voyeurism, and sometimes, death' (Phelan 1993: 10–11). Moreover, Phelan suggests (and Card's account of the 'bisexual' woman would appear to confirm this) that 'the economy of representation' uses the other as a cipher for the self and in doing so, perceives similarity and erases 'dissimilarity and negat[es] difference' (Phelan 1993: 150). Phelan concludes that only a revaluation of a belief in 'subjectivity and identity which is not visibly representable' (Phelan 1993: 1) could enable the other to be something other than a vehicle through which the self is established. Unlike Walker, Phelan argues that: 'This is not the same thing as calling for greater visibility of the hitherto unseen' (Phelan 1993: 1).

Despite the difference between Walker's and Phelan's suggested strategies for 'dealing' with the relation between visibility and identity, Phelan nevertheless assumes, as Walker does, that identities inhere in the self even when they are not immediately visible. Adrian Piper for example, is understood to be 'Black' even when she is passed off as 'White' (the purpose of the calling cards is to confirm the existence of her identity *as* Black). Indeed, Phelan writes of 'an *active* vanishing, a deliberate and conscious refusal to take the payoff of visibility' (Phelan 1993: 19) which itself presupposes a pre-existing subject who is able to refuse the payoff.[18] In other words, the issue in these analyses is not whether identities are *possible* outside of the arena of visible representation, but that given that they *are*, how, and with what implications (both desirable and undesirable), they come to be misrecognised or invisibilised. In short, the issue for both Walker and Phelan is more about recognition and less about identification *per se*. By contrast, I would suggest that the 'problem' of bisexuality cannot be solved either, as Walker suggests, by expanding the field of the visible in order that it might be recognised as an authentic identity (by which I mean that it might be claimed as one's 'own' in the way that lesbian and heterosexuality, either explicitly or implicitly, often are), or by including it among those identities that Phelan argues have refused to take the payoff of visibility. In the following section I will recap briefly on the position of bisexuality as it is produced in the texts I have analysed here, in order to illustrate why this is so.

Identity without selfhood

Although bisexuality is present in biographical representations of de Beauvoir, this 'visibility' does not serve as a guarantee of identity-as-selfhood (as Walker's analysis of the relation between visibility and identity suggests that it might). In Crosland's analysis for example, de Beauvoir's 'bisexuality' is confined to androgyny. By suggesting that de Beauvoir's admirers loved her 'as passionately as if she were a man' (Crosland 1992: 233), Crosland implies that these relationships are more heterosexual (where de Beauvoir assumes the role of the man to her female lovers) than either lesbian or bisexual. Ironically, since it is the gender of object choice which defines sexuality in Crosland's account, 'bisexuality' only serves to confirm de Beauvoir as heterosexual. Her 'elusive (bisexual) nature' (Crosland 1992: 229) is also transformed into an integral part of a narrative quest in which de Beauvoir attempts to discover – perhaps not accidentally, given the emphasis on de Beauvoir's 'manly' role in her same-sex relationships – the extent to which she is or is not a woman (ibid.). The contradictory elements in this narrative are to some degree resolved insofar as Crosland assures the reader of de Beauvoir's femininity by positioning her as 'mother' to her young lovers. Sartre's role as 'father' completes the portrait of a heterosexual nuclear family in which de Beauvoir's same-sex relationships are no more than an extension of her 'near-motherly instinct' (Crosland 1992: 224).

Unlike in Crosland's representation, where bisexuality-as-androgyny anchors bisexuality to the issue of de Beauvoir's gender, Fullbrook and Fullbrook embrace it as a feature of de Beauvoir's sexual identity. However, de Beauvoir's pleasurable emotional and sexual relationships with women (as well as men) does not, in their biography, constitute her as bisexual. Rather, bisexuality is just one aspect of de Beauvoir *and* Sartre's heterosexuality. As in Moi's account, where de Beauvoir's relationships with women are not understood to be significant *in themselves* (but are rather produced out of a fear of heterosexual emptiness), so in Fullbrook and Fullbrook's biography their value lies elsewhere; specifically, in their contribution to her relationship with Sartre and, in particular, to their 'singular bond' (Fullbrook and Fullbrook 1993: 95). In each of these representations therefore, as well as in Margaret Simons' account of de Beauvoir's sexuality (where bisexuality is configured not merely as heterosexuality but also, as in Card's analysis – which she applies to her own – as inauthentic lesbianism), various narrative techniques preclude bisexuality from being a constitutive feature of de Beauvoir's sexual-narrative-identity. Bisexuality is not a 'durable property', or identity-as-sameness, which lasts from the start to the finish of de Beauvoir's life.

Although Ricoeur suggests that identity-as-selfhood remains even when there is a crisis of identity-as-sameness, this does not appear to be the case in the context of bisexuality (as it is constructed in the biographies). In the first instance, bisexuality is not constituted as an identity-as-sameness which might subsequently *be* lost or 'put into crisis'. Secondly, although bisexuality is present in these texts (it is both identifiable and nameable) it is nevertheless not coupled with a bisexual 'she' (de Beauvoir). This suggests not merely that the question 'who is de Beauvoir?' is not answerable with a bisexual 'what' (the 'what' referring to identity-as-sameness), but also that bisexuality is not intelligible in terms of the question 'who'. Bisexuality is not perceived to inhere in the self of de Beauvoir and, in this respect, it exceeds the individuality ascribed to de Beauvoir through the production of her sexual-narrative-identity.

In the newspaper representations of the sexuality ascribed to de Beauvoir, the 'source' of her relationships with both men and women is perceived to reside not within de Beauvoir herself (where it might express the truth of the self), but rather in existentialism, the historical accident of her bohemian lifestyle and in unhappy heterosexuality. Constructed as *external* to the self bisexuality, in this context, cannot be produced as a property *of* the self. In these representations then, the very possibility of bisexuality as an identity which expresses the 'truth' of the self is displaced. De Beauvoir is neither passed off as something other than bisexual nor is bisexuality invisibilised; bisexuality does not 'exist' to even potentially be 'framed' inside or outside the field of visibility. Unconstituted, it is 'beyond representation'.

As in the biographical accounts of de Beauvoir's sexuality outlined in chapter 4, Card acknowledges the presence of bisexuality (approximately one fifth of her analysis is given over to it) but this presence, or visibility, does not guarantee that it is an identity *such as lesbian and heterosexuality are*. And as in chapter 5, where I argued that there is no constituted bisexuality, so there is no 'bisexual' woman who passes as an authentic lesbian (instead, it is an inauthentic lesbian who passes as an authentic one). Bisexuality is constructed, by Card, as inauthenticity itself which, unlike taking responsibility for oneself or for others, or making choices for instance, is not constructed as a technique of the self.[19] Bisexuality is understood to constitute the deception itself, the moments during which the inauthentic lesbian passes as an authentic one. Only when discussing the nature of this deception, this inauthenticity, does Card employ the term 'bisexual'. Having established 'inauthenticity', the term 'bisexual' appears no longer to be necessary: the 'bisexual' woman is redefined as an inauthentic lesbian and the notion of bisexuality as an identity (an identity able to be claimed by the subject) is erased. This, as I have argued, recuperates the woman in the example into a model of identity based on sameness. Failing to pass, the inauthentic lesbian is facialised; defined as a lesser version of the authentic lesbian, she is recognised and identified.

In none of these accounts therefore, is there a constituted, bisexual subject of representation who exists either to be misrecognised or to be invisibilised. Equally, there is no bisexual self who would be in a position to take the payoff of visibility that Phelan advocates. It is possible to conjecture therefore, that the difference between bisexuality and lesbianism and heterosexuality is not a difference which is established 'under the rule of the negative' (Foucault 1977: 185). If this were the case, then bisexuality would signify a degree of deviation from what remained an essential similarity – perhaps that they are all identities which may be possessed (or may be perceived to be possessed) by the self. However, given that bisexuality is clearly not an identity in the conventional sense, the similarity between bisexuality and lesbianism and heterosexuality may be understood to be produced not as a result of an essential sameness, but as an effect of difference, as difference is understood by Deleuze. Explaining Deleuze's difference with reference to simulacra, Patton writes:

the difference between a simulacrum and what it simulates, by contrast [to a copy and its imitation of the original], is of another order altogether. The simulacrum is not in essential respects the same as what it simulates, but different. Although it reproduces the appearance of the original, it does so as an effect. Here, the apparent identity of the two is the secondary, derived relation, while it is their difference that is primary.   (Patton 1994: 154)

A simulacrum, according to this interpretation, is *not* a copy of a copy since this would maintain an essential similarity: 'The simulacrum would then be a second-order copy, the difference between copy and original redoubled' (Patton 1994: 153). Equally, bisexuality cannot be seen as an imitation of either heterosexual or lesbian inauthenticity since this would presuppose that it participated, albeit in a lesser way, of the original (self-present) identity. Since bisexuality is not understood to participate in such an identity, its resemblance may be understood as secondary, as an effect derived of a primary difference.

Difference

By way of example, it is worth exploring the difference between the inauthenticity that characterises bisexuality and theories of identity as masquerade or queer theories of performativity. At first glance, there appear to be similarities. Insofar as bisexuality 'is' inauthenticity, for example, it can be likened to Riviere's analysis of womanliness. She writes:

The reader may now ask how I define womanliness or where I draw the line between genuine womanliness and the 'masquerade'. My suggestion is not, however, that there is any such difference; whether radical or superficial, they are the same thing.
                                                                    (Riviere 1986: 38)[20]

Unlike Frye and Card, who have an investment in the 'genuine' (Card 1985: 213) lesbian, Riviere rejects the very idea that 'genuine' womanliness is possible. Her argument instead invites us to agree that there is no difference between womanliness and the masquerade, to agree that 'they are the same thing'. Thus to say that the woman is 'masked' is not to misrecognise her since the masquerade is constitutive of womanliness, just as inauthenticity is constitutive of bisexuality.

However, both Riviere's masquerade and, as I have argued in chapter 2, queer theories of performativity account not only for signifiers of identity (the name 'woman' for example, and the image), but also material corporealities ('real' women to which those signifiers refer).[21] Thus even though the 'woman' produced through masquerade or performativity may never possess her identity (as Card and Frye suppose that an identity may be claimed as one's own), it may *appear* that she is possessed of it. As noted in chapter 2, for Judith Butler the subject appears to 'have' an identity because discourse 'conceals or dissimulates the conventions of which it is a repetition' (Butler 1993: 12). Nevertheless, Tyler argues that to all intents and purposes the difference between those who are 'naive' enough to believe that representation and identity, sign and signifier, are the same (as Card and Frye appear to do) and those who 'know' that they are not (but who still 'come out' and claim the signifiers of identity as their own) is slight. To quote her again on this point:

No matter how self-consciously we deconstruct identities, no matter how self-reflexively we perform our selves, we are still 'doing' them. What's more, we demand that the Other recognize both our identities and our 'cynicism' about them – the Other is at once our credulous dupe and the 'subject supposed to know' that we know better.   (Tyler 1994: 222)

Thus even though 'identity' is understood to be a fiction or error, identity theorists are often, for the most part, concerned with bodies which are already, as Deleuze and Guattari would put it, organised, stratified and regulated (without such stratification, there would be nothing to theorise). Deleuze and Guattari's objection to stratification is that it places limits on what a body can *do*. As noted in chapter 2, for Deleuze a body is defined 'not in terms of its organs and their functions, but rather more inventively and rhizomatically as a site of affectation' (Ansell Pearson 1997: 227).[22] Although it is not possible to anticipate what affects a body will be capable of, where molar entities – such as the binaries of men and women – are concerned, the flow of forces is limited and ordered by the three strata of organism, signifiance[23] and subjectification: their capacity both to affect and be affected is circumscribed. Indeed, as I outlined in the first chapter, the self itself is folded and stabilised force, its interiority no more than a mirror which reflects the self back to its self. Deleuze and Guattari write:

Let us consider the three great strata concerning us, in other words, the ones that most directly bind us: the organism, signifiance, and subjectification . . . You will be organized, you will be an organism, you will articulate your body – otherwise you're just depraved. You will be signifier and signified, interpreter and interpreted – otherwise you're just a deviant. You will be subject, nailed down as one, a subject of the enunciation recoiled into the statement – otherwise you're just a tramp.

(Deleuze and Guattari 1988: 159)

Organised into human corporeality, the subject 'woman', possessed of and by her gender identity, is available to be analysed and interpreted (most frequently, as a huge body of feminist literature shows, as 'lack'). As Deleuze and Guattari put it, molar entities are 'know[n] from the outside and recognise[d] through experience' (Deleuze and Guattari 1988: 275).

Drawing on Foucault, I suggested at the beginning of the book that contemporary Western concepts of the self are often the product of the theories which seek to explain them. The analysis of both the ways in which a self is ascribed to de Beauvoir and the ways that 'bisexuality' is erased as a property of that self illustrates how this is so. In order to explain 'who' de Beauvoir is, commentators draw on a number of techniques of the self (some of which are practices, such as self-reflection, others which are narrativised, such as individuality and sexuality). The preclusion, displacement and erasure of bisexuality serves to assure commentators that the self is indeed produced in this way. In other words, the self that is constructed is built upon the very assumptions which preceded it. Deleuze unravels the implications of producing knowledge based on that which is already representable in thought:

History, subjectivity, and the meaning of Being are products in consciousness; to take any particular form of these as the starting point for interpretation and understanding fails to attain the underlying level of the processes by which such forms of consciousness are produced.   (Goodchild 1996: 13)

For Deleuze what we may 'know' is always static and therefore prevents 'forces from acting, so that we only deal in inverted and flattened representations. Life is replaced by an image' (Goodchild 1996: 31. See also MacKenzie 1997). Thus whether the identities, bodies and selves which are described and analysed are assumed to be a 'fiction' or not, they are always already images – molar entities located in the field of conscious expression rather than unconscious production – and, as such, inevitably seal flows of energy within them.

The inauthenticity of bisexuality however, is not productive of a molar entity, nor is it a molar entity itself. Defined as wholly inauthentic, the moments during which the inauthentic lesbian passes as an authentic one (perhaps bisexuality is passing itself), bisexuality is neither entirely visible nor invisible. Similarly, although present in the biographical accounts analysed in chapter 4, bisexuality is nevertheless not constructed as a sexual-narrative-identity. In this respect bisexuality exceeds facialisation. Relatedly, in Card's analysis, as in press representations of de Beauvoir (where the source of 'bisexuality' is perceived to be external to the self ascribed to her), bisexuality does not cohere in the body of the woman or, as in Simons' analysis also, in the body of de Beauvoir. However, this is not necessarily to suggest that bisexuality (as it is constituted in these texts), because it is not possessed by the self which it might have expressed, and because it is not embedded within material corporeality, is not a body at all.[24] Instead, it may be understood as a different kind of body, a body without the organs which would stratify and regulate it.[25]

A Body without Organs of bisexuality

The Body without Organs [BwO] is 'what remains when you take everything away' (Deleuze and Guattari 1988: 151) from the three strata of organism, subjectification and signification:[26]

> no longer an organism that functions but a BwO that is constructed. No longer are there acts to explain, dreams or phantasies to interpret, childhood memories to recall, words to make signify . . . There is no longer a Self [*Moi*] that feels, acts and recalls.   (Deleuze and Guattari 1988: 162)

Neither 'a place nor a plane, a scene or a fantasy' (Grosz 1994: 202), the BwO cannot be pinned down to an 'organised' or embodied individual. Instead, it is a field for the production of the immanence of desire, where desire is understood as 'a process of production without reference to any exterior agency, whether it be a lack that hollows it out or a pleasure that fills it in' (Deleuze and Guattari 1988: 154). If desire is betrayed (if a BwO is made into an organism, a signification or a subject), it is uprooted from its immanence: 'The BwO howls: "They've made me an organism! They've wrongfully folded me! They've stolen my body!"' (Deleuze and Guattari 1988: 159).

The BwO of bisexuality, like all bodies without organs, is not a representational figure (Boyne 1990: 43); 'Nothing here is representative', Deleuze and Guattari write (Deleuze and Guattari quoted in Boyne 1990: 37). What is instead privileged is a 'history of connections and disconnections' (Boyne 1990: 43), the molecular lines of flight which are inscribed onto and construct the BwO. The effect is one of conjugation and continuance rather than stratification and subjectification. In the newspaper representations for instance, the BwO of bisexuality is produced as a connecting force or *movement between* existentialism, Sartre and de Beauvoir. In this context, bisexuality is not fused to the self (in a semblance of stasis), but is rather a mobile assemblage which has the effect of bringing existentialism, Sartre and de Beauvoir together in a relation which is neither mediated by a single subjectivity nor necessarily subject to the disciplinary processes of individualisation. Desire spread *over* and across objects, the BwO is a conjunction of parts, rather than an 'organised and integrated being' (Grosz 1994: 203).

As with a line of flight, bisexuality neither sets out from nor arrives at any given terminus; instead it arises from the middle. Chapter 5, for example, saw bisexuality emerge at the centre of the narrative quest ascribed to de Beauvoir. However, despite this seeping through the narrative, bisexuality is not constituted as a narrative identity – and this is precisely because there is no initial bisexual 'potential', a beginning, which could be actualised by the end of the narrative (so providing narrative continuity). In these biographical representations of de Beauvoir, de Beauvoir is neither possessed of bisexuality nor is she possessed by it: like all Bodies without Organs, the BwO of bisexuality is never subordinated to property, it is always *a* body, it 'is never yours or mine' (Deleuze and Guattari 1988: 164). The effect of the BwO of bisexuality is not simply to destratify the narrative ascribed to de Beauvoir however; it also deterritorialises the very theory which seeks to explain narrative identities. Ricoeur's theory of narrative suggests that identity-as-selfhood will always remain even without identity-as-sameness: yet bisexuality defies the logic which justifies this account by making its presence felt and simultaneously escaping the confines of a narrative identity.

Cutting across molar entities, the effect of the BwO is to deterritorialise the lines which stratify and produce identities organised around individuality, possession (of identity), material corporeality, visibility and sameness. Hence the BwO of bisexuality cannot be understood to be different from lesbianism and heterosexuality simply because it is not the same as them (this is the difference between 'x' and 'y'). As illustrated, the molecular BwO of bisexuality is not a copy of a copy, but a simulacrum: if it resembles lesbianism, then this resemblance is produced as an effect of a more fundamental difference. For example: it is *precisely* resemblance that ensures that bisexuality is recognised *just enough* to be in a position to intervene in processes of recognition and identification. Passing through the lesbian community, the BwO of bisexuality disrupts the molar line which suggests that the relation between representation and identity is mimetic. Deleuze and Guattari write, in relation to the BwO:

> You have to keep enough of the organism for it to reform each dawn; and you have to keep small supplies of signifiance and subjectification, if only to turn them against their own systems when the circumstances demand it, when things, persons, even situations, force you to; and you have to keep small rations of subjectivity in sufficient quantity to enable you to respond to the dominant reality. Mimic the strata. You don't reach the BwO . . . by wildly destratifying [. . .] the worst that can happen is if you throw the strata into demented or suicidal collapse, which brings them back down on us heavier than ever.   (Deleuze and Guattari 1988: 160–1)

The BwO of bisexuality is not an imitation of molar entities (which would suggest that it was basically the same as these molar entities). Rather, its effect is to mimic the stratifications which produce them and, in doing so, it *comes* to resemble them. Bisexuality appears, for instance, to be a part of the narrative ascribed to de Beauvoir by the biographers but then, *because* it is not produced as a narrative identity, it deterritorialises the very theory on which narrative identity is based. Similarly, bisexuality appears to be an identity that may be possessed but then, *because* it is not, it destratifies the presupposition that the relation between representation and identity is a smooth one.

Deleuze argues that it is not possible to anticipate in advance what a body is capable of, or what it will be able to do. It would not have been possible to anticipate that the resemblance between bisexuality and lesbianism, rather than pertaining to a basic sameness, is produced as an effect of a primary and unrecuperable difference, a simulation:

> Simulation is the production of an effect rather than the reproduction of an appearance. The effect in question may be an effect of resemblance, or may be produced by means of an effect of resemblance, but these have no particular privilege in the world of simulacra.   (Patton 1994: 155)

It is significant that the BwO of bisexuality is a field of production rather than expression. As Philip Goodchild notes, in Deleuze's thought: 'the unconscious processes [such as the BwO] that produce meaning will be of a different nature from the meanings produced – the unconscious is a place of production, not expression . . . meaning is purely a surface effect' (Goodchild 1996: 13–14). To create further meanings through the interpretation of what it is that we already 'know' cannot in itself transform thought.[27] As a simulacrum, by contrast, the BwO of bisexuality refers to 'gestures which develop before organised bodies [and] . . . masks before faces' (Deleuze 1994: 10).

If bisexuality *were* wholly destratified, then it would not be present in the texts I have analysed here at all, it would not be a BwO. Conversely, if bisexuality were not a BwO, it would not have the effect, as it does, of deterritorialising the presuppositions on which intelligible selfhood rest. This deterritorialisation occurs amid the specific formations that I have explored throughout this book, from the encounters between bisexuality and the techniques which contribute to the production of intelligible selfhood. These are encounters which serve to destabilise that production. These are the affects of which a Body without Organs of bisexuality is capable.

Conclusion

> The theory of thought is like painting: it needs that revolution which took art from representation to abstraction. This is the aim of a theory of thought without image.
>
> Gilles Deleuze, quoted in Paul Patton, 'Anti-Platonism and art'

In keeping with Foucault's genealogy, which examines not the history of the self but the historical processes by which the self comes to be established, I have outlined a number of techniques which serve to render the figure of de Beauvoir intelligible: individuality, narrative continuity, interiority, the ability to take responsibility for others as well as for oneself, materiality and visibility are among the techniques which have been explored here. Some of these techniques are understood, in a strict Foucauldian sense, to be practices through which the self establishes a particular relation to the self in the service of a desired state (such as authenticity). Others constitute the self through textually mediated narratives. Hence this study of bisexuality has illustrated not only how it is that bisexuality is produced through discourse, but also how the self itself is constituted and how the individuality ascribed to de Beauvoir is constructed. I have argued that it is precisely the production of de Beauvoir *as* an individual which precludes bisexuality from being produced as a property of the self. As it is constituted in the texts analysed here, bisexuality cannot be articulated in terms of 'selfhood' because in all manner of ways it exceeds the individuality conferred on de Beauvoir.

Given that bisexuals have frequently had to defend not merely, as Merl Storr argues, a bisexual politics and theory, but the very viability of bisexuality as a subject position (see chapter 1), it would be tempting to dispute the production of bisexuality outlined here, and to assert that Simone de Beauvoir is deserving of a place in an expanding gallery of bisexual figures. The move to claim bisexuality as an inhabitable, even desirable, subject position is compelled not only by psychic and social investments in identity (Dollimore 1996: 524), but also by political investments. For while the 'deconstruction' of identity and selfhood continues apace, identity nevertheless remains a key vehicle through which political battles are fought. This chapter thus returns to the debate which opened the book: how is it possible to highlight the contingency of processes of subjectification, without abandoning the subject entirely? It is in this context that Foucault's analytic has been deployed by theorists of identity and, indeed, I have used it throughout my own research to explore the different ways in which bisexuality is erased as a property of the self.

Although Foucault's work has been central to this study of selfhood and identity, and although I have repeatedly referred to his analysis of techniques of the self to explore both the construction of de Beauvoir and the erasure of bisexuality, I have not chosen to use either Foucault's notion of an aesthetics of the self, nor his brief mention of bodies and pleasures, in drawing my conclusions. This is because I have found the ethical value that Foucault, in his later work, accords to (an aesthetics of) the self problematic. Foucault's accent on the self in this regard sits uneasily with analyses such as my own, which seek to illustrate the high costs that processes of subjectification may incur. There is a tension here then, insofar as Foucault's 'solution' to the 'problem' of the self appears to be bound by the very theory (his own) which precedes it. It is worth exploring this tension briefly, and considering what a Deleuzian ethics might offer this analysis of bisexuality by comparison.

Making things do things

In his earlier works, Foucault describes the processes by which the self is disciplined and regulated, subject to and of techniques of individualisation and normalisation. Additionally, the self is tied to its own identity through conscience or self-knowledge: ceaselessly searching for the 'truth' of its self, the self binds itself still further to regimes of power/knowledge. Modern secular ethics are all the more horrifying, Foucault argues, because they are grounded not in religion but in the 'so-called scientific knowledge of what the self is, what desire is, what the unconscious is' (Foucault quoted in McNay 1994: 142).

One of the ways that Foucault attempts to negotiate the historical processes of normalisation is by advocating an aesthetics of existence, an aesthetics which obliges the individual endlessly to invent itself anew. As Lois McNay summarises it:

For the individual, freedom from normalizing forms of individuality consists in an exploration of the limits of subjectivity. By interrogating what are held to be necessary boundaries to identity or the limits of subjectivity, the possibility of transgressing these boundaries is established and, therefore, the potential of creating new types of subjective experience is opened up.   (McNay 1994: 145–6)

A question that the analysis of bisexuality and of de Beauvoir raises is whether the very technique which *delimits* and confines the self – individuality – can be held up as the vehicle through which the limits of the self are to be explored. As this study of the figure of de Beauvoir highlights, individuality has its costs: 'the costs of breeding an animal that could feel guilty and bear responsibility for itself and its conduct, against which it must pledge itself as guarantor' (N. Rose 1996: 322). It is difficult to imagine how a concept of the individual could be established without incurring such costs: self-knowledge, conscience, responsibility – as Foucault illustrates in his work and my own examples confirm – are profoundly bound up with processes of individualisation. Moreover, how would bisexuality, for example, which is not necessarily *intelligible* in terms of the self, fit into such a schema?

Although Foucault's notion of the individual who reinvents his or her self does not necessarily require that that individual, or its experiences, be privileged (for Foucault subjectification is a historically and culturally specific process which precedes interiority), Rosalyn Diprose (1994) argues that there is nevertheless a fundamental problem with Foucault's aesthetics of existence which illustrates the extent to which he confers primacy on the sovereign self. This problem is illustrated with reference to Foucault's analysis of the Ancient Greek techniques of the self which disqualified women from participating in an aesthetics of the self on two counts. Diprose argues that women were excluded, firstly, because moderation (perceived to be a necessary prerequisite for self-mastery) had an 'essentially masculine structure of active virility' (Diprose 1994: 30). Since the very notion of self-mastery depended upon a struggle to subordinate the womanly characteristic of *immoderation*, the value attributed to the male Greek body as a work of art was gained precisely through the denigration of the other. As Diprose's analysis highlights, the exclusion of women from the Ancient Greek ethics of the self is not simply an omission, but rather a *structural* necessity (Diprose 1994).

Women were also disqualified from participating in an aesthetics of existence because their use of pleasure was (and arguably, often still is) understood to be derived not from their own selves, but from their role as wife and mother. Women are again excluded then, since Foucault's aesthetics prioritises and maintains the relation with the self *over* the relation with others. As he says: 'One must not have the care for others precede the care for self. The care for self takes moral precedence on the measure that the relationship to self takes ontological precedence' (Foucault quoted in McNay 1994: 152).[1] The privileging of the self's relation to the self is problematic: it can be advocated, Beverley Skeggs argues, only by those who 'occupy the economic and cultural conditions which enable them to do the work on the self' (Skeggs 1997: 163):

> Yet the caring self, as it is lived and produced on a daily basis, is a gendered (classed and raced) self . . . The ontological precedence, outlined by Foucault, in the care of the self, is evidence of a bourgeois individualist practice. It is the prerogative of someone who does not have to care for others to be seen as worthy of respect.
> (Skeggs 1997: 64)

The White working-class women that Skeggs interviewed for example, do not 'feel a possessive relationship to their subjectivity . . . Their care of the self and the technologies they work on the self are not for self-mastery, as Foucault would suggest, but to generate dignity, deflect degradation *and* help others' (Skeggs 1997: 163).

Diprose and Skeggs, among other theorists, illustrate that the relation to the self described by Foucault is neither available to everyone, nor available to everyone in the same ways.[2] I would add that not only does Foucault privilege the relation with the self over the relation with others, but he additionally valorises this relation over any intrasubjective – or indeed non-subjective – experience. In other words, Foucault's intention appears not to be to deterritorialise the self, or the boundaries which divide self and other, so much as to realise the conditions under which the self would be 'free' to dominate itself.

Deleuze and Guattari recognise that sign and subject are the basis for systems of thought but, for them, they are not privileged terms but rather 'effects or consequences of processes of sedimentation, the congealing or coagulation of processes' (Grosz 1994: 191). Sedimentation or stratification gives rise to molar entities, such as the binary division of the sexes into men and women. Thus although, for example, they acknowledge that it is 'indispensable for women to conduct a molar politics', they add that 'it is dangerous to confine oneself to such a subject, which does not function without drying up a spring or stopping a flow' (Deleuze and Guattari 1988: 276).[3] To put that another way, while Deleuze and Guattari acknowledge that molar politics are, in some instances, necessary (as my account, in chapter 1, of the context in which a Euro-American bisexual politics has emerged and developed illustrates), they are also concerned with the effects of such a politics insofar as it might stifle the capacity of a body to affect and be affected, it might block what a body can *do*.[4] For Deleuze and Guattari, 'texts, concepts and subjects' *should* be 'put to work, made to do things' (Grosz 1994: 200). 'Making things do things' is therefore not simply a method but also an ethical objective (Grosz 1994; Mackenzie 1997). Elizabeth Grosz expands on the relation between Deleuze and Guattari's understanding of a body and ethics. She writes:

In the wake of Spinoza's understanding of ethics, ethics is conceived of as the capacity for action and passion, activity and passivity; good and bad refer to the ability to increase or decrease one's capacities and strengths and abilities . . . the question of ethics is raised whenever the question of a being's, or an assemblage's, capacities and abilities are raised.   (Grosz 1994: 196)

The ethics towards which Deleuze and Guattari gesture then is not, as in Foucault's aesthetics of existence, based on the self (a molar entity which is *already* organised). Instead, it concerns the effects of and on forces which *may or may not* have been regulated by the three strata. It is an ethics which is elastic enough to *address* identity politics, but which is not ultimately mediated by, or confined to, subjectivity and selfhood.

Foucault's privileging of the care of the self in his aesthetics appears to be too bound up with the very self that he seeks to critique: it is an ethics born of that self, a reinterpretation perhaps, but one that does not move far enough away from the analysis that Foucault himself began. For McNay, if the contemporary boundaries of subjectivity are to be transgressed, it will not take place by means of a philosophy that: 'posits an active self acting on an objectified world and interacting with other subjects who are defined as objects or narcissistic extensions of the primary subject' (McNay 1994: 153).

The perils of such a subject/object relationship have been outlined in some detail at the start of chapter 7 which also, along with chapter 2, has tried to show that theorisations of inter-, and even intra-, subjectivity frequently rely on some notion of a discrete entity and, consequently, an other upon whom it must depend to distinguish itself. As I noted in the second chapter, Diana Fuss introduces *Inside/Out* by claiming that the boundaries between inside and outside cannot be dispelled (Fuss 1991: 1). Both Butler and Braidotti suggest that, even though identity is relational, the 'I' must be understood to be a distinct existent. All these theorists rely on some notion of boundedness and subsequently introduce an other which resides 'outside' or beyond those boundaries. This frequently uneasy relation between self and other is no doubt exacerbated by the 'confusion' of communication and representation; it is a relation characterised most often by lack. Roy Boyne summarises the consequences of the split between subject and object thus:

Firstly, the disjunction between subject and object means that modern consciousness tends not to experience the world in its immediacy, inclining instead to understand it as a simulation or representation of something radically other . . . The second consequence is that . . . [i]f the subject can never directly experience the object, the desiring subject can never be truly satisfied: wanting and waiting constitute its interminable condition.   (Boyne 1990: 34)

Sharing similar concerns about the implications that follow from the subject/object divide, Elspeth Probyn argues that 'gay and lesbian theory' (Probyn 1995: 6) too frequently confines desire to the individual body, a body which is perceived to be both the source of desire and 'the place where it is incarnated' (Probyn 1995: 7). Indeed, she argues that to conceptualise desire as lack 'as the longing for an impossible object, is the condition of possibility for constructing desire as encapsulated within an [individualised] object' (Probyn 1995: 8). By contrast, Probyn advocates 'a difference in kind, a movement that cannot be founded, condensed in *a* lesbian body, *a* lesbian being, *a* lesbian experience or, even, *a* lesbian aesthetic' (Probyn 1995: 14).

Probyn's Deleuzian understanding of desire, as that which 'disconnects images and things' and which does not point 'to a person . . . [or] an individual' (ibid.), is realised in the BwO of bisexuality. The BwO of bisexuality has the effect of deterritorialising the proprietorial relation between sexuality and selfhood, of disrupting the assumption that identity necessarily inheres 'within' an organism and/or that it is necessarily immured to an individual. In this respect the notion of the BwO, and of desire as pure productivity – because it 'in no way privilege[s] the human, autonomous, sovereign subject; the independent other; or the bonds of communication and representation between them' (Grosz 1994: 197) – might well offer an alternative route, a line of flight, away from contemporary conceptions of the self. 'At stake is the end of the representational order, and the advent of machinic connection . . . flowing from one connection to the next, from one uninterrupted link to the next' (Boyne 1990: 42). This is the aim of a theory of thought without image that the epigraph at the start of this chapter called for:

The body without organs is not the proof of an original nothingness, nor is it what remains of a lost totality. Above all, it is not a projection; it has nothing whatsoever to do with the body itself, or with an image of the body. It is the body without an image.   (Deleuze and Guattari 1994: 8)

I have drawn on Deleuze and Guattari's work in the context of this study of de Beauvoir and of bisexuality because they not only render the implications of stratification available for analysis and critique but also, because of their accent on *flows* of forces, open up new ways of thinking about identity.[5] In other words, while a molar identity politics is *possible* within a Deleuzo-Guattarian framework, it is not the *only* option available to those concerned with the production of identity. The accent on forces which have *not* been territorialised offers the opportunity to explore alternative avenues of transformation and change, avenues which do not, necessarily, require recourse to subjectification (with all its attendant costs). While the BwO is neither inhabitable nor representable (which precludes any immediate 'access' to it), the deterritorialising effects that this assemblage produces are nevertheless available for scrutiny. What, then, does this body offer? Tracing a molecular path away from the presuppositions on which theories of identity based on representation rest, the BwO of bisexuality suggests that identities will not always be confined to the individual nor must relations always be constituted through a dependence on the other. Lesbianism and heterosexuality are not the 'other' through which a BwO of bisexuality is produced nor is the BwO of bisexuality itself an other against which another subjectivity is defined. Stratified neither by organism, significance or subjectification, a BwO of bisexuality cannot be conceived of in isolation (as a sovereign subject, for example) nor is there an 'outside' in which an external other might reside. However, although without an other, the BwO *always* exists in a relation (arising, as it does, from the middle).

There are gains to be had then, by following a line of enquiry which, firstly, seeks to explore the violence of identity (on self and other) and, secondly, considers the effects of decoupling identity and selfhood. The concept of the BwO enables the analysis of bisexuality to be moved along just such a path, one in which desire is no longer confined to the self and to the disciplinary exercises of subjectification. In short, a BwO of bisexuality destabilises the centrality accorded to self and other, subject and object, in theories of sexuality.

I chose an extract from Kathy Acker's *In Memoriam to Identity* to frame my account of bisexuality because Acker longs for something 'new'. This may be possible because, as the production of bisexuality in these texts illustrates, the BwO has the capacity to intervene in arenas which appear to be highly stratified. As Deleuze writes, 'there is no diagram that does not also include, besides the points which it connects up, certain relatively free or unbound points, points of creativity, change and resistance, and it is perhaps with these that we ought to begin' (Deleuze 1988: 44). It may ultimately be a BwO of bisexuality, rather than a bisexual self, that will begin to be able to *do* things or to make things happen.

Notes

Introduction

1 The analysis was confined to English language texts and covered the period
   1980–94.

2 This indicates that it is possible to identify discursive features which *transverse*
   the individual genres and subsume the specificity of de Beauvoir within them.
   It remains the case however, that de Beauvoir is a woman and therefore that the
   representations of bisexuality which are analysed here are specifically gendered.
   As I will illustrate, a number of techniques of the self are themselves affected,
   to a greater or lesser degree, by gender. This is certainly the case with Foucault's
   author-function for example. I will be arguing (in chapter 3) that the status of
   the author is mediated by, and will vary according to, the author's gender.

3 By 'West' and 'Western' I broadly mean what Marilyn Strathern calls 'Euro-
   American'. This term, as she says, is 'both wider and narrower than anything
   one might wish to attribute to the citizens of Northern Europe and North
   America' (Strathern 1997: 40) and refers not to the citizens *per se*, but to Euro-
   American discourses.

4 See M. Fraser (1998) for an analysis of the implications of the often competing
   ways in which identities are perceived to be produced.

1 Identity and selfhood

1 I am sketching out this complex debate between 'essentialism' and 'constructionism'/'constructivism' in very broad brush strokes. By contrast, in *Essentially
   Speaking,* Diana Fuss illustrates how and why there may be considerable overlap
   between these apparently polarised positions. She argues for example, that:
   'there is no compelling reason to assume that the natural is, in essence, essentialist and that the social is, in essence, constructionist . . . In other words, it may be
   time to ask whether essences can change and whether constructions can be normative' (Fuss 1989: 6).

2 The reflexivity of this 'identity-work' goes some way to account for the fact that

so many of the texts on de Beauvoir are also feminist texts. Not only does de Beauvoir's work contribute to these debates – *The Second Sex*, for example, is often understood to be a landmark in the theorisation of women as 'other' – but her life, too, is source of considerable interest (as well as the relation, as I will illustrate, between her life and work). However, given the recent debates which have emerged between feminists who focus on sexual difference and those who prefer to theorise gender (Butler 1994: 15–22 and Braidotti with Butler 1994: 27–61), perhaps it is more accurate to suggest not, as Braidotti does, that a history of Western feminism has focused on sexual difference, but that one strand of European feminism, as distinct from some American feminisms, have centred their analyses on sexual difference. It is difficult however, to mark out clear theoretical and political differences between feminists and feminisms. Unlike Braidotti, Elizabeth Grosz argues that de Beauvoir, for instance, is a feminist of equality rather than a feminist of difference (Grosz 1995: 50–4).

3 Although, as Fuss notes, it is possible to see politics itself rather than the category 'woman' as the basis for, or, as she puts it, the 'essence' of, a feminist politics (Fuss 1989: 37).

4 See Lury (1997) who situates reversals of this kind within a broader cultural context, one in which, notably, the concept 'I think therefore I am' is replaced by 'I can therefore I am' with all its attendant privileging of choice in the construction of identity and selfhood.

5 Elizabeth Grosz usefully distinguishes between essentialism, biologism, naturalism and universalism as they have been applied to the category 'woman' (Grosz 1995: 47–9). Although there are important differences between these positions, they all 'refer to necessarily ahistorical qualities . . . confuse social relations with fixed attributes . . . see these fixed attributes as inherent limitations to social change; and . . . refuse to take seriously the historical and geographical differences between women' (Grosz 1995: 49).

6 Although the relation between 'what we see and what we know' (Berger 1972: 7) is contested, thought in Western philosophy has been largely guided by a visual paradigm (Jay 1992, 1993). As Chris Jenks puts it: 'Looking, seeing and knowing have become perilously intertwined' (Jenks 1995a: 1). Broadly speaking then, we know only what we think we can see and are able to see only what we are able to know. Foucault is not the first to acknowledge the role of the visible in Western societies and, as Martin Jay (1994) points out, he shares with a number of French thinkers a tendency both to privilege visibilities and at the same time to 'denigrate' them. Nevertheless, Foucault's work contributes to an understanding of the importance of the visible in a number of ways, including scientific representations of the human body (Foucault 1976). His notion of the Panopticon, a 'dark inspection tower' (Jenks 1995b: 149), has come to signify 'the metaphoric import of standing for a regime of rapid, mobile, calculating power that transforms from an external reality to an internalised phantasmagoria – the ideology of modernity – "a vision"' (ibid.). Foucault's politics of surveillance sits alongside a large body of literature on 'the gaze' which has been developed in psychoanalysis and by feminists (Mulvey 1975; Doane 1982; Dyer

1982; hooks 1993; Neale 1983; Stacey 1988). I will consider some of the implications of Foucault's analysis of the visible, as they have been drawn out by feminists, in the following chapter.

7 Referring to Foucault's point in *The Order of Things* (1994), that 'we do not speak of what we see, or see that of which we speak' (Deleuze 1988: 67), Deleuze notes that the visible and the articulable are irreducible to each other (see Deleuze 1988: 58–69 on the relation (or non-relation) between systems of language and systems of light and also Foucault 1983).

8 Where the first volume of *The History of Sexuality* (1990a) is concerned with 'a history of the experience of sexuality, where experience is understood as the correlation between fields of knowledge, types of normativity, and forms of subjectivity' (Foucault quoted in Probyn 1993: 121), the second and third volumes – *The Use of Pleasure* (1992b) and *The Care of the Self* (1990b) – focus on the relation of the self to the self, and the theories and practices which organize this relation. The first volume of this work may thus be viewed as part of a shift from the analysis of external techniques of control (the prison, the asylum) to techniques of self-management (Hutton 1988: 130. But see also Valverde (1996) who argues that ethical liberal self-governance is characterised by unevenness and frequently includes 'despotic', non-liberal and even illiberal modalities).

9 Foucault argues that history does not progress as a smooth process of maturation, but is rather marked by discontinuities. His aim however, is not to emphasise discontinuity as an end in itself – '[m]y problem was not at all to say, "*Voilà*, long live discontinuity . . . and a good thing too"' – but rather to employ it as a means to consider how 'at certain moments and in certain orders of knowledge, there are these sudden take-offs, these hastenings of evolution, these transformations which fail to correspond to the calm, continuist image that is normally accredited' (Foucault 1991c: 54).

10 Although this analysis of subjectification appears to fall back on the two axes of knowledge and power, Deleuze argues that while folds 'are apt to unfold and merge' (Deleuze 1988: 105) with knowledge and power, they do not do so 'without new foldings being created in the process' (ibid.). Constantin V. Boundas writes: 'the outside is never exhausted; every attempt to capture it generates an excess or a supplement' (Boundas 1994: 115). Consequently, '[t]here never "remains" anything of the subject, since he is to be created on each occasion' (Deleuze 1988: 105).

11 This is not least because, if power passes 'through the dominated forces no less than through the dominating' (Deleuze 1988: 27) (as it must, if it is expressed as a *relation* between forces rather than being understood as emanating from a central source), then there can be no 'authentic' sexuality which lies, uncontaminated, beyond the bounds of discourse and which, by implication, is able to 'oppose' or 'resist' power. Resistance, Foucault argues, 'is never in a relation of exteriority in relation to power' (Foucault 1990a: 95).

12 This notion, that the bisexual subject/bisexuality has existed 'continuously' throughout history, is especially clearly demonstrated in Garber's book *Vice*

Versa (1996) which documents 'bisexuality' in 'everyday life' across a range of centuries. See Storr for a critique of Garber's 'totalising and reductive' (Storr 1997a: 13) approach to bisexuality.

13 In this respect, Foucault's ontology is historical because, although the relations of knowledge, power and self do not vary historically, they do, given certain conditions, 'vary *with* history' (Deleuze 1988: 114):

> This is why he [Foucault] calls his work historical research and not the work of a historian . . . He does not write a history of private life but of the conditions governing the way in which the relation to oneself consti-tutes a private life.   (Deleuze 1988: 116)

Hence it is not the fold itself, but the way it comes to be folded, which is of interest.

14 An interesting interpretation, if it is the case that many 'contemporary bisexual theorists have been eager to locate bisexuality as a *sexual* orientation rather than as a *gendered* identity, and in particular to distinguish bisexuality from androg-yny' (Storr 1997a: 19). Storr goes on, rightly I think, to query the distinction between the sexual and the gendered (see chapter 4, this volume).

15 Which is not to suggest that identity and desire are in opposition: not *all* iden-tities will necessarily have the effect of sedimenting desire.

16 Hostility towards bisexuals, perhaps as a result of increased visibility, was demonstrated by Labour MP David Blunkett who voted against an equal homo-sexual age of consent specifically because he disapproved of bisexuality. See Storr (1998) for more details of this and other examples.

17 Deleuze specifies four folds altogether 'whose variations constitute irreducible modes of subjectivation' (Deleuze 1988: 104–5).

18 It is ironic that Ricoeur's distinction between identity-as-selfhood and identity-as-sameness should enable me to illustrate this point since he assumes that iden-tity-as-selfhood cannot be displaced. It is this assumption, I will argue, that reveals an over-arching individualism in his work (see chapter 4). In order to negotiate this, it should be noted that I am taking narrative identity to be *only one* of the practices by which a relation to the self is established (see also note 19).

19 Indeed, the very concept of narrative will be understood as a product of dis-course.

20 The year 1990 saw the publication of de Beauvoir's letters to Sartre in French, followed by an English translation of the same in 1991. Covering the period 1930–63, these letters document de Beauvoir's relationships with women as well as with men.

21 Four biographies were chosen from those published between 1980 and 1994. Francis and Gontier's (1987), which was published before de Beauvoir's letters to Sartre were in print, was chosen as a representative of accounts aimed at a popular audience, while Margaret Crosland's (1992) biography has a popular feminist slant and incorporates de Beauvoir's letters into the narrative.

Fullbrook and Fullbrook's (1993) biography bridges the popular and the academic and is distinguished by its explicit concern with de Beauvoir's letters to Sartre. Finally, Toril Moi's study of de Beauvoir (1994), which is little concerned with the letters, is an academic 'personal genealogy' rather than a biography and, as such, provides a fruitful point of contrast and comparison.

22 To suggest that commentaries on de Beauvoir's life and work are as productive of ('her') selfhood as the work of the author herself, is to displace the hierarchy between de Beauvoir's 'primary' texts and 'secondary' criticism. Indeed, I have chosen not to examine de Beauvoir's own production of the self at all.

23 Given that bisexuality is not produced, in the texts explored here, in the same way that lesbianism and heterosexuality are, I will not initially offer a definition of what it 'is'. But based on the analysis throughout, I will draw some conclusions as to the 'difference' of bisexuality in chapters 7 and 8.

2 Identity and embodiment

1 It should be noted however, that even if Foucault's analysis is not universalistic, it is nevertheless Eurocentric. Although Deleuze suggests that Foucault 'never considered himself sufficiently competent to treat the subject of Oriental forms of development' (Deleuze 1988: 148n), he still (despite not considering 'Oriental' techniques) posits an ontology (even if historical) which implies that the processes of subjectification are the same the world over. The very term 'Oriental' has a long history which Edward Said charts in *Orientalism* (1978). He writes: 'I refer my reader to my study of what I have called Orientalism for details and for an account of a long, consistent history which culminates today in the fact, for example, that practically the *only* ethnic group about whom in the West racial slurs are tolerated, even encouraged, is the Arabs' (Said 1992: 26).

2 Feminists who draw on Foucault, in varying degrees, include, for example, Rosi Braidotti (1991, 1994), Judith Butler (1993), Lois McNay (1992, 1994), Elspeth Probyn (1993) and Jana Sawicki (1991). Although these writers find much that is productive in Foucault's work, none of them are without their criticisms of it.

3 See Fraser (1998) where I explore the implications of this in more detail.

4 In a footnote immediately following a similar definition of a performative act in the introduction to *Bodies That Matter*, Butler acknowledges her debt to J. L. Austin (Butler 1993: 246). Austin argues that speech has both a constative and a performative element. The former describes the world, while the latter enacts the activity that the speech signifies.

5 Notably, neither power, nor the subject 'acts'; rather there is 'only a reiterated acting that is power in its persistence and instability' (Butler 1993: 9).

6 Rosemary Hennessey (1995) argues that Butler does not in fact 'historicise' the signifier, but rather merely situates it in an historical context. I will return to Hennessey's critique below.

7 Butler herself acknowledges that 'a regime-theory of sexuality . . . would include

psychoanalysis itself as one of its regulatory modes' (Butler 1994: 13). I will explore some of the ways in which psychoanalysis preserves the notion of the individual in more detail in chapter 3.

8 The notion of a self-sufficient self, independent of others, is a feature of the Cartesian formulation of subjectivity which psychoanalysis, among other theories of the self, has sought to displace. Descartes believed that mind and body are different 'substances' and that, because the mind is located within the body, it is only available through introspection: 'The very assumptions that underpin this question [as to how one may know any mind other than one's own exists] somewhat preempt the answer that can be given: if minds can only be known from within then each mind can only know itself for certain' (Crossley 1995: 142).

9 See Butler 1993, pages 3 and 8, for her definition of abjection. In a footnote Butler refers the reader to Kristeva's notion of abjection which offers a 'different but related' (Butler 1993: 244) approach to 'this problematic of exclusion, abjection, and the creation of "the human"' (ibid.).

10 It is as difficult to identify a body of 'queer texts' as it is to identify a queer body. I have chosen to focus on the edited collection *Inside/Out* largely because it was the first 'showcase' (Fuss 1991: 1) for this kind of theorising.

11 I will return to this point and explore it in more detail in chapters 7 and 8.

12 Foucault contrasts the identification of the homosexual as a species to the notion of homosexuality as acts whereby the perpetrator is 'nothing more than the juridical subject of them' (Foucault 1990a: 43).

13 Which is not to suggest that bisexuality is absent from these texts, only that it is not produced as an identity which coheres in a self.

14 Huck Gutman makes the relation between boundaries and the self clear. He writes:

> For a 'me' to emerge, a distinction must be made between the 'me' and the 'not-me'. The boundaries of the self are those lines that divide the self from all that which is not the self, which is beyond the self. The first, and essential, move in the constitution of the self is division.
>
> (Gutman 1988: 107)

15 Although Elspeth Probyn argues that it is precisely Butler's use of psychoanalysis which reinstates the centrality of the individual. Probyn suggests that while 'Butler does an admirable job of dislodging sex as origin she does not quite manage to shift desire from its Lacanian position as that which circulates endlessly and compulsively around its constituted object' (Probyn 1995: 4). Hence desire is confined to an unfulfilled longing for 'one individual-object' (Probyn 1995: 8). (See chapters 7 and 8 for an alternative, Deleuzian, conception of desire, one which is neither characterised by lack nor anchored around an individual-object.)

16 Which is often perceived to 'end' at the skin. As Jackie Stacey notes: 'the skin [is] a particularly significant part of the body in its role as interface between

inside and outside; [Kristeva] writes of the skin that it is "the essential if not the initial boundary of biological and psychic individuation"' (Stacey 1997: 254n. But see Haraway 1991).

17 Although Butler is an influential queer theorist, the accent on embodiment and the contemporary focus on material corporeality has a broader context, as Braidotti (see below) illustrates.

18 This is not to suggest however, that either the visible or the material are reducible to the seeable. As noted in the first chapter, the visible constitutes an important (if fraught) part of Foucault's materialist analysis of discourse and refers not merely to empirical bodies and things, but also to 'knowledges – discourses, significations, modes of intelligibility – by which identity is constituted' (Hennessey 1995: 148). Equally, the seeable does not constitute the whole of the material. For Marx, the material refers to the human labour which goes into the production of objects but which is 'not visible in the objects themselves as a physical property' (Hennessey 1995: 161). In this respect the material exceeds the seeable.

19 Queer activism, and particularly the emphasis on the queer body, may be seen to be continuing the tradition of 'making visible' which has characterised a number of political movements (especially those based around identity) since the 1960s. Slogans such as 'Out and Proud' or 'Black is Beautiful' bear witness to the belief that visibility is a source of power. The catchword 'Visi**BI**lity', which was printed on T-shirts and badges at the recent 11th National Bisexual Conference in Britain, encapsulates the investment in visible representation in a word.

20 Whereas in Christian moral systems modes of subjectification were established through the individual's relation to externally imposed moral codes, in Ancient Greek systems the accent lay on self-mastery. Domination is an issue in each, but in the latter, the emphasis lies on self-domination. Boundas writes: 'When the Greeks decided that the mastery of others must go through the mastery of oneself, the folding of outside forces by means of a series of practical exercises was already on its way' (Boundas 1994: 114).

21 This suggests that the notion of 'freedom' cannot necessarily be easily transposed from one age to another. The Greek ethics of the self, for example, depended on a clear separation between those selves who were free to dominate the self and the rest of society 'who were totally dominated' (Thacker 1993: 17). As Braidotti points out, women were excluded from these practices since they were neither desiring subjects nor civil subjects (Braidotti 1991: 96). Thus, 'the theoretical distinction that Foucault wishes to uphold between power and domination might only make sense in a Greek world' (Thacker 1993: 17). This is also a significant issue in the context of the argument presented throughout this book because it indicates the extent to which Foucault's aesthetics of existence is dependent upon a division between self and other. I will return to this point in chapter 8, in the context of my own critique of Foucault.

22 Nancy Fraser, similarly, suggests that Butler's theory of performativity is:

not well suited to the crucial work of articulation, contextualization, and provisional totalization. It does not, for example, help us to map the links among various discrete discursive regimes and thus to theorise the construction of hegemony. Nor does it help us to contextualize – and thereby to realistically assess – the seemingly expansive, gender-bending performative possibilities of everyday life in relation to structural dynamics involving large-scale institutions, such as states and economies.

(N. Fraser 1995b: 163)

(But see M. Fraser (1998) where I argue that Butler's more recent work, and particularly her use of Bourdieu's notion of the habitus (1997), could go some way to addressing the relation between large-scale issues of 'social and economic justice' (Butler 1995b: 141) and the production of subjectivities.)

23 It should be noted however, that Butler displaces any notion of individual intentionality. In *Gender Trouble* she explicitly states that her analysis does not represent 'a return to an existential theory of the self as constituted through its acts, for the existential theory maintains a pre-discursive structure for both the self and the acts' (Butler 1990: 142).

24 Which is not to suggest that poorer segments of society do not participate in consumer culture (Lury 1996). Mike Featherstone (1991) also demonstrates the relation between lifestylisation and class while Susan Willis (1990) and Les Back and Vibeke Quaade (1993), for example, have documented its relation to race. Janice Winship (1983) and Rachel Bowlby (1985) look at the implications of consumer culture in the production of feminine identities.

25 The 'American mythos' sits particularly well with lifestylisation insofar as both imply that there is no aspect of the self which cannot in some way be altered or 'overcome'. Celia Lury (1996) shows how Benetton, for example, figures skin colour as a choice comparable and equal to the choice of cloth colour. Although this implies that identities are not bound by 'essences', given that it is the self who must work at itself and who must 'choose', the notion of an essential 'core' (who works, who chooses) is reinscribed.

26 Mike Featherstone *et al.* (1995), Chris Shilling (1994) and Bryan Turner (1992, 1995) all explore the implications of this shift in thinking for sociology.

27 Judith Butler criticises Foucault's analysis of bio-power, arguing that he seeks to replace kinship as the organising structure of sexuality in favour of state-sponsored efforts to control the population and medicalise sexuality (Butler 1994: 13). Her critique of this shift in emphasis is (at least) threefold (Butler 1994: 12–15). She argues, firstly, that it is a sweeping generalisation to suggest that the role of kinship in organising sexuality has been entirely superseded; secondly, that state-sponsored controls of sexuality themselves deploy and reconfigure forms of kinship; and thirdly, that the move away from kinship is coupled with a turn from psychoanalysis and, as such, represents: 'the desire to desire beyond the psyche, beyond the traces of kinship that psyches bear' (Butler 1994: 15). In short, Butler is arguing that a radical separation of kinship and sexuality is not only implausible but also politically undesirable.

28 The pregnant body is particularly troublesome in the eyes of an economy where 'to *see* is the primary act of knowledge and *the gaze* the basis of all epistemic awareness' because it is 'capable of defeating the notion of fixed *bodily form*, of visible, recognizable, clear, and distinct shapes . . . which marks the contour of the body' (Braidotti 1994: 80).

29 Braidotti is playing on Deleuze and Guattari's notion of Bodies without Organs.

30 Barbara Creed (1987) and Mary Ann Doane (1990) also offer fascinating accounts of the relation between new (reproductive) technologies, the female body and visibility in popular films. Doane and Braidotti (explicitly) and Creed (implicitly) link the anxiety surrounding this new technology to the post-modern fear and fascination with the loss of origins.

31 For other points of agreement and disagreement between Braidotti and Butler, see their discussion in the special edition of *differences* on feminism and queer theory (Braidotti with Butler 1994).

32 Making this point explicit, Braidotti writes: 'Identity bears a privileged bond to unconscious processes – which are imbricated with the corporeal' (Braidotti with Butler 1994: 40; and also, for example, Braidotti 1994: 103).

33 'Affects' may be understood in terms of a body's potentiality, what it may potentially do. For instance:

> Deleuze cites the example of a tick, an insect with only three capacities: to climb upwards towards the light into the branches of trees; to smell a passing mammal and fall upon it; and to seek the warmest area of the mammal in order to suck its blood . . . If there is no tree available, or if no mammal arrives on time, the tick will die. Such potentials or habits are called 'affects'.   (Goodchild 1996: 34)

The difference between affects and forces may be understood as one of connotation: in the former, implied agency, or a sense of 'good' and 'bad', is displaced.

34 The plane of immanence may be understood, in this context, as the level at which things are able to be affected. For a more thorough and detailed explanation however, see MacKenzie (1997).

35 Although feminists might be included among those who have focused on the body at the expense of other aspects of selfhood, they have nevertheless offered, within this context, a weighty critique of Foucault's work often arguing, for example, that Foucault ignores the differences between *bodies* in favour of an analysis which rests on the unity of *the* body. Sandra Bartky suggests that Foucault 'is blind to those disciplines that produce a modality of embodiment that is peculiarly feminine . . . even though a liberatory note is sounded in Foucault's critique of power, his analysis as a whole reproduces that sexism which is endemic throughout Western political theory' (Bartky 1990: 65). Braidotti suggests that Foucault's gender blindness 'constitutes a scientific error, an unsatisfactory, inaccurate theory' (Braidotti 1991: 96). It is indeed remarkable, as Braidotti argues, that Foucault has focused so intensely on power, the

body and sexuality and yet simultaneously has so little to say about pregnancy, birth control or lesbianism (Braidotti 1991: 86).

3 Telling tales

1 My use of the terms preclusion and displacement specifically are employed to refer to the different ways in which bisexuality is constituted through discourse: preclusion recalls temporality, which befits the analysis of narrative, while displacement, which I employ in the chapter on 'framing', finds resonance with spatial techniques of identity.

2 The author-function, narrative and a theory of frames (see chapter 5) are the three modes of analysis which will be *systematically* employed throughout this study of bisexuality and of de Beauvoir.

3 Not all texts have an author (indicating that the name of the author does not function in the same way as a proper name), nor is the author-function constant or manifest in all discourses (Foucault 1979a: 19–20).

4 The author, in this context, does not denote 'an actual individual' (Foucault 1979a: 23) however. Rather, the author-function makes three independent subject positions or 'egos' available in discourse: the 'real' individual, the author and the fictional narrator. None of these can be collapsed with each other.

5 But see my qualifications and critiques of Ricoeur's theory of narrative identity in chapters 1 and 4.

6 A characteristic which can be traced back to feminism's problematization of the self, as noted in chapters 1 and 2.

7 The role played by 'History' in negating this responsibility, and thereby itself assuming the role of 'author', will be explored in chapters 5 and 6.

8 That is, prior to the author's death. The issue here is material which was not published during de Beauvoir's lifetime and which, therefore, she is assumed not to have had a hand in editing. I will return to this point below.

9 Significantly, Simons draws attention to the fact that these manuscripts, which covered the period 1928–45, were made available exclusively to scholars (Simons 1992: 140). This serves to emphasise her own authority and expertise as a commentator, an issue to which I will return below.

10 Fullbrook and Fullbrook's title, *Simone de Beauvoir and Jean-Paul Sartre: The Remaking of a Twentieth Century Legend*, refers both to what the biographers believe was de Beauvoir's conscious creation of a 'legend' out of Sartre as well as to their own 'correction' of it.

11 Notably, both Simons (see above) and Francis and Gontier refer to the 'style' of de Beauvoir's handwriting which confers a note of 'authenticity' on their evidence. Moreover, each description of de Beauvoir's script corresponds to the point the biographer is making: Simons, concerned with the subterfuge and intrigue of de Beauvoir's lesbian relationships, finds her writing 'illegible'. Francis and Gontier, in the context of love letters, describe it as 'delicate' which suggests innocence, fragility and vulnerability.

12 Evans also comments however that:

> To write is to assert oneself, one's Self. It implies, therefore, authority, a sense of justification. But what if the Self one wishes to assert turns out to be confused, guilty and soiled? In that case, writing becomes an exhibition of just those qualities one wishes most to hide.   (Evans 1986: 84)

For Evans then, de Beauvoir's writings signify *both* a technique of the self (where, as in the newspaper extracts above, 'to write' enables her to 'assert', 'justify' and establish a relation to the self) *and* the vehicle through which the 'truth' of her self is inadvertently revealed.

13 It is arguable that even though Moi rejects the conventional biographical genre, her account of de Beauvoir's life and work is nevertheless loosely structured by a biographical narrative. For example: in Part I of her book, she explores the 'subjective' and 'objective ... factors' (Moi 1994: 19) in de Beauvoir's childhood that resulted both in the decision to become a writer rather than a philosopher and that led her to 'define herself as second only to Sartre' (ibid.). In Part II, although Moi does not chart each 'factual' event in de Beauvoir's life, many of these emerge through her analysis of how the tensions described in Part I are played out in de Beauvoir's major texts. The final part of Moi's book does not examine de Beauvoir's 'actual' death, but rather examines her lifelong attitudes to death and depression.

14 Psychoanalysis has a particular link with writing insofar as it perceives the unconscious to be structured by language.

15 Freud's primary method: the interpretation of dreams, jokes, slips of the tongue.

16 Given the role conferred on sex and sexuality in expressing the 'truth' of the self, it is surely fitting that it is de Beauvoir's 'flawed' virginity *specifically* which is perceived to threaten the entire edifice of the de Beauvoir/Sartre myth.

17 My summary of what these accounts perceive de Beauvoir to 'be' (a feminist, a lover, a superior thinker, a philosophical Other) is somewhat reductive: this is obviously not *all* that de Beauvoir 'is' in these books. However, they are the dominant features ascribed to de Beauvoir in each account and therefore, for the sake of brevity, I will be focusing almost exclusively on these particular representations.

18 According to the terms of this pact, de Beauvoir and Sartre 'agree' (although the nature of this agreement is in question) that, while their love is 'essential', they would also be 'free' to have 'contingent' loves. Because the pact has two parts, it is sometimes referred to as though there were two pacts.

19 Which is not to suggest that the biographies are without ruptures in the narrative.

20 This is the second time in this chapter that letters have played a resuscitating role after death. See above, where Crosland argues that the posthumous publication of de Beauvoir's letters to Sartre allows for a 'deeper' understanding of her life.

21 Francis and Gontier are not alone in using the mirror metaphor to describe de Beauvoir's relationships with others. I will be returning to a very different use of this metaphor, in the context of same-sex relationships, in the following chapter.

22 By the end of the book this imputed individuality transcends almost *every* social grouping. The final words, echoing those in the first chapter, read: 'When she was a little girl she had insisted that she was not a "child", like other children, she did not want to be a member of a group, a race, or like other people. *J'étais moi,* she insisted, and repeated the phrase years later. "I was myself". She was unique' (Crosland 1992: 429).

23 Crosland generally downplays the role of the family, except insofar as it provides the focus for de Beauvoir's 'feminist' rebellion (see for example Crosland 1992: 41). This slant on feminist 'rebellion' however, which requires a rejection of the family, says more about Crosland than it does about feminism *per se*. The role of the family as a support network for black women has been documented, for example, in Toubia (1988) and Shaaban (1988).

24 Foucault notes that contemplation of the self is an important technique of the self (see chapter 1).

25 In a number of commentaries, as in this extract, Sartre is almost always present even when his influence is supposedly being negated.

26 As noted in chapter 2, '[t]he first, and essential, move in the constitution of the self is division' (Gutman 1988: 107). This division encompasses 'self and other, me and not-me, individual and society' (Gutman 1988: 116).

27 See above in this chapter and Foucault (1979a: 22) on this point and its relation to the author-function.

28 The conscious existent, or transcendent self, is called *Being-for-Itself* and is distinguished from *Being-in-Itself* which simply and unambiguously 'exists' without consciousness. While for-itself and in-itself are not in opposition (since the former, in order to come into being, is dependent on the latter to the extent that it 'is' only what it distinguishes itself from), the gap between them is unbridgeable: the for-itself destroys the in-itself in order to exist. Hence being is negatively constituted (it is 'nothing' but what it is not) and conscious and nonconscious beings are fundamentally divided by 'being able and not being able to conceive of *what is not the case*' (Warnock 1967: 21).

29 See Butler (1986) for an account of the differences between Sartre and de Beauvoir's existentialisms.

30 Where Freud writes of unconscious repression, Sartre writes of falsehoods (Tong 1989: 199) which enable people to deny their responsibility.

31 Fullbrook and Fullbrook's biography also only goes up to the 1940s, although this is because it is the first volume of two. At the time of writing, the second had yet to be published.

32 The communal act of narrative repetition illustrates that the transmission of a heritage of potentialities occurs not only from the self to the self, but also 'from *another* to the *self*' (Ricoeur 1980: 188).

4 Preclusion

1 Moi's account is the exception here, although even without reciprocity, de Beauvoir appears to be possessed of a heterosexual identity.

2 This calls Monique Wittig's (1992) analysis of sex as gender to mind. Wittig argues that heterosexuality itself produces the categories 'man' and 'woman' and that a lesbian, because she is not engaged in the heterosexual economy, cannot be understood to be a woman 'either economically, or politically, or ideologically' (Wittig 1992: 20). As will be clear below though, Crosland does not share the complexity of Wittig's analysis, nor her political intentions. Indeed, her question is more closely aligned to a common fear, as Barbara Creed puts it, that 'the lesbian is really a man trapped in a woman's body' (Creed 1995: 88). In this respect, her narrative finds some resonance with the 'narrative of the tomboy . . . in which feminine sexuality is put into crisis and finally recuperated into the dominant patriarchal order' (ibid.). See the section on sex and gender, below, for more details on this.

3 I have defined androgyny in terms of both male and masculine and female and feminine characteristics because Crosland never quite makes clear what she perceives the difference to be.

4 The only occasion, in a same-sex relationship, where de Beauvoir is portrayed as the more emotionally dependent partner is with Elizabeth Lacoin (better known as Zaza in her memoirs). De Beauvoir's 'violent passion' (Crosland 1992: 38) for Zaza not only alienates her sister who she was reportedly extremely close to (Crosland 1992: 39), but also threatens her individuality (Crosland 1992: 96). However, Crosland insists that although the relationship was 'intense', this intensity was only 'on Simone's side' (Crosland 1992: 36); de Beauvoir's 'admiration . . . was not reciprocated' (Crosland 1992: 38). Given that Zaza does not appear to reciprocate de Beauvoir's feelings in any way, it is possible ('acceptable', as Ricoeur might put it), for Crosland to assert that this was 'no quasi-sexual relationship' (Crosland 1992: 37); 'there were no kisses, except at the end of letters' (Crosland 1992: 36). Hence while de Beauvoir's relationship with Zaza is distinguished from other same-sex relationships insofar as it is *de Beauvoir* who is 'subjugated' (Crosland 1992: 96) by another woman, like her other same-sex affairs it is characterised by a lack of reciprocity of feeling. A similar portrait of this relationship can be found in Francis and Gontier's account (see Francis and Gontier 1987: 40–1, 56, 60, 83 for example).

5 This is also witnessed in Moi's account where she writes (with near disbelief) that de Beauvoir 'denies that Nathalie Sokorine is a lesbian, in spite of the fact that she herself carried on an unusually tempestuous relationship with [her]'. (Moi 1994: 201). What Moi is arguing here is that Sokorine could be perceived as lesbian even though she had relationships with men, and that de Beauvoir should acknowledge this, particularly given that she herself had an affair with her. Significantly, Moi refers to *Sokorine* rather than de Beauvoir in order to illustrate her argument, even though her point could have been demonstrated with reference to de Beauvoir herself. In other words, even though de Beauvoir was involved in the very same relationship which supports Moi's point (that one can be lesbian and also have relationships with men), Moi nevertheless chooses to attribute a lesbian identity to Sokorine. The story thus 'belongs' to Sokorine and is constitutive of her, rather than de Beauvoir's, sexual-narrative-identity.

6 This is not to suggest that Crosland is not engaged in acts of appraisal. The production of what is 'good', as Ricoeur puts it, emerges through the very process by which de Beauvoir is constituted as heterosexual. In other words, while any sexuality other than heterosexuality is not directly condemned, the preclusion of either bisexuality or lesbianism as a possibility itself appears as a judgement. This supports the notion that Ricoeur 'adopts the deeply unfashionable position that narrative is prescriptive . . . and permits a direct transition to the realm of ethics: "Every well-made story teaches something"' (S. H. Clark 1995: 2).

7 The complex relationship between conscious choice, responsibility and appraisal/evaluation will be explored in more detail in chapter 6.

8 As above, the notion that de Beauvoir had to 'submit' to these women suggests that these relationships took place almost against her will. At the very least, it suggests that she passively accepted them.

9 See Crosland on de Beauvoir's relationship with Jacque-Laurent Bost for example, or Francis and Gontier's representation of her affair with Claude Lanzmann.

10 It is notable that Moi finds an almost direct expression of de Beauvoir's relationship with Algren in a single text. Indeed, a distinguishing feature of Moi's account of de Beauvoir's sexuality is that she draws substantially on the 'facts' of de Beauvoir's 'personal' life (see for example pages 200–1). It seems to be sexuality, and sexuality alone, which disrupts both Moi's epistemology and her methodology and justifies a prioritisation of one text over another – a method of reading which Moi rejects and otherwise successfully avoids.

11 Although it has been documented that Le Bon had been involved, in some way, with de Beauvoir since the 1960s, she gets short shrift in both Francis and Gontier's and Crosland's biographies. Le Bon is also barely mentioned in Fullbrook and Fullbrook's and Moi's accounts, although this is likely to be because neither is concerned with de Beauvoir's life after the 1940s.

12 As I outlined in chapter 2, a number of feminists have sought to 'denaturalise' the apparently 'natural' correlation between sex, gender, sexuality and desire (see especially Butler 1990, 1993). These critiques apply to homosexuality as well as to heterosexuality. Eve Sedgwick for example, points out that although the creation of 'the homosexual' as a species appears to have solidified the definition of sexuality on the basis of the gender of object choice, there is no reason to believe either that this has always been the case or that sexuality should continue to be defined in this way (Sedgwick 1991: 8). The following analysis is situated in the context of these debates: I will address the different ways that Crosland negotiates the 'troubled' relationship between de Beauvoir's 'ambiguous' sexuality and her gender.

13 The implication here is that de Beauvoir and the women in whom she is reflected (and whom she reflects) are the 'same' (thus the accusations of narcissism). I will be returning to the themes of reflection, mirroring, narcissism and, particularly, the role of the other in the production of the self, in chapter 7.

14 Although de Beauvoir, perhaps more famously, also argues that lesbian relationships may be narcissistic (de Beauvoir 1988: 437).

15 A common charge against lesbians in a 'patriarchal heterosexual culture' (Creed 1995: 88).

16 Interestingly, even though, according to Moi, de Beauvoir perceived not only Sartre but also Le Bon to be 'her double' (Moi 1994: 242), she does not mention narcissism in this context. Perhaps this is because de Beauvoir's relationship with Le Bon is itself seen to reflect or 'mirror' her primary relationship with Sartre (tying it therefore, to heterosexuality and reciprocity). Moi writes: 'Sartre protected [de Beauvoir] against solitude in her youth, Sylvie Le Bon was to do so in her old age' and notes that de Beauvoir and Le Bon's 'way of life also mirrors that of Sartre and de Beauvoir' (ibid.). This privileging of de Beauvoir's relationship with Sartre over Le Bon cannot be explained merely by reference to chronological events (which would suggest that the 'facts' speak for themselves). In Margaret Simons' interpretation of de Beauvoir's life for example (see below), all de Beauvoir's relationships, including with Sartre, are understood as 'trial runs' for her relationship with Le Bon.

17 See Lawler (1999) for a detailed discussion of the organisation and construction of motherhood around needs and, in particular, the 'needs' of children.

18 Frequent references to 'The Family' *as* a family support this image not only in Crosland's account (see for example Crosland 1992: 160, 249, 283) but also in press representations (see for example the *Guardian,* 15 April 1986b).

19 Which again (see chapter 3) both suggests and confirms that that which is hidden is perceived to be most 'true' to the self.

20 Motherhood by no means has to be anchored to heterosexuality; this representation says more about Crosland's understanding of it, than about motherhood *per se.*

21 Even Moi produces an intelligible, if fragmented, representation of de Beauvoir.

22 In this respect, Ricoeur makes explicit the commonly assumed trope that the statement 'I am' is constituted and governed by temporality. As John Berger puts it: '"I am" includes all that has made me so. It is more than a statement of immediate fact: it is already an explanation, a justification, a demand – it is already autobiographical' (Berger quoted in Probyn 1993: 117).

23 See chapter 6 for more details of Simons' 'defence' of de Beauvoir's rejection of a lesbian identity during her life.

24 Again, I am referring to bisexuality specifically in terms of object choice (rather than androgyny) since this is how lesbianism and heterosexuality are defined.

25 Ricoeur's analysis is not situated in the context of post-structuralist theories of the self nor does he use his thesis to critique contemporary theoretical trends. Nevertheless, it may act as a pertinent reminder of the implications of the use of the 'I' even when mapping its supposed breakdown. While it may be the case that narratives which are characterised by clear beginnings, middles and ends have recently been challenged (see Plummer 1995 for an account of some of the ways in which what might be called 'post-modern' stories differ from 'modern' stories), this does not necessarily result in the 'death' of the subject. Judith Butler, whose work is situated more firmly in the context of these debates, makes a similar point to Ricoeur. She writes: 'what is the status of the utterance that announces its passing? What speaks

now that the subject is dead? That there is a speaking seems clear, for how else could the utterance be heard?' (Butler 1995a: 48).

26 Both are possible because, as Ricoeur writes, 'this awkward vocabulary of the self' applies equally to the first, second and the third person in narrative, as well as to possessive pronouns and adverbs of time and place (Ricoeur 1991b: 191).

5 Displacement

1 Although I develop the notion of 'framing' most explicitly in this chapter, I have also drawn attention to it in my analysis of the biographies (see chapter 3).

2 Which is not to suggest that either the naked female body, de Beauvoir or bisexuality somehow exist prior to, or transcend, cultural framing. Instead, all three are constituted through this discursive framing itself.

3 Among others, Nead draws on Derrida's essay 'The parergon' in *The Truth in Painting*. In his critique of Kantian aesthetics – in which a 'disinterested attitude' is understood to be the 'essence of aesthetic experience' (Derrida 1987: 39) – Derrida argues that it is not the object of contemplation but the frame itself which produces meanings. In other words, meanings are made at the limits or boundaries rather than in the centre.

4 And is frequently compared to other 'eccentric' women writers such as Virginia Woolfe (*Sunday Telegraph*, 20 December 1992), Dame Edith Sitwell (*Independent on Sunday*, 2 February 1992a), George Sand and Madame de Staël (*Sunday Telegraph*, 26 January 1992). These women are additionally distinguished by their sexuality, over which a question mark might be perceived to hang.

5 Sontag, describing August Sander's 1930s collection of photographs, notes that the middle and upper classes were usually photographed indoors, without the use of props. 'Laborers and derelicts', by contrast, were often pictured outdoors which furnished them with a setting: 'as if they could not be assumed to have the kinds of separate identities normally achieved in the middle and upper classes' (Sontag 1979: 61). Sontag's analysis might also be applied to gender: de Beauvoir is usually considered to be bourgeois, but she seems to me to be shown with pen and paper to hand more frequently than Sartre is.

6 I found only one reference to de Beauvoir, a short obituary, in the British tabloids between October 1984 and December 1992.

7 This 'revelatory' capacity of photography, which contributes to an impression of depth, is ironic given that the photograph is composed of an entirely bounded surface from which nothing 'emerges'.

8 Jackie Stacey shows how film stars may become so associated with a specific outfit that the spectator 'takes pleasure in the fulfilment of the expectation that [a star] would appear in her films wearing [a] particular item of clothing' (Stacey 1994: 200). Similarly, the turban is a source of much media interest. However, newspapers are not necessarily de Beauvoir's 'fans' and the turban is frequently employed as the vehicle through which de Beauvoir is criticised or even ridiculed. As noted above, the *Independent on Sunday* describes the turban as 'a

cleaning lady's scarf' (*Independent on Sunday*, 2 February 1992b). Notably, the 'joke' is informed by class: de Beauvoir's 'high' cultural status is 'reduced' to that of a cleaning lady. Fascination with the turban follows de Beauvoir to the grave: 'After her own death she was dressed in a long red bathrobe and matching red turban' (*Independent on Sunday*, 2 February 1992a). Taking spectacle to its limits, de Beauvoir is aesthetically displayed in the coffin: the reader can visualise her body and clothes, arms folded, colour co-ordinated with turban intact in the earth.

9 This is the first example of a British newspaper signalling and amplifying national differences. The heavily ironic tone suggests that 'we' ('British') are aligned with the 'Americans' who are not actually naïve so much as 'perfectly sensible' in their attitudes to relationships. I will consider press manipulation of British and French national identities in more detail below.

10 De Beauvoir's 'French' identity does not constitute the whole of her self, just as sexuality does not sum into a self.

11 In this respect the papers play a key role in producing and reproducing national identities. As Michael Billig notes, 'nationalism' is not 'removed from everyday life, as some observers have supposed' (Billig 1995: 6), but is rather routinely (in 'banal' circumstances and in 'banal' ways) invoked: 'Daily, the nation is indicated, or "flagged", in the lives of its citizenry' (ibid.).

12 The notion of a 'postcard' is also relevant here insofar as this chapter especially focuses on the 'aestheticization of everyday life' (Featherstone 1991). Naomi Schor suggests that the rise, in the 1900s, of the 'iconic face of the illustrated postcard . . . can be considered a sign of the rise of the culture of the image' (Schor 1992: 213).

13 John Tagg argues that photographs 'are never "evidence" of history; they are themselves the historical' (Tagg 1988: 65).

14 Schor argues that 'more so than in any other country, to promote the nation in France is to promote its capital, and vice versa' (Schor 1992: 213). Although referring to the French promotion of themselves, this postcard will illustrate that Schor's analysis may be equally well applied to British newspaper representations of Paris/France.

15 As Schorr points out, nostalgic 'souvenirs' (such as the images impressed upon the reader here) serve to 'authentic a past or otherwise remote experience' (Stewart quoted in Schor 1992: 200).

16 A survey in the *Guardian* included de Beauvoir among a number of other well-known 'stars', and claimed that she 'outscore[d]' Marilyn Monroe for example 'for student appeal' (*Guardian*, 17 August 1992).

17 Again, it is de Beauvoir's gender that threatens her status as an existential thinker. The *Sunday Telegraph* too, writes: 'An austere individual, supposedly above frivolity [de Beauvoir], cared a lot about clothes, but later denied it' (*Sunday Telegraph*, 26 January 1992). This suggests that de Beauvoir has to deny some aspect of her identity (her 'feminine' care for clothes which is equated with 'frivolity') in order to be taken seriously as a thinker/author etc.

18 Sadie Plant, drawing on the Situationists, notes that this is a key feature of a

process of commodification which 'presents all aspects of experience – events, goods, roles and issues – with an equivalence which denies their peculiarity' (Plant 1990: 4).

19 As noted in chapter 1, Foucault argues that, in the modern era, self-revelation is often allied to a violent disassociation from a 'past' self. Although de Beauvoir is not actively revealing herself to the public here, her letters are nevertheless received as a form of confession wherein the journalist occupies the position of 'interpreter'. De Beauvoir's 'confession' reveals the 'truth' of her self insofar as she is perceived to have disassociated her self from her bohemian past. There is an implicit tone of 'relief' in these later representations, the relief, perhaps, that follows from confession and remorse (Gutman 1988: 105).

20 Hence, as in the biographical accounts, de Beauvoir's and Sartre's contingent relationships appear to confirm rather than threaten their 'essential' love (see for example *Financial Times*, 19 January 1991; *The Times*, 15 April 1986; *Guardian*, 24 July 1987).

21 That de Beauvoir's 'scandalous reputation' is largely rooted in her perceived 'guilt' and 'self-recrimination' provides an acute demonstration of Foucault's notion of self-surveillance so familiar to the disciplinary technics of modernity (see also chapter 7 where I discuss the part played by shame in the production of the sexuality ascribed to de Beauvoir). The criticisms levelled against de Beauvoir might be partially put down to the degree to which she embodies a set of values around which there exists serious cultural anxiety (an anxiety, in particular, which centres around sexuality and gender). The 1990s have witnessed the language of the 1960s liberation movements (feminism, lesbian and gay liberation and the civil rights movements) – which spoke of 'rights' and 'choice' – turned upon itself (McNeil 1991). The conservative fear that such groups demand 'more' than a fair share of 'equality' has inspired a reactive 'back-to-basics' discourse. Thus when representations of de Beauvoir repeatedly constitute her as 'at some level sorry' (*Sunday Telegraph*, 8 December 1991) for her actions, she is an eerie embodiment of a social desire to 'make amends' and take (a specific kind of) 'responsibility'.

22 It is ironic that the journalists should bemoan de Beauvoir's self-promotion when, as Deleuze argues, they play such a significant role in encouraging the promotion of writers (Deleuze and Parnet 1987: 27).

23 De Beauvoir's perceived 'excesses' are often characterised in such specifically gendered terms. Newspaper representations frequently draw on the image of a woman nagging, speaking or showing 'too much'. De Beauvoir's taped conversations with Sartre, for instance, are seen to go into 'obsessive detail' and her endearments to him are 'tedious . . . with constant repetition' (*Sunday Telegraph*, 8 December 1991). Again, Nelson Algren captures what a number of the newspaper portrayals of de Beauvoir imply: 'in the aftermath of a nuclear holocaust, one small voice would emerge from "the ancestral ocean's depths", that of Simone de Beauvoir, whom nothing could make "quit talking"' (Algren quoted in the *Financial Times*, 15 August 1987).

24 Nead, writing from a feminist perspective, notes that for women: 'To write, or more generally to represent, is to take power; it is to tell your own stories and draw your own lines, rather than succumb to the tales and images of others' (Nead 1993: 82). It is perhaps partly for this reason that de Beauvoir is so harshly criticised for attempting to manage her own self image.

25 As Rose notes, 'morality' is 'a form of licensed pleasure in itself' (J. Rose 1992: 6).

26 Featherstone writes: 'the new conception of self which has emerged, which we shall refer to as the "performing self" places greater emphasis upon appearance, display and the management of impressions' (Featherstone 1982: 27. See also N. Rose 1992).

27 This cheapening might also have implications for the status of the author. Andrew Goodwin points out however, that popular bands such as ABC or the Pet Shop Boys reassert their authorial status and lay claim to originality and creativity by 'promoting themselves as the authors of their own *image*' (Goodwin 1988: 268).

28 In chapter 3 I explored how, for a number of similar reasons, de Beauvoir's unpublished texts acquired a truth-value that eluded the published material. Given that this is one of the ways in which the author-function is reinscribed into discourse, perhaps Dyer's analysis suggests the possibility of a 'star-function' which has similar effects. This analogy cannot be pushed too far however. Celia Lury (1993) analyses the breakdown of the author-function, through branding and copyrighting for example, in a postmodern and consumer culture (of which stars are a significant part).

29 I will return to the relation between the self and visibility in chapter 7.

6 Erasure

1 Interestingly, Frye suggests that questions of choice and responsibility, which are here produced as techniques of *sexual* identities, could be transposed to other issues. She writes: 'The very important and interesting issues about deter-minism and responsibility could just as well be discussed, for instance, in terms not of what we do with our bodies but what we do with our money' (Frye 1985: 215). It is this broad application which enables Frye to discuss not only sexual-ity but also women's liberation more generally. For the most part, I will be confining the analysis to the implications of these techniques for the production of sexuality and selfhood.

2 Others might disagree with Ferguson's reading, and claim that it was de Beauvoir who qualified Sartre's notion of total freedom of choice in *The Second Sex* by arguing that women, under patriarchy, are *more* split between transcen-dence and immanence, subject and object, than men are (Moi 1994: 155). In this respect, de Beauvoir takes account of the social, political and historical cir-cumstances that are responsible for women's 'bad faith'.

3 Other writers who broadly adopt this approach include Lilian Faderman (1981), Sheila Jeffreys (1985) and Jeffrey Weeks (1985).

4 Ferguson's perspective may be identified as largely social constructionist in that it assumes that same-sex experiences are universal, although

> only some individuals in some societies organize their lives around homoeroticism. A social analyst who assumes constructionist premises may wish to trace the social factors which have transformed this universal homoerotic desire into a homosexual identity.
>
> (Seidman 1995: 126)

The notion that same-sex experiences are universal suggests that social constructionism shares something with essentialist views of sexuality (cf: Sedgwick 1991). Perhaps it is useful therefore, to see essentialist and social constructionist perspectives as a part of a spectrum rather than in opposition.

5 The notion of lesbianism as a lifestyle reinscribes the centrality of the individual who must necessarily pre-exist the choices she makes. Ironically, in this respect Ferguson's argument is closer to the 'individualistic' approach that she seeks to criticise than it might at first appear (see also chapter 2).

6 Biographical accounts of de Beauvoir seem to be less concerned with confining the author to her historical context. Instead, she is often seen to be either ahead of history (Crosland 1992: 370) or she changes its course (Francis and Gontier 1987: 251). Most striking is Fullbrook and Fullbrook's account in which de Beauvoir appears to evaluate the limitations of her own historical context (concluding that a woman could not be taken seriously as a philosopher), and subsequently (consciously) uses the novel *She Came to Stay*, and Sartre, as no less than an elaborate ruse through which to publicise her own philosophy. The biographers further suggest that de Beauvoir intended this manoeuvre to be disclosed after her death. In this respect, 'knowledge' transcends history and, because de Beauvoir possesses knowledge, she is able to conquer history itself. That the biographies, more so than the academic analyses, emphasise de Beauvoir's individuality over and above her historical context is not surprising given that their *raison d'être* is to cast a spotlight on 'great individuals' demonstrating that their subjects '"make a difference" to social life' (Stanley 1992: 8).

7 Felstiner shapes history into a *narrative* wherein events, such as *The Second Sex*, receive their definition from their contribution to a plot. Although history appears to unfold as though it were a natural 'progression' or *forward* development, it is only the *backward* glance – from this 'particular vantage point', as Felstiner puts it – that enables significance to be conferred on the book. Ironically, Felstiner accuses de Beauvoir of taking 'for granted a momentum in one direction known as progress' (Felstiner 1980: 258).

8 This suggests that the author is reinscribed through a 'history-function'.

9 Frye, Card and Ferguson all point out that de Beauvoir's position on lesbianism served as a radical counter to psychoanalytic interpretations of homosexuality as *always* 'inauthentic' since homosexuality was understood to be (among other things) a neurosis (Ferguson 1985: 206; Card 1985: 209; Frye 1985: 215).

10 Card suggests that the only instance where de Beauvoir *does* treat heterosexuality as a choice is in relation to *lesbian* rejections of heterosexuality (rather than heterosexual women's acceptance of it) (Card 1985: 210. See also Frye 1985: 215).

11 I will return to the implications of evaluating identities on an 'equal basis' at some length in the following chapter.

12 The reason for de Beauvoir's failure to consider heterosexuality as a choice might be because, according to the existential doctrine, 'an act', to qualify as such, must be intentional (Blackham 1978: 127). Hence even if Card is correct in suggesting that heterosexual women make choices (although they may not be aware of them), from de Beauvoir's existential perspective, this might not be properly considered a choice.

13 I have illustrated this myself in chapters 4 and 5, where I argued that by providing 'reasons' for de Beauvoir's same-sex relationships (where none are required for her heterosexual liaisons), the biographies and press portray heterosexuality as 'inherent' and 'natural' (to de Beauvoir) while same-sex relationships are figured as unusual and (therefore) in need of explanation.

14 There is something of a blurred area here, between the two definitions of 'techniques of the self' that I am using. The notion that the self should reflect on, and take responsibility for, itself and its attitudes (in order to 'better' itself) has already been identified as one of the techniques of the self that Foucault describes (see chapter 1). In this context however, Card appears to be suggesting that such a practice is one of a series of related techniques through which a subject might 'put together', narrativise, or, as she says, 'develop', their sexuality. As a result, sexuality is itself perceived to be a 'real activity and not just an attitude' (Foucault 1988b: 24) which contributes to the creation of selfhood.

15 Arguably however, it is only *after* a lesbian 'identity' is defined that lesbian 'practices' may also be identified (calling the social constructionist position, as defined by Seidman above, into question). I made a similar point in chapter 2, when I suggested that the boundaries of 'the homosexual' can only be worked over, by queer, insofar as it has *already* been defined as a species.

16 This illustrates, as Celia Lury puts it, that individuation and individuality 'have joined forces in paradoxical ways, insofar as the exercise of *self*-surveillance (an extension of individuation) is linked to, or, indeed, rendered an aspect of self-development or self-actualisation (conventionally part of the cultivation of individuality)' (Lury 1995: 6).

17 The notion that, over a period of fifteen years, Frye has transformed her potential – or 'aptitude' as she puts it – for 'passionate connection with women' into an 'actuality' bears a striking resemblance to Ricoeur's analysis of narrative identity (see chapters 3 and 4). To recap, Ricoeur suggests that the end of the story 'is what equates the present with the past, the actual with the potential' (Ricoeur 1980: 186). I will be returning to Frye's story in the following chapter.

18 Which accords with Card's analysis of attitude as a 'disposition' which may or may not be chosen to be developed.

19 Her continual emphasis on choice and the active process of identity construction and acquisition suggests that Frye perceives herself to be more possessed *of* than *by* sexuality.

20 Frye discusses and ultimately, somewhat dismissively, rejects some of these arguments during the course of her paper. Her conclusion that women should take responsibility for others as well as themselves – a 'behalf-ism' of sorts – rests on the implicit assumption that women are more alike than different from each other. That women are *not* all alike has been an important criticism targeted at White, middle-class feminists. Frye's own ability to choose (continually) to develop both her lesbianism into an identity and to make choices about her lifework for example, is a privilege that not all women share. Further, the notion that more freedom to choose is desirable is a particularly Western concept which is frequently imposed on women who do not share this belief. Some feminists' (especially White feminists') anxieties and moral outrage over arranged marriages is a case in point. See chapter 2 also, for a more detailed critique of theories of the self which privilege choice and the relation between these and the 'American mythos' of self-invention.

21 This is not the only reason though. Further reasons for associating (and indeed conflating) bisexuality with inauthenticity, and the implications that follow, will be explored throughout this and the next chapter.

22 The relation that Crosland formulates between pleasure, responsibility and choice for example is only implicitly developed. See chapter 4 for details.

23 Which is not to suggest that inauthenticity could never be a technique of the self. One could, for example, be a 'master of insincerity'.

24 Card distances the notion of bisexuality throughout her article by keeping it in inverted commas. Almost a decade later, it appears that she will still not concede to any concept of bisexuality as a proper object of analysis. In her introduction to a special edition of *Hypatia* on lesbian ethics (Card 1992), Card suggests that an article by Elizabeth Däumer – which is entitled 'Queer Ethics, or The Challenge of Bisexuality to Lesbian Ethics' – 'raises the question . . . whether a political understanding of "lesbian" makes possible *male lesbians*' (Card 1992: 4). Although Däumer does discuss male lesbians, this is by no means the central emphasis in her article.

25 I am taking this phrase from Lisa Walker's (1993) article 'How to recognize a lesbian: The cultural politics of looking like what you are' which will be considered in more detail in the following chapter.

7 Lose your face

1 I chose the title of this chapter in the light of this analysis. 'Lose your face' is a phrase I have taken from *Dialogues* (Deleuze and Parnet 1987: 47).

2 The brevity of the extract cited here may imply that Frye *is* able to 'be' a lesbian without 'acting' like one 'early' on (she argues that during this period '[i]t would

have been "inauthentic" to act the lesbian'). As noted in chapter 6 however, Frye writes that: 'In my case, being lesbian is an attitude evolved over perhaps fifteen years – from my earliest awareness of aptitude for passionate connection with women to a way of being which actualises that possibility' (Frye 1985: 217). This suggests that 'earlier' Frye is not so much 'being' a lesbian, as being in the process of 'actualising' a lesbian identity (which, until actualised, cannot be claimed as an authentic identity).

3 As in Plato's Forms which are 'nothing other than what they are' (Patton 1994: 147).

4 See chapter 2 for examples of this.

5 Although Tyler argues that Piper herself falls prey to the very assumptions she seeks to critique: in handing out calling cards to those she *assumes* are White, Piper inverts the relation that has erased her own racial identity. Now, Piper assumes that everyone who is not Black is White.

6 'Male models' in this context refers to 'Latino and African-American gay men, transvestites, and transsexuals' (Phelan 1993: 93).

7 It is arguable that most dominant identities, as Skeggs point out with respect to middle-classness, are 'invisibilised'. That Piper is passed off as White for example, illustrates the unmarked – and therefore assumed – nature of Whiteness. Similarly, Phelan notes that passing as heterosexual (by choice or not) is relatively easy because heterosexuality is also assumed. Passing in this context, she argues, makes visible 'the unmarked nature of heterosexual identity. The one who passes then does not "erase" the mark of difference, rather the passer highlights the invisibility of the mark of the Same' (Phelan 1993: 96) (against which all differences are measured).

8 Insofar as Phelan appears to be unwilling to admit that there may be other ways in which the subject might 'see' itself, her evaluation of the gaze is framed in terms of an apparently inevitable 'loss' and 'failure'. The very negativity of this evaluation suggests that Phelan continues to privilege the role of the visible in the production of identity even as she attempts to move away from it. In this respect, Phelan shares what Martin Jay, in relation to Foucault, has described as a profound mistrust of the visible: 'the ocularcentrism of those who praised the "nobility of sight" [is] not so much rejected as reversed in value. Vision [is] still the privileged sense, but what that privilege produce[s] in the modern world [is] damned as almost entirely pernicious' (Jay 1994: 384).

9 Skeggs notes that the pressure of the gaze of the other does not have to be imaginary. She writes: '[Jane M] is very conscious that she is in a very different social class. This is not induced by an imaginary other, the product of representations, but from her experiences of middle-class women' (Skeggs 1997: 88).

10 Sartrean existential philosophy is perhaps most famous for its claim that: 'it is in fear, shame, pride, vanity and the like that we experience our existence for others' (Blackham 1978: 119).

11 The concept of self-surveillance is important because it signals a difference between a singular gaze (as in Foucault's account of the medical gaze), which implies a unified coherent position from which one might look, and a visual

episteme which does not require the implied presence of an actual individual: 'It's a machine in which everyone is caught, those who exercise power just as much as those over whom it is exercised' (Foucault 1980a: 156). The notion of a visual *episteme* in Foucault's work replaces, Martin Jay argues, his account of both the absent spectator of Cartesianism and the 'observed spectator' of humanism (Jay 1994: 406).

12 Even in the biographies the perceived 'similarity' (the 'double mirror') between de Beauvoir and Sartre is hardly transparent. Francis and Gontier write of the 'cutting edge' (Francis and Gontier 1987: 106) (de Beauvoir and Sartre's difference?) at the heart of their relationship which disrupts the narrative of sameness that the biographers attempt to construct.

13 Although Card argues that the 'bisexual' woman is 'basically heterosexually oriented' (Card 1985: 213), this does not preclude her from (re)defining this woman as an inauthentic lesbian. This does not mean that *all* heterosexual women are inauthentic lesbians(!). Presumably it is *because* the 'bisexual' woman resembles the authentic lesbian (while authentic heterosexuals do not) that such a (re)definition is possible.

14 As 'pure Matter-Function' (Deleuze and Guattari 1988: 141), the abstract machine, like Foucault's analysis of power, has no independent form or content of its own: it operates by distributing matter rather than substance and function rather than form. Matter in this context pertains to substance that is neither physically nor semiotically formed (substance is formed matter) while functions are not 'semiotically' formed.

15 'There is a whole social system which might be called the white wall/black hole system. We are always pinned against the wall of dominant significations, we are always sunk in the hole of our subjectivity' (Deleuze and Parnet 1987: 45). Deleuze and Guattari point out that the sign and the subject do not precede or construct the wall and hole, instead faces are 'their condition of possibility' (Deleuze and Guattari 1988: 180). Since only certain assemblages of power require the production of a face, it cannot be said that the face is universal (Deleuze and Guattari 1988: 175).

16 Deleuze and Guattari write: 'European racism as the white man's claim has never operated by exclusion, or by the designation of someone as Other . . . Racism operates by the determination of degrees of deviance in relation to the White-Man face' (Deleuze and Guattari 1988: 178).

17 Which suggests that Phelan's privileging of the role of the other in the production of identity is perhaps overstated. There may be other ways in which the subject 'sees' itself and is 'seen'.

18 The notion of an 'active' vanishing does not necessarily imply an active subject. However the role Phelan confers on individual performance artists (see her final chapter especially) implies that while the economy of representation, which produces women as an 'absence' or as 'not-all', is an active system which does not require a subject to 'drive' it, as it were, an artist/subject *is* required to disrupt it.

19 Although again, this is not to suggest that inauthenticity could never be such a technique.

20 Although Riviere talks about 'bisexuality' (Riviere 1986: 33), she configures it as androgyny. My comparison of bisexuality with masquerade makes use of Card's definition of sexuality (where sexuality is defined through object choice) as she is the focus of my analysis.

21 Although this is a similarity between Riviere's masquerade and queer theories of performativity, they cannot be collapsed for a number of reasons. Not least among them is that Judith Butler's notion of performativity for example, unlike Riviere's analysis of masquerade, exploits the gap between the performance and the identity in order to 'rework' the signifier of that identity. It is not Riviere so much as Mary Ann Doane's 'fine-tuning' of Riviere's work, as Kim Michasiw points out, that injects similar political possibilities into the theory of woman-liness as masquerade (Michasiw 1994: 149).

22 All things therefore, 'regardless of their type, have the same ontological status' (Grosz 1994: 200). Deleuze and Guattari do not distinguish between natural or artificial bodies, or between human, animal or textual bodies (and so on).

23 Significance refers not to 'acts' of signification, but to the general tendency of *thought* towards producing significations.

24 Why, then, retain the notion of 'the body'? Keith Ansell Pearson, in his Deleuzo-Guattarian analysis of Stelarc, provides an explanation:

> The claim that 'the body is redundant' fails to specify the body that is being referred to. Worse it is in danger of falling back on the assumption of an isolated monadic body . . . When the body is situated on a plane of immanence any literal claim about the obsolescence of the body becomes nonsensical: there are only different kinds of bodies, human, animal, non-organic . . .   (Ansell Pearson 1997: 233)

And, one might add, bodies without matter.

25 It may seem odd to be concluding with a Body without Organs of bisexuality given Deleuze and Guattari's views on bisexuality (see chapter 1). However, the conclusions that I am drawing here are based on my own analysis of bisexuality where, in the texts I have analysed, it does not refer to the male/female binary. Nor does it, as Diana Fuss implies in the introduction to *Inside/Out*, refer to the dualism of homosexual/heterosexual. Fuss suggests that sexualities other than hetero and homosexuality – such as 'bisexuality, transvestism, transsexualism . . . ' (Fuss 1991: 2) – rather than being 'left out' of the homosexual/heterosexual equation, might themselves be assimilated into the inside/outside opposition so securing its logic ever more tightly. Although she does not expand at any length, presumably Fuss is referring to the feature that bisexuality, transvestism and transsexualism are sometimes perceived to have in common: that they 'are' the opposition, they 'hold' it within themselves and, as a consequence of this definition, reinforce (rather than deconstruct) that opposition.

26 Although Deleuze and Guattari note that: 'The BwO is not opposed to the

organs but to that organization of the organs called the organism' (Deleuze and Guattari 1988: 158).

27 As Iain MacKenzie puts it: 'Philosophy gives rise to transcendence whenever it confuses the concept it creates with the plane of immanence instituted by the concept; or, to put it another way, whenever it confuses the image it creates of what it is to think with thought itself' (MacKenzie 1997: 9).

Conclusion

1 Indeed the fold is a 'doubling' movement whereby it relates back to itself. In this way, a relation to the self is always established in the first instance.

2 See also M. Fraser (1998) for a further critique of the accent on aesthetics in Foucault's work and also in queer political campaigns and strategies.

3 Criticising their work partly on this basis, Braidotti asks: 'Can feminists, at this point in their history . . . actually afford to let go of their sex-specific forms of political agency? Is the bypassing of gender in favour of a dispersed polysexuality not a very masculine move?' (Braidotti 1991: 120 and 1993). I have considered this debate in some detail in chapters 1 and 2.

4 See chapters 2 and 7 for more details on Deleuze (and Guattari's) concept of a body.

5 Nevertheless, there is an ambivalence in the conclusions that I have drawn about bisexuality. An apparently affirmative BwO of bisexuality emerges from an analysis based unremittingly on preclusion (chapter 4), displacement (chapter 5) and erasure (chapter 6). A critique which focuses almost entirely on negativity finds, finally, a positive, if unrepresentable, role for bisexuality. And I have argued this even though, as Michael Hardt notes, Judith Butler and others criticise Deleuze precisely because the 'power' of the negative is erased. Describing the terms of such critiques, Hardt writes: 'philosophies of affirmation remain impotent because they have deprived themselves of the power of negation, they have lost the "magic" of the labor of the negative' (Hardt 1993: 115). The BwO of bisexuality illustrates however, that affirmation is not opposed to critique. Indeed, Deleuze refers to a 'total critique', 'an unrestrained attack on the established values and the ruling powers they support' (Hardt 1993: 116). Hardt adds – and the BwO of bisexuality demonstrates this point – that: 'This is not to say that all that is present is negated, but simply that what is negated is attacked with unrestrained force' (ibid.).

References

Acker, K. 1993. *In Memoriam to Identity.* London: Flamingo.

Ahmed, S. 1996. Tanning the body: Skin, colour and gender. Paper presented at the Women's Studies Dayschool on Passing, Lancaster University.

Ansell Pearson, K. 1997. Life becoming body: On the 'meaning' of post human evolution. In *Cultural Values*, 1 (2), pp. 219–40.

Back, L. and Quaade, V. 1993. Dream utopias, nightmare realities: Imaging race and culture within the world of Benetton advertising. In *Third Text,* 22, pp. 65–80.

Baker, K. 1992. Bisexual feminist politics: Because bisexuality is not enough. In E. R. Weise, ed. *Closer to Home: Bisexuality and Feminism.* Seattle: Seal.

Barthes, R. 1981. *Camera Lucida: Reflections on Photography.* Trans. R. Howard. New York: Hill and Wang.

1992. The death of the author. Trans. and ed. S. Heath. In P. Rice and P. Waugh, eds. *Modern Literary Theory: A Reader.* New York: Routledge.

Bartky, S. L. 1990. *Femininity and Domination: Studies in the Phenomenology of Oppression.* London: Routledge.

Benhabib, S. 1995a. Feminism and postmodernism: An uneasy alliance. In L. Nicholson, ed. *Feminist Contentions: A Philosophical Exchange.* New York: Routledge.

1995b. Subjectivity, historiography, and politics: Reflections on the 'feminism/postmodernism exchange'. In L. Nicholson, ed. *Feminist Contentions: A Philosophical Exchange.* New York: Routledge.

Berger, J. 1972. *Ways of Seeing.* London: BBC and Penguin.

Bernstein, J. M. 1990. Self-knowledge as praxis: Narrative and narration in psychoanalysis. In C. Nash, ed. *Narrative in Culture*. London: Routledge.

Bi Academic Intervention, eds. 1997. Introduction. In Bi Academic Intervention, eds. *The Bisexual Imaginary: Representation, Identity and Desire*. London: Cassell.

Billig, M. 1995. *Banal Nationalism*. London: Sage.

Blackham, H. J. 1978. *Six Existential Thinkers: Kierkegaard. Nietzsche. Jaspers. Marcel. Heidegger. Sartre*. London: Routledge and Kegan Paul.

Blasingame, B. M. 1992. The roots of biphobia: Racism and internalized heterosexism. In E. R. Weise, ed. *Closer to Home: Bisexuality and Feminism*. Seattle: Seal.

Boundas, C. V. 1994. Deleuze: Serialization and subject-formation. In C. V. Boundas and D. Olkowski, eds. *Gilles Deleuze and the Theater of Philosophy*. New York: Routledge.

Bowlby, R. 1985. *Just Looking: Consumer Culture in Dreiser, Gissing and Zola*. New York: Methuen.

Boyne, R. 1990. War and desire. In *The Polish Sociological Bulletin,* 1, pp. 33–46.

Braidotti, R. 1991. *Patterns of Dissonance*. Trans. E. Guild. Cambridge: Polity.

   1993. Discontinuous becomings. Deleuze on the becoming-woman of philosophy. In *Journal of the British Society for Phenomenology,* 24 (1), pp. 44–55.

   1994. *Nomadic Subjects: Embodiment and Sexual Difference in Contemporary Feminist Theory*. New York: Columbia University Press.

Braidotti, R. with Butler, J. 1994. Feminism by any other name. In *differences: A Journal of Feminist Cultural Studies,* 6 (2+3), pp. 27–62.

Brewer, M. 1991. Two-way closet. In L. Hutchins and L. Kaahumanu, eds. *Bi Any Other Name: Bisexual People Speak Out*. Boston: Alyson.

Butler, J. 1986. Sex and gender in Simone de Beauvoir's *Second Sex*. In *Yale French Studies,* 72, pp. 35–49.

   1990. *Gender Trouble: Feminism and the Subversion of Identity*. New York: Routledge.

   1993. *Bodies That Matter: On the Discursive Limits of 'Sex'*. New York: Routledge.

   1994. Against proper objects. In *differences: A Journal of Feminist Cultural Studies,* 6 (2+3), pp. 1–27.

   1995a. Contingent foundations: Feminism and the question of 'postmodernism'. In L. Nicholson, ed. *Feminist Contentions: A Philosophical Exchange*. New York: Routledge.

1995b. For a careful reading. In L. Nicholson, ed. *Feminist Contentions: A Philosophical Exchange.* New York: Routledge.

1997. *Excitable Speech: A Politics of the Performative.* London and New York: Routledge.

Card, C. 1985. Lesbian attitudes and *The Second Sex.* In *Hypatia/Women's Studies International Forum,* 8 (3), pp. 209–14.

1992. Introduction. In *Hypatia,* 7 (4), pp. 1–5.

Clark, D. 1991. Commodity lesbianism. In *Camera Obscura,* 25–6, pp. 181–201.

Clark, S. H. 1995. Narrative identity in Ricoeur's *Oneself as Another.* Paper presented at the 2nd *Theory, Culture and Society* Conference.

Creed, B. 1987. From here to modernity – feminism and postmodernism. In *Screen,* 28 (2), pp. 47–69.

1995. Lesbian bodies: Tribades, tomboys and tarts. In E. Grosz and E. Probyn, eds. *Sexy Bodies: The Strange Carnalities of Feminism.* London: Routledge.

Crosland, M. 1992. *Simone de Beauvoir: The Woman and Her Work.* London: Heinemann.

Crossley, N. 1995. Body techniques, agency and intercorporeality: On Goffman's *Relations In Public.* In *Sociology,* 29 (1), pp. 133–49.

Däumer, E. 1992. Queer ethics; or, the challenge of bisexuality to lesbian ethics. In *Hypatia,* 7 (4), pp. 91–105.

de Beauvoir, S. 1988. *The Second Sex.* Trans. H. M. Parshley. London: Picador.

1991. *Letters to Sartre.* Trans. Q. Hoare. London: Radius.

Debord, G. 1977. *Society of the Spectacle.* Detroit: Black and Red.

Deleuze, G. 1988. *Foucault.* Trans. S. Hand. London: Athlone.

1992. Ethology: Spinoza and us. Trans. R. Hurley. In J. Crary and S. Kwinter, eds. *Incorporations.* New York: Zone.

1994. Introduction: Repetition and difference. *Difference and Repetition.* Trans. P. Patton. London: Althone.

Deleuze, G. and Guattari, F. 1988. *A Thousand Plateaus: Capitalism and Schizophrenia.* Trans. B. Massumi. London: Athlone.

1994. *Anti-Oedipus: Capitalism and Schizophrenia.* Trans. R. Hurley, M. Seem and H. R. Lane. Minneapolis: University of Minnesota Press.

Deleuze, G. and Parnet, C. 1987. *Dialogues.* Trans. H. Tomlinson and B. Habberjam. London: Athlone.

Derrida, J. 1987. The parergon. Trans. G. Bennington and I. McLeod. In *The Truth In Painting.* Chicago and London: The University of Chicago Press.

Dietz, M. G. 1992. Introduction: Debating Simone de Beauvoir. In *Signs: Journal of Women in Culture and Society,* 18 (1), pp. 74–88.

Diprose, R. 1993. Nietzsche and the pathos of distance. In P. Patton, ed. *Nietzsche, Feminism and Political Theory.* London: Routledge.

1994. *Ethics, Embodiment and Sexual Difference.* London: Routledge.

Doane, M. A. 1982. Film and the masquerade – theorizing the female spectator. In *Screen,* 23 (3/4), pp. 74–89.

1990. Technophilia: Technology, representation, and the feminine. In E. Weed, ed. *Coming to Terms.* London: Routledge.

Dollimore, J. 1996. Bisexuality, heterosexuality, and wishful theory. In *Textual Practice,* 10 (3), pp. 525–39.

Dyer, R. 1982. Don't look now – the male pin up. In *Screen,* 23 (3/4), pp. 61–74.

1988. White. In *Screen,* 29 (4), pp. 44–64.

1991. *A Star is Born* and the construction of authenticity. In C. Gledhill, ed. *Stardom.* London: Routledge.

Eadie, J. 1993. We should be there bi now. In *Rouge,* 12, pp. 26–7.

1997. 'That's why she's bisexual': Contexts for bisexual visibility. In Bi Academic Intervention, eds. *The Bisexual Imaginary: Representation, Identity and Desire.* London: Cassell.

The Economist, 20 October 1984. Life is a café. p. 103.

19 April 1986. Castor and martyr: Obituaries of Simone de Beauvoir and Jean Genet. p. 100.

Evans, M. N. 1986. Murdering *L'Invitée*: Gender and fictional narrative. In *Yale French Studies,* 72, pp. 67–86.

Faderman, L. 1981. *Surpassing the Love of Men.* London: Junction.

Featherstone, M. 1982. The body in consumer culture. In *Theory, Culture and Society*, 2, pp. 18–33.

1991. *Consumer Culture and Postmodernism.* London: Sage.

Featherstone, M. Hepworth, M., and Turner, B. S., eds. 1995. *The Body: Social Process and Cultural Theory.* London: Sage.

Felstiner, M. L. 1980. Seeing *The Second Sex* through the second wave. In *Feminist Studies,* 6 (2), pp. 247–76.

Ferguson, A. 1985. Lesbian identity: Beauvoir and history. In *Hypatia/Women's Studies International Forum*, 8 (3), pp. 203–8.

Financial Times, 15 August 1987. Sadness of Simone de Beauvoir. J. Wullshlager, London Page XII.

19 January 1991. Chronicler of the low life – Geoffrey Moore on the unfulfilled career of the lover of de Beauvoir. G. Moore, London Page xiv.

1 February 1992. De Beauvoir, still a centre of industry. A. C. Grayling, London Page xii.

Foucault, M. 1976. *The Birth of the Clinic: An Archaeology of Medical Perception.* Trans. A. M. Sheridan. London: Tavistock.

1977. Theatrum philosophicum. Trans. D. F. Bouchard and S. Simon. In D. F. Bouchard, ed. *Michel Foucault: Language, Counter-Memory, Practice: Selected Essays and Interviews.* Oxford: Blackwell.

1979a. What is an author? Trans. D. F. Bouchard. In *Screen* 20 (1), pp. 13–35.

1979b. *Discipline and Punish: The Birth of The Prison.* Trans. A. Sheridan. London: Peregrine.

1980a. The eye of power. Trans. C. Gordon, L. Marshall, J. Mepham and K. Soper. In C. Gordon, ed. *Power/Knowledge: Selected Interviews and Other Writings 1972–1977.* Brighton: Harvester.

1980b. The history of sexuality. Trans. C. Gordon, L. Marshall, J. Mepham and K. Soper. In C. Gordon, ed. *Power/Knowledge: Selected Interviews and Other Writings 1972–1977.* Brighton: Harvester.

1981. The order of discourse. Trans. I. McLeod. In R. Young, ed. *Untying the Text: A Post-Structuralist Reader.* Boston: Routledge and Kegan Paul.

1983. *This Is Not a Pipe.* Trans. J. Harkness. Berkeley: University of California Press.

1988a. Truth, power, self: An interview with Michel Foucault with R. Martin. In L. H. Martin, H. Gutman and P. H. Hutton, eds. *Technologies of the Self: A Seminar with Michel Foucault.* London: Tavistock.

1988b. Technologies of the self. In L. H. Martin, H. Gutman and P. H. Hutton, eds. *Technologies of the Self: A Seminar with Michel Foucault.* London: Tavistock.

1990a. *The History of Sexuality, Volume I: An Introduction.* Trans. R. Hurley. Harmondsworth: Penguin.

1990b. *The History of Sexuality, Volume III: The Care of the Self.* Trans. R. Hurley. Harmondsworth: Penguin.

1991a. What is enlightenment? In P. Rabinow, ed. *The Foucault Reader: An Introduction to Foucault's Thought.* London: Penguin.

1991b. Nietzsche, genealogy, history. In P. Rabinow, ed. *The Foucault Reader: An Introduction to Foucault's Thought.* London: Penguin.

1991c. Truth and power. In P. Rabinow, ed. *The Foucault Reader: An Introduction to Foucault's Thought.* London: Penguin.

1991d. What is an author? In P. Rabinow, ed. *The Foucault Reader: An Introduction to Foucault's Thought.* London: Penguin.

1992a. *The Archaeology of Knowledge.* Trans. A. M. Sheridan Smith. London: Routledge.

1992b. *The History of Sexuality, Volume II: The Use of Pleasure.* Trans. R. Hurley. Harmondsworth: Penguin.

1994. *The Order of Things: An Archaeology of the Human Sciences.* London: Routledge.

Francis, C. and Gontier, F. 1987. *Simone de Beauvoir.* Trans. L. Nesselson. London: Sidgwick and Jackson.

Fraser, M. 1998 forthcoming. Classing Queer: Politics in Competition, *Theory, Culture and Society.*

Fraser, N. 1995a. False antitheses: A response to Seyla Benhabib and Judith Butler. In L. Nicholson, ed. *Feminist Contentions: A Philosophical Exchange.* New York: Routledge.

1995b. Pragmatism, feminism, and the linguistic turn. In L. Nicholson, ed. *Feminist Contentions: A Philosophical Exchange.* New York: Routledge.

Frye, M. 1985. History and responsibility. In *Hypatia/Women's Studies International Forum*, 8 (3), pp. 215–17.

Fullbrook, K. and Fullbrook, E. 1993. *Simone de Beauvoir and Jean-Paul Sartre: The Remaking of a Twentieth Century Legend.* Hemel Hempstead: Harvester Wheatsheaf.

Fuss, D. 1989. *Essentially Speaking: Feminism, Nature and Difference.* London: Routledge.

1991. Inside/Out. In D. Fuss, ed. *Inside/Out: Lesbian Theories, Gay Theories.* New York: Routledge.

Garber, M. 1996. *Vice Versa: Bisexuality and the Eroticism of Everyday Life.* London: Hamish Hamilton.

Goodchild, P. 1996. *Deleuze and Guattari: An Introduction to the Politics of Desire.* London: Sage.

Goodwin, A. 1988. Sample and hold: Pop music in the digital age of reproduction. In S. Frith and A. Goodwin, eds. *On Record.* London: Routledge.

Grosz, E. 1994. A thousand tiny sexes: Feminism and rhizomatics. In C. V. Boundas and D. Olkowski, eds. *Gilles Deleuze and the Theater of Philosophy.* New York: Routledge.

1995. Sexual difference and the problem of essentialism. In E. Grosz. *Space, Time and Perversion.* London: Routledge.

Guardian, 15 April 1986a. De Beauvoir dies at 78/French novelist and feminist. P. Webster, p. 1.

15 April 1986b. Turbanned guerrilla/Obituary of Simone de Beauvoir, French feminist writer. P. Webster, p. 23.

16 April 1986. The hind that gave feminists the sight. J. Tweedie, p. 23.

24 July 1987. Triste topic. M. Walters, p. 13.

6 December 1989. Second coming. L. Appignanesi, p. 19.

17 August 1992. De Beauvoir outscores Marilyn for student appeal. A. Milligan, p. 3.

22 December 1992. Witness to my life: The letters of Jean-Paul Sartre to Simone de Beauvoir, 1926–1939. J. Evans, p. 8.

Gutman, H. 1988. Rousseau's *Confessions*: A technology of the self. In L. H. Martin, H. Gutman and P. H. Hutton, eds. *Technologies of the Self: A Seminar with Michel Foucault.* London: Tavistock.

Hall, D. E. 1996. BI-ntroduction II: Epistemologies of the fence. In D. E. Hall and M. Pramaggiore, eds. *RePresenting Bisexualities: Subjects and Cultures of Fluid Desire.* New York: New York University Press.

Hall, D. E. and Pramaggiore, M. eds. 1996. *RePresenting Bisexualities: Subjects and Cultures of Fluid Desire.* New York: New York University Press.

Hall, S. 1993. Encoding, decoding. In S. During, ed. *The Cultural Studies Reader.* London: Routledge.

Haraway, D. 1991. *Simions, Cyborgs, and Women: The Reinvention of Nature.* London: Free Association Books.

Hardt, M. 1993. *Gilles Deleuze: An Apprenticeship in Philosophy.* London: University College of London Press.

Heath, S. 1986. Joan Riviere and the masquerade. In V. Burgin, J. Donald and C. Kaplan, eds. *Formations of Fantasy.* London: Methuen.

Hemmings, C. 1993. Resituating the bisexual body. In J. Bristow and A. R. Wilson, eds. *Activating Theory: Lesbian, Gay, Bisexual Politics.* London: Lawrence and Wishart.

1997. Bisexual theoretical perspectives: Emergent and contingent relationships. In Bi Academic Intervention, eds. *The Bisexual Imaginary: Representation, Identity and Desire.* London: Cassell.

Hennessey, R. 1993. Queer theory: A review of the *differences* special issue and Wittig's *The Straight Mind.* In *Signs: Journal of Women in Culture and Society*, 18 (4), pp. 964–74.

1995. Queer visibility in commodity culture. In L. Nicholson and S. Seidman, eds. *Social Postmodernism: Beyond Identity Politics.* Cambridge: Cambridge University Press.

hooks, b. 1993. The oppositional gaze: Black female spectators. In M. Diawara, ed. *Black American Cinema.* New York: Routledge.

Hutchins, L. and Kaahumanu, L. eds. 1991. *Bi Any Other Name: Bisexual People Speak Out.* Boston: Alyson.

Hutton, P. H. 1988. Foucault, Freud, and the technologies of the self. In

L. H. Martin, H. Gutman and P. H. Hutton, eds. *Technologies of the Self: A Seminar with Michel Foucault.* London: Tavistock.

Independent, 9 June 1990. Dutiful daughter in a birds nest. P. O'Brian, p. 31.

Independent on Sunday, 10 June 1990. Book review of *The Long Road to Freedom: 'Simone de Beauvoir'* by Deirdre Bair. A. Brookner, p. 15.

2 February 1992a. Turban guerrilla: Simone de Beauvoir. S. Mackay, p. 30.

2 February 1992b. Lentils for lunch again little one? H. Mantel, p. 30.

Independent Weekend, 23 November 1991. Letters from a radical lover – in which Simone tells her beloved Jean-Paul what she gets up to while he's away, p. 31.

Jardine, A. 1985. *Gynesis: Configurations of Woman and Modernity.* London: Cornell University Press.

Jay, M. 1992. Scopic regimes of modernity. In S. Lash and J. Friedman, eds. *Modernity and Identity.* Oxford: Blackwell.

1993. *Force Fields: Between Intellectual History and Cultural Critique.* London: Routledge.

1994. *Downcast Eyes: The Denigration of Vision in Twentieth-Century French Thought.* Berkeley: University of California Press.

Jeffreys, S. 1985. *The Spinster and Her Enemies: Feminism and Sexuality 1880–1930.* London: Pandora.

Jenks, C. 1995a. The centrality of the eye in western culture: An introduction. In C. Jenks, ed. *Visual Culture.* London: Routledge.

1995b. Watching your step: The history and practice of the *flâneur.* In C. Jenks, ed. *Visual Culture.* London: Routledge.

Kaloski, A. 1997. Returning to the lesbian *bildungsroman*: A bisexual reading (of) Nancy Toder's *Choices.* In Bi Academic Intervention, eds. *The Bisexual Imaginary: Representation, Identity and Desire.* London: Cassell.

Kaufmann, D. 1989. Autobiographical intersexts: Les mots de deux enfants rangés. In *L'Esprit Créateur,* xxix (4), pp. 21–32.

Kember, S. 1995. Medicine's new vision? In M. Lister, ed. *The Photographic Image in Digital Culture.* London: Routledge.

Lawler, S. 1997. 'Getting out and getting away': Women's narratives of class mobility. Paper presented to the Women's Studies Research Group, Loughborough University.

1999. *Mothering the Self.* London: Routledge.

Le Doeff, M. 1980. Simone de Beauvoir and existentialism. In *Feminist Studies,* 6 (2), pp. 277–89.

LeVay, S. 1996. *Queer Science: The Use and Abuse of Research into Homosexuality.* London: Massachusetts Institute of Technology.

Lury, C. 1993. *Cultural Rights: Technology, Legality and Personality.* London: Routledge.

1995. The possessive individual. Unpublished manuscript, later published in: Lury, C. 1997. *Prosthetic Culture: Identity, Memory and Photography.* London: Routledge.

1996. *Consumer Culture.* New Brunswick, New Jersey: Rutgers University Press.

1997. *Prosthetic Culture: Identity, Memory and Photography.* London: Routledge.

MacKenzie, I. 1997. Creativity as criticism: The philosophical constructivism of Deleuze and Guattari. In *Radical Philosophy,* 86, pp. 7–18.

Maffesoli, M. 1991. The ethic of aesthetics. In *Theory, Culture and Society,* 8, pp. 7–21.

McNay, L. 1992. *Foucault and Feminism: Power, Gender and the Self.* Cambridge: Polity.

1994. *Foucault: A Critical Introduction.* Cambridge: Polity.

McNeil, M. 1991. Making and not making the difference: The gender politics of Thatcherism. In S. Franklin, C. Lury and J. Stacey, eds. *Off-Centre: Feminism and Cultural Studies.* London: Harper Collins Academic.

Michasiw, K. 1994. Camp, masculinity, masquerade. In *differences: A Journal of Feminist Cultural Studies,* 6 (2+3), pp. 146–73.

Moi, T. 1990. *Feminist Theory and Simone de Beauvoir.* Oxford: Blackwell.

1994. *Simone de Beauvoir: The Making of an Intellectual Woman.* Oxford: Blackwell.

Morris, S. and Storr, M. 1997. Bisexual theory: A Bi Academic Intervention. In *Journal of Gay, Lesbian and Bisexual Identity,* 2 (1), pp. 1–5.

Mulvey, L. 1975. Visual pleasure and narrative cinema. In *Screen,* 6 (3), pp. 11–12.

Nead, L. 1993. *The Female Nude: Art, Obscenity and Sexuality.* London: Routledge.

Neale, S. 1983. Masculinity as spectacle. In *Screen,* 24 (6), pp. 2–18.

Nietzsche, F. 1956. *The Genealogy of Morals.* Trans. F. Golffing. New York: Doubleday and Company.

O'Sullivan, S. 1994. Girls who kiss girls and who cares? In D. Hamer and B. Budge, eds. *The Good, The Bad and The Gorgeous.* London: Pandora.

Patton, P. 1994. Anti-Platonism and art. In C. V. Boundas and D. Olkowski, eds. *Gilles Deleuze and the Theater of Philosophy.* New York: Routledge.

Phelan, P. 1993. *Unmarked: The Politics of Performance.* London: Routledge.

Plant, S. 1990. The Situationist International: A case of spectacular neglect. In *Radical Philosophy,* 55, pp. 3–10.

    1992. *The Most Radical Gesture: The Situationist International in a Postmodern Age.* London: Routledge.

Plummer, K. 1995. *Telling Sexual Stories: Power, Change and Social Worlds.* London: Routledge.

Pramaggiore, M. 1996. BI-ntroduction II: Epistemologies of the fence. In D. E. Hall and M. Pramaggiore, eds. *RePresenting Bisexualities: Subjects and Cultures of Fluid Desire.* New York: New York University Press.

Probyn, E. 1993. *Sexing the Self: Gendered Positions in Cultural Studies.* London: Routledge.

    1995. Queer belongings: The politics of departure. In E. Grosz and E. Probyn, eds. *Sexy Bodies: The Strange Carnalities of Feminism.* London: Routledge.

Ricoeur, P. 1980. Narrative time. In *Critical Inquiry,* 7 (1), pp. 169–90.

    1991a. Life in quest of narrative. In D. Wood, ed. *On Paul Ricoeur: Narrative and Interpretation.* London: Routledge.

    1991b. Narrative identity. In D. Wood, ed. *On Paul Ricoeur: Narrative and Interpretation.* London: Routledge.

Riley, D. 1988. *Am I that Name? Feminism and the Category of Women in History.* London: Macmillan.

Riviere, J. 1986. Womanliness as a masquerade. In V. Burgin, J. Donald and C. Kaplan, eds. *Formations of Fantasy.* London: Methuen.

Rose, J. 1992. *The Haunting of Sylvia Plath.* London: Virago.

Rose, N. 1989. *Governing the Soul: The Shaping of the Private Self.* London: Routledge.

    1992. Governing the enterprising self. In P. Heelas and P. Morris, eds. *The Values of the Enterprise Culture: The Moral Debate.* London: Routledge.

    1996. Authority and the genealogy of subjectivity. In P. Heelas, S. Lash and P. Morris, eds. *Detraditionalization: Critical Reflections on Authority and Identity.* Oxford: Blackwell.

    1997. Identity, genealogy, history. In S. Hall and P. Du Gay, eds. *Questions of Cultural Identity.* London: Sage.

Rose, S. and Stevens, C. *et al.* (The Off Pink Collective), 1996. *Bisexual Horizons: Politics, Histories, Lives.* London: Lawrence and Wishart.

Saalfield, C. and Navarro, R. 1991. Shocking pink praxis: Race and gender on the ACT UP frontlines. In D. Fuss, ed. *Inside/Out: Lesbian Theories, Gay Theories.* New York: Routledge.

Said, E. 1978. *Orientalism.* Harmondsworth: Penguin.

1992. *The Question of Palestine.* London: Vintage.

Sawicki, J. 1991. *Disciplining Foucault: Feminism, Power and the Body.* New York: Routledge.

Scheff, T. J. 1994. Emotions and identity: A theory of ethnic nationalism. In C. Calhoun, ed. *Social Theory and the Politics of Identity.* Oxford: Blackwell.

Schor, N. 1992. *Cartes Postales*: Representing Paris 1900. In *Critical Inquiry,* 18, pp. 188–244.

Sedgwick, E. K. 1991. *The Epistemology of the Closet.* Hemel Hempstead: Harvester Wheatsheaf.

1992. Epidemics of the will. In J. Crary and S. Kwinter, eds. *Incorporations.* New York: Zone.

1994. *Tendencies.* London: Routledge.

1996. Queer performativity: Warhol's shyness/Warhol's whiteness. In J. Doyle, J. Flatley and J. E. Muñoz, eds. *Pop Out: Queer Warhol.* Durham and London: Duke University Press.

Seidman, S. 1995. Deconstructing queer theory or the under-theorization of the social and the ethical. In L. Nicholson and S. Seidman, eds. *Social Postmodernism: Beyond Identity Politics.* Cambridge: Cambridge University Press.

Shaaban, B. 1988. *Both Right and Left Handed: Arab Women Talk About Their Lives.* London: The Women's Press.

Shilling, C. 1994. *The Body and Social Theory.* London: Sage.

Simondon, G. 1992. The genesis of the individual. Trans. M. Cohen and S. Kwinter. In J. Crary and S. Kwinter, eds. *Incorporations.* New York: Zone.

Simons, M. 1992. Lesbian connections: Simone de Beauvoir and feminism. In *Signs: Journal of Women in Culture and Society,* 18 (1), pp. 136–61.

Skeggs, B. 1997. *Formations of Class and Gender.* London: Sage.

Sontag, S. 1979. *On Photography.* Harmondsworth: Penguin.

Spivak, G. 1984/1985. Criticism, feminism and the institution. Interview with E. Grosz. In *Thesis Eleven,* 10/11, pp. 175–87.

Stacey, J. 1988. Desperately seeking difference. In L. Gammon and L. Marchment, eds. *The Female Gaze.* London: The Women's Press.

1994. *Star Gazing: Hollywood Cinema and Female Spectatorship.* London: Routledge.

1997. *Teratologies: A Cultural Study of Cancer.* London: Routledge.

Stanley, L. 1992. *The Auto/Biographical I: The Theory and Practice of Feminist Auto/biography.* Manchester: Manchester University Press.

Steedman, C. 1992. Culture, cultural studies, and the historians. In L. Grossberg, C. Nelson and P. Treichler, eds. *Cultural Studies.* London: Routledge.

Storr, M. 1997a. Bisexuality and its discontents: Some problems with current bisexual theory. Paper given at the 'Heretical Theory' seminar series, University of North London.

1997b. The sexual reproduction of 'race': Bisexuality, history and racialization. In Bi Academic Intervention, eds. *The Bisexual Imaginary: Representation, Identity and Desire.* London: Cassell.

1998. 'New sexual minorities', oppression and power: Bisexual politics in the UK. In T. Jordan and A. Lent, eds. *Storming the Millennium: The New Politics of Change.* London: Lawrence and Wishart.

Strathern, M. 1992. *Reproducing the Future: Anthropology, Kinship and the New Reproductive Technologies.* Manchester: Manchester University Press.

1997. Enabling identity? Biology, choice and the new reproductive technologies. In S. Hall and P. Du Gay, eds. *Questions of Cultural Identity.* London: Sage.

Sunday Telegraph, 8 December 1991. The bourgeois heart of de Beauvoir. M. Marrin, p. 116.

26 January 1992. Nice girls didn't – de Beauvoir did. R. Mayne, p. 111.

20 December 1992. Private Sartre's tangled sex life. J. Shilling, p. 11.

The Sunday Times, 2 August 1987. Free-loving, free-loading and free-wheeling. F. Raphael, p. 45.

Tagg, J. 1988. *The Burden of Representation: Essays on Photographies and Histories.* London: Macmillan.

Thacker, A. 1993. Foucault's aesthetics of existence. *Radical Philosophy,* 63, pp. 13–21.

The Times, 15 April 1986. Obituary of Simone de Beauvoir, exponent of revolutionary feminism. p. 18.

19 April 1986. Vive la differance: Simone de Beauvoir and the death of Parisian left bank culture, p. 9.

Tong, R. 1989. *Feminist Thought: A Comprehensive Introduction.* London: Unwin Hyman.

Toubia, N. ed. 1988. *Women of the Arab World.* London: Zed.

Turner, B. S. 1992. *Regulating Bodies: Essays in Medical Sociology.* London: Routledge.

 1995. Recent developments in the theory of the body. In M. Featherstone, M. Hepworth and B. S. Turner, eds. *The Body: Social Process and Cultural Theory.* London: Sage.

Tyler, C-A. 1994. Passing: Narcissism, identity, and difference. In *differences: A Journal of Feminist Cultural Studies,* 6 (2+3), pp. 212–48.

Valverde, M. 1996. 'Despotism' and ethical liberal governance. In *Economy and Society,* 25 (3), pp. 357–72.

Walker, L. 1993. How to recognize a lesbian: The cultural politics of looking like what you are. In *Signs: Journal of Women in Culture and Society,* 18 (4), pp. 866–91.

Warnock, M. 1967. *Existential Ethics.* London: Macmillan.

Waugh, P. 1992. Postmodern theory: The current debate. In P. Waugh, ed. *Postmodernism: A Reader.* London: Edward Arnold.

Weeks, J. 1985. *Sexuality and its Discontents.* London: Routledge.

Weinberg, M. S., Williams, C. J. and Pryor, D. W. 1994. *Dual Attraction: Understanding Bisexuality.* New York: Oxford University Press.

Weise, E. R. ed. 1992. *Closer to Home: Bisexuality and Feminism.* Seattle: Seal.

Wernick, A. 1991. *Promotional Culture.* London: Sage.

White, H. 1987. *The Content of the Form: Narrative Discourse and Historical Representation.* Maryland: John Hopkins University Press.

 1991. The metaphysics of narrativity: Time and symbol in Ricoeur's philosophy of history. In D. Wood, ed. *On Paul Ricoeur: Narrative and Interpretation.* London: Routledge.

Willis, S. 1990. I want the black one. In *New Formations,* 10, pp. 77–97.

Winship, J. 1983. Options – for the way you want to live now. In *Theory, Culture and Society,* 1 (3), pp. 44–65.

Wittig, M. 1992. One is not born a woman. In *The Straight Mind and Other Essays.* Hemel Hempstead: Harvester Wheatsheaf.

Yanay, N. 1990. Authenticity of self-expression: reinterpretation of female independence through the writings of Simone de Beauvoir. In *Women's Studies and Interdisciplinary Journal,* 17, pp. 219–33.

Yingling, T. 1991. AIDS in America: Postmodern governance, identity and experience. In D. Fuss, ed. *Inside/Out: Lesbian Theories, Gay Theories.* New York: Routledge.

Zita, J. N. 1992. Male lesbians and the postmodernist body. In *Hypatia,* 7 (4), pp. 106–27.

Index

Cambridge Cultural Social Studies